C000056246

'Opinions are proffered with the same enthu... McLintock's rise from the Gorbals to the marbled halls of Highbury ... It has been a hell of a ride'   *The Times*

'McLintock is of the generation of footballers that has a tale worth telling ... Interesting anecdotes aplenty'   *FourFourTwo*

'An entertaining autobiography'   *Independent on Sunday*

'Brutally honest ... intriguing and effortless reading ... highly recommended'   *Scotland on Sunday*

'An educational book'   *Scotsman*

'His behind-the-scenes stories spice up the tale'
                                              Leicester Mercury

Frank McLintock made his debut for Leicester City at 19 and played over 200 games. In 1964 he moved to Arsenal for a British record fee of £80,000 where, after being appointed captain, he made history when he led the team to victory against Anderlecht in the Fairs Cup in 1970 and the following season to the League and FA Cup double. In 1971 he was named Player of the Year and cemented his place as one of Arsenal's most respected captains of all time. He was awarded the MBE in 1972.

For such an outstanding player he won only nine caps for Scotland, perhaps as a result of a bias against players based south of the border. For the Gunners he played over 400 games before moving to QPR, where he stayed for four years.

After retiring as a player, he managed at Leicester and Brentford and was youth team coach at QPR and assistant manager at Millwall before becoming an agent. He continues to retain a high profile in the game, appearing regularly as a Sky Sports pundit, and is a highly regarded after-dinner speaker.

Rob Bagchi, who worked with Frank on his book, was a director of Sportspages bookshop for ten years and is a freelance writer who has worked for numerous newspapers and magazines. This is his second book.

TRUE GRIT

The Autobiography

Frank McLintock

with Rob Bagchi

headline

First published in 2005
by HEADLINE BOOK PUBLISHING

First published in paperback in 2006
by HEADLINE BOOK PUBLISHING

1

ISBN 0 7553 1413 1

Typeset in Bembo by Palimpsest Book Production Limited,
Polmont, Stirlingshire

Printed and bound in Great Britain by
Mackays of Chatham plc, Chatham, Kent

Headline's policy is to use papers that are natural, renewable
and recyclable products and made from wood grown in sustainable forests.
The logging and manufacturing processes are expected to conform to the
environmental regulations of the country of origin.

HEADLINE BOOK PUBLISHING
A division of Hodder Headline
338 Euston Road
London NW1 3BH

www.headline.co.uk
www.hodderheadline.com

To Barbara

CONTENTS

ACKNOWLEDGEMENTS

Although this book is dedicated to Barbara, I would like to pay further tribute to my wife for the tremendous support and love she has given me since the day we met forty-five years ago. She managed with great grace the sometimes lonely lot of the footballer's wife and she brought up our family of four terrific boys with such skill, affection and diligence. Neil, Iain, Jamie and Scott, I hope you know how much you and your families mean to me and I hope I've made up in recent years for the long absences caused by work over the last few decades. Also to my sister Jean, who bore the brunt of my mother's occasionally difficult nature, and my brother-in-law Andy and their children. My life is all the better for having them in it.

Without the help of so many people, it is doubtful whether

my career would have taken the shape it did. I would like to pay my warmest respects to Matt Gillies, Bert Johnson, Alex Dowdells, George Dewis, Bertie Mee, Alec Forbes, Alf Fields and Gordon Jago and offer my most heartfelt gratitude to my twin mentors Dave Sexton and Don Howe.

A vast cast list of names comprising scores of friends and former team mates who have inspired, entertained and contributed so much to my life over the years also springs to mind but I am aware of the need to keep this part brief so I'd just like to make special mention of two wonderful companions the game so graciously gave me – Davie Gibson and George Graham. Long may the laughs continue.

For their specific and important contributions to this book, I would like to thank Alex Fynn, who helped get the ball rolling and asked some provocative questions; David Luxton, whose tenacious good humour, skill and constant cajoling saw me through to publication; and all at Headline, especially David Wilson, Lorraine Jerram, Rona Johnson and Adrian Morgan, and Jack Rollin. Thanks for your patience, dexterity and wise guidance.

Rob Bagchi, who helped me put the book together over several months of tea-fuelled conversations in my conservatory, would also like to offer his own profound thanks to Alison Kirby, Saral and Angela Bagchi.

1

LITTLE BIG MAN

As you get on, your memory starts to play tricks on your emotions so that experiences that at the time were grisly and difficult to endure now become bittersweet at best, romantically nostalgic at worst. But I look back fondly on my childhood and trust that those instincts that always drew me home long after I had left for England were not simply sentimental.

There was a growl to Glasgow when I was young. It was not a quiet place. A city of extremes, it was tough and rough and warm and angry. In the decade before I was born, the city had become notorious as the 'Chicago of Europe' and though conditions had improved since the depths of the depression that my parents had barely survived, it was still a place where brutal hardship was commonplace and violent men thrived.

I was born in Sandyfaulds Street in the heart of the Gorbals at the end of 1939. My mother Catherine, father Archie and elder sister Jean lived in a typical Gorbals tenement. Our flat had two small rooms, known as a 'room and kitchen'. The tiny kitchen put us one step up from the even smaller single-end dwellings, which had just the one multi-purpose room. Most of our time indoors was spent in the larger 'room' that doubled up as bedroom and living area. There was a curtained-off bed recess in the wall where my parents slept and I shared the pull-down settee with my sister. We didn't have electricity but still relied on gas lamps for light. They had filaments like gossamer that used to break so easily if accidentally touched when putting a match to them and the whole building always had the hint of an acrid, gassy smell.

We were on the ground floor and shared an outside toilet with two other families. In the winter I would try to hang on as long as possible before venturing out to use it because it was so damp and dark and cold in there. Winters in general were miserable. The constant bugbear of tenement life in those days was burst pipes cutting off the water supply and flooding your flat, and it seemed to happen almost every year when I was a child.

Our only source of hot water was the kettle on the stove, and with no other form of heating we were reliant on the coal fire to protect us from the Siberian-like draughts; but once it went out late at night you had to make sure you were wearing your balaclava and had piled enough coats on the bed to prevent hypothermia setting in while you slept. Some mornings I would wake up and there would be ice on the inside of the windows, so it's not hard to understand why the cold remains an abiding memory for kids of my generation.

My friend, Tommy Docherty, who is also a Glasgow boy, has a funny story about both the poverty and the arctic conditions of our youth: 'The wind used to howl through our tenement and one day it blasted so hard that it blew the padlocks off the gas-meter. Well at least that's what my mother told the police, anyway.'

While it's a good line, I am sure Tom's mother did not really fiddle her meter, and mine, certainly, would never contemplate such monkey business.

She could be very awkward towards my sister, Jean. My mum had been brought up to believe that the daughter should be like a servant to her mother and would often be very curt, almost cruel, in letting Jean know what her duties were. But I remained my mother's blue-eyed boy right up to her death last year at the age of ninety-eight. With my father sometimes out of work, she was the main breadwinner for the family, working long hours as a cleaner – usually down on her knees scrubbing floors in well-to-do families' homes.

Now I can appreciate the sacrifices she made just to get us enough to eat and I still feel guilty that I was not much help to her. Because she was out all day I was supposed to rush straight home after school to light the fire and lay the table for our tea, but I always tried to squeeze in an extra game of football before it got too dark and would leave the chores right up to the last minute. This usually entailed me sprinting the 800 yards home from the playground, dousing the sticks with fat from the chip pan to get them to light quickly and furiously kennelling the fire with newspaper to get it roaring just as she came through the door. Sometimes it would work but I made a poor arsonist and more often than not would get into a terrible muddle; the newspaper would catch fire and I would still be trying to swat the burning slivers of paper flying around the room just as she walked in. However many times she told me off, it didn't seem to make any difference to me. The after-school match, the first of the evening, was more important to me than helping to alleviate my poor mother's daily burden.

My father, Archie, was just an average, working-class guy happy to get through another day unscathed. I'm glad that he had adopted the shortened version of his name, otherwise it would have been very embarrassing for me at school because Archibald used to draw the incomprehensible playground taunt: 'Archibald, bald, bald, King of the Jews'.

Not having a trade meant that he took whatever work he could get but my father never again found the same satisfaction he had enjoyed as a wireless operator in the Merchant Navy during the war. Sometimes he would work on the railways, at other times he would be labouring, or in a factory, or on the dole. Like a lot of people in Glasgow back then – and like his wife – my father was less than five feet tall. The malnutrition in the first few decades of the twentieth century seemed to have spawned this midget race whose size camouflaged their aggression. I know it's become a Glaswegian cliché to insist that 'wee barras' are more lethal in fights than 'big yins' but it held true for that generation. They had learned to be vicious to protect themselves from all the bullying they suffered.

My father was very fiery. Most of it was verbal not physical but, if provoked, he had the sort of temperament that would lead him to fight King Kong rather than back down. For all that, he was well liked in our neighbourhood and was very easy-going, almost nonchalant, most of the time. As long as he had enough money left over from what he gave my mother to have a couple of pints a night, five Woodbines and the odd bet, he was satisfied.

Compared to my experiences as a parent with a bit of money

behind me, mine stumbled through life. Their only priorities were paying the rent and making sure there was enough food on the table. And thanks to my mother there was always something: porridge and broth when she was scraping coppers together; egg, meat and chips when there was more money about. Through my parents' hard work, love expressed itself in actions rather than words. There was a lot of love present but we spent most of our time shouting and bawling at one another.

I get on very well with my sister but we were always fighting when we were kids and my mother, as inflamed as her bright red hair, used to break it up by wielding her cloot or dish-cloth and skelping us across the face to shut us up. Money was always tight and one of my greatest regrets is the time I threw the salt dish at my sister to get her to belt up and it missed, smashed straight through the brand new sunshine window in the kitchen and landed out in the back yards where the middens were. We quickly concocted a story about some young hooligan throwing a stone and, though the shards of glass were not on the inside of the window, as she would expect, my mother stoically accepted our lie and, I am ashamed to say, had to take on extra cleaning shifts to save up for the repairs.

Although we could never afford proper holidays we always had a trip out in the summer to Saltcoats or Largs – seaside resorts just a few miles down the Clyde. There was always a great deal of excitement on the bus journey there and as soon as we arrived I would race into the sea. The swimwear at that time was usually made of wool – quite often hand-knitted – and we pale, white as ghost Glaswegians would emerge from the icy North Atlantic or North Sea in violent shivering fits with the gussets of our swimming trunks around our knees. I'd dry myself off with a flimsy, skinny towel and quickly try to get some tea in me to thaw myself out. It does sound bleak but that's not the whole story as our expectations were significantly lower then. I genuinely used to love those days and I was always chuffed to bits to enjoy any one of the small treats that my mum and dad sweated blood to give us.

I hope that they knew how grateful I was because I used to have a real problem showing it. No self-respecting Glasgow boy would be lovey-dovey with his parents lest he be thought a bit of a nancy and that attitude has marked me to this day. If I ever bought flowers for my mother, or later for my wife, Barbara, I would hide them under my coat to prevent any embarrassment in case someone spotted and mocked me in the street. I know it's ridiculous but it is deeply ingrained and for a long time I thought everyone behaved like that.

I remember staying overnight with a pal at his house and it was like a scene from *The Waltons*. The whole family was so polite to each other and it reached a climax when we all went to sleep in the big room. One by one they all took turns saying 'Goodnight, God bless! Pleasant dreams! Sleep well!' to each other. It went on for about five minutes as they worked their way down their lengthy list. Needless to say I didn't join in. I couldn't believe my ears and even as I squirmed with embarrassment I thought that they must be acting out some sort of charade for my benefit. It wasn't really until I met Barbara's family in Leicester many years later and saw how even-tempered, affectionate and benevolent their behaviour was that my sarcasm about being 'nice' was punctured.

Contrary to most people's assumptions, sectarian hatred was not all that rampant in my youth. It would rear its ugly head largely at weekends, when most men would go out drinking. The Gorbals, and nearby Oatlands where we later moved, was pretty mixed and everyone attempted to get on but there were a few exceptions.

Babs McCormack, for example, who lived in our street was a very pleasant guy most of the time but on Thursday nights you would often see him around midnight, drunk as a sack, staggering like he was shadow-boxing a lamp-post and screaming 'Fuck the Pope!' at one of our neighbours. You rarely got much sleep on Thursday nights because his target, the very devout Mrs McCartney, a proper Holy Joe or, more correctly Josephine, in Glaswegian parlance, would throw up her window and threaten to come down and tan his backside with her broom for his impertinence. The same performance was played out every Thursday night for years, yet for the other six days of the week there was never any bother between them.

My family was Catholic but, though you could call me a dutiful observant during my youth, when I really had little say in the matter, I've always seen it as something that is a small part of me but doesn't define me. If you want to be a good Catholic, good for you, get on with it. The same goes for those who want to be good Protestants. I applaud and respect you but why the hell your choice of faith should be of any consequence to anyone else, I genuinely fail to see.

It wasn't a popular view back then but I hated the divisive hold that religion had on Glasgow. Dogma and bullshit were everywhere. A lot of vital charitable work was done by the churches and in 1955, Billy Graham's six-week crusade to the city – when he packed 90,000 into Hampden Park to watch him preach – turned around a lot of people's lives. But surely it would have been better all round if both sides had explicitly disowned the 'us versus them' mentality that caused so much strife and corruption.

Most Catholics were sent to church schools and I was no different. We had a couple of good teachers at St Bonaventure's but we also had more than our fair share of visits from old, tyrannical Irish priests. I suppose many of them had suffered appallingly rough upbringings in rural seminaries and had consequently become decidedly odd in their behaviour; many were misfits who showed no sympathy at all to terrified kids. They would thunder out their spittle-enhanced admonishments about purgatory and damnation totally oblivious to the effect they were having on their petrified audience of eight-year-olds.

The worst by far was Father Gilmartin. If ever a man took such sadistic pleasure from 'putting the fear of God' into children it was that swine. We would quake in his presence even at the age of fifteen. The whole school, about 150 of us, would trudge up to St Francis's for confession every Friday. There they would split us into groups and allocate the priest. The relief you felt if you didn't get Gilmartin was immense but was never worth the dread that you might or, of course, the actual bowel-churning hell of being stuck with him. You would be in turmoil just walking into the confessional and then stutter through the routine: 'Forgive me Father for I have sinned. It has been three weeks since my last con—'

'Three weeks? Three weeks?' he would yell for all the church to hear.

'Impure thoughts? Impure thoughts?' he'd bellow. So by the time you staggered out with your gargantuan penance you would be crimson with embarrassment and everyone would be staring at you. Once I had a match on a Sunday and missed mass. I don't know what possessed me to inform him of this but for once he was speechless, or at least he was for a considerable time, before he almost burst my eardrums with his screech to: 'Get out of my church!'

What surprises me now is that I kept going back instead of seeing him for the semi-educated bloodsucker he actually was. Since those days I've always hated bullies and will always try to stand up to them. I still regret that I felt helpless to stand up to Father Gilmartin.

St Bonaventure's was a pretty hopeless school. We had fifty-six in our class and any teacher unable to control us soon came unstuck. I was no tearaway, I was too busy thinking about football to bother, but there were plenty – game for anything – who made the teachers' lives miserable and you would quite often see one of the weaker teachers assaulted if he tried, belatedly, to impose his authority.

The hygiene, too, wasn't up to much and there was always a terrible smell. Some of the kids didn't even have a monthly bath and so they were always scratching themselves. One kid was so infested with bugs and lice, and had a filthy neck from carrying the bags of coal he used to steal, that the metalwork teacher tried to make an example of him, but he only ended up humiliating the poor lad in front of the braying class. Cruelty, I suppose, was often the teachers' only recourse.

Corporal punishment was doled out regularly. Our head-master, Mr Ribchester, was a big devotee of the strap. If you were sent to his office, you had to stand in front of his desk and wait while he bollocked you. Because it was so cold in winter, and school policy demanded we wear shorts up to the age of fifteen, you couldn't stop yourself from edging towards the radiator as his tirade went on. This would make him go bananas. He used to draw his arm so far back behind his head as he wound up to strike you that he looked like a fast-bowler at cricket. Instinct would make you flinch and withdraw your hand slightly, but this would make him miss and he'd get even more furious because you'd embarrassed him. He would then make you sit on his desk with your hand out above your lap – a position from which there was no escape. If he missed your hand, or you took it away, he would get you across your bare legs. A session with him and you would have strap marks all over your thighs and up to your elbows.

The worst time of all was when I did succumb to being a bit of a jack-the-lad and shoplifted some brooches from Woolworths on a school trip to Prestwick. I only did it for the dare, but at the back of the bus on the way home I was bragging about these worthless trinkets and was overheard by a teacher. Not only did it not impress him, which I had foolishly thought it might, but he also gave me a severe dressing-down and sent me in to see Ribchester. This time his words were more hurtful than the blows and I felt so ashamed that I resolved never again to get involved in such stupidity.

I used to get into trouble for fighting and, though I was often scared, the word that I was a handy boxer quickly got round so I would often be challenged to fight older kids, one-on-one, after school. I would be approached at lunchtime and spend the afternoon lessons sweating over what awaited me once the bell rang. I knew what I was doing – my mother and father had saved up and bought me a speed-ball when I was younger – but it was still a very daunting prospect to face lads who were so much older than me. Luckily, few of my challengers could even hold up their hands and those that could weren't used to southpaws so I was always on top before the fight was broken up – usually by my sister who would drag me home to face my mother's wrath.

Apart from football and the occasional punch-up, there was little else on offer in the form of entertainment. A trip to the pictures, quite literally flea-pits in those days, fell into the treat category; something to be saved up for and savoured. We used to spend most of our time outdoors. Walking was a big pastime and a group of us – John and Billy MacDougall, Jim Bree, Francie Cunningham, Davie Moffat, Joe and Brynie Kelly, Tom Breslin and I – would tramp all around Glasgow. It was a time when simple pleasures meant so much; if you could scrape enough together for a penny dainty, a huge sweet toffee, then that alone would make your day. I also used to go to my friend Joe Winters' house on the way to school most mornings and we would play the only record in his collection, Frankie Laine's *I Believe*, ad nauseam until the lyrics became so engrained that I can still recite them almost sixty years on.

But I loved winter best, when the same pals and I would go out to the snow-covered hills surrounding the city, running so hard to get there that our Wellingtons would chaff our shins raw. We didn't have proper sledges so we would slide down these hills aboard tin trays or, riskier, sit on the blades of shovels that someone would have managed to pinch. The shovels were death-traps, sharp as butchers' cleavers, and with a thick wooden handle which would clout you round the head if you fell off or hit anything. I shudder looking back and wonder how we escaped from cutting off our balls or slicing ourselves in two. How no one was ever killed, never mind suffered a serious injury, on our lethal sleighs was a miracle.

Apart from those times when it was too cold to get the ball out, we played football – morning, noon and night. From an early age I was enthralled by the game and have always felt lucky to have been born in a city of football fanatics. I was captain of the school team by the age of ten and was responsible for looking after the school's big old leather 'T ball'. That meant that we could have a kick-about pretty much whenever we wanted, though I'd have to spend hours each night coating it in dubbin to hide the scars it picked up on the improvised pitches we used by the 'steamies' or tenement wash-houses.

A few years later we moved the stadium to the top of our street where a tenement had been demolished. It had left a space about eighty yards long by forty yards wide and, with a pair of goals we scratched with a stone on the walls of the adjoining buildings, it proved ideal for our twenty-a-side matches. Those informal games were usually enlivened by commentary from the lad in possession of the ball and, more often than not, our chosen scenario would be Scotland v England at Hampden Park. I'd be racing up the wing pretending simultaneously to be both Willie Waddell and Raymond Glendenning, describing with glee the humiliation I was inflicting on my pal, the left back, who was doubling up as England's George Hardwick. It won't surprise you to learn that we always played on until Scotland won our imaginary internationals, waste-ground games I can still recall in vivid detail.

I did not spend too much time running up the wing in school games, however, as I was stuck at right back in the old 'WM' formation, which had defensive frailties that could be easily exploited if you moved too far out of position. Our matches were played on Glasgow Green, which was a hell of a piece of fanciful labelling as there wasn't a blade of grass on it. The Green was a vast park where women would hang out their washing to dry so that scores of sheets could be seen flapping in the breeze as you played on any one of the dozens of ash and cinder pitches.

Studs, if you were foolish enough to wear them, would last no more than ten minutes before snapping off on the stones and chunks of smooth glass embedded in the surface. We wore meaty leather ankle boots that had three leather horizontal bars on the soles. It was the only way you could get any purchase at all. The dire state of the pitches almost put paid to my career as my mother grew increasingly concerned at the large number of scratches I was picking up from slide tackles. I'd get home and she'd scrub the cuts on my thighs and hips with Dettol and urge me to 'pack this bloody game in' before I was crippled, but I managed to persuade her to let me continue.

The first time I played on grass was when I was fifteen and had a trial for Scotland schoolboys at Celtic Park. I did not play as well as I had hoped because they put me at outside right; they thought I was too short to play at the back. It would have been even worse if the kit man had not spotted my old-fashioned, Glasgow Green boots and lent me a pair with studs. Had he not come to my rescue I'd have spent most of the match on my arse, when I wasn't skating around like Bambi on ice.

I represented the school from the age of eight until I was fifteen when I joined the affiliated St Bonaventure's Boys' Guild run by Father Cunningham. Fifteen is the age when most promising youth footballers usually give up the game and I started to panic as my schooldays drew to a close. I had become so used to playing at least two organised games a week that I began to go nuts at the thought of having to stop.

I decided to ask our local club, Shawfield Juniors, if they would let me train with them. Junior football in Scotland is the equivalent of the semi-pro level in England and has nothing to do with age. Shawfield Juniors, based on the banks of the Clyde, had been one of the top teams of the 1930s and continued to flourish in the immediate post-war period, though they eventually folded in the late sixties. I wasn't confident enough to ask to play for them, and even I thought that at just five feet I was way too small to play alongside grown men – but I thought that the manager, Wattie Johnson, might let a Scotland schoolboy triallist train with them.

'Go away, son!' he said on my first trip up there. 'Come back when you're bigger.' Four months later his words were the exact headline they used in the evening paper after I'd made my debut.

I wasn't put off by Johnson's put-down and continued to pester him until he relented. We trained two evenings a week on the club's pitch – a great setting on the river's edge, mist rolling in off the Clyde – which was illuminated by two massive arc lamps. Most professionals love evening games and I think it stems from those first, wonderfully romantic experiences playing under lights. It was such a rarity back then that, for me, the atmosphere it generated was tangible; I would tingle with excitement and it's a thrill that's never really left me.

The training wasn't particularly sophisticated but it was much more intense than anything I'd done before. We started with a few laps of the pitch followed by a spurt of doggy sprints from one eighteen-yard box to the other. At first, I was miles behind everyone else, my little legs comprehensively out-powered by the rest of the squad, but after about two months I had improved beyond all expectations. My team mates – men like Jimmy Dickie, John Hepburn and Hennie Flanagan – were all very kind to me and with the encouragement of these grizzled ex-professionals my confidence started to grow. They were fifteen years older, yet they treated me as an equal. And even if I couldn't overcome my embarrassment enough to jump in the bath with them after training – afraid they would laugh at my skinny, hairless body – it was their praise and generosity that first made me begin to think that I had a future in the game.

One evening the physiotherapist, a great guy called Willie Ross, asked if I fancied a game that weekend for Stephens Shipyards and I jumped at the offer. Stephens later became part of Upper Clyde Shipbuilders but were still independent then and played in a flourishing works' league. The ground was miles away and I had to take three tram 'caurs' to get over to Broomielaw on the Sunday morning. Seeing I hadn't played a proper game in months, and knowing I wouldn't see much of the ball in my usual right-back position, I told a white lie and insisted I was a right half. We won 7–2 and I scored five times, and as I came off the pitch this chap sidled over to me and said: 'Don't turn professional too early, son.'

I thought he was being facetious but his warning was soon to make more sense to me. The following week Mr Ross absent-mindedly asked me at the end of training: 'Didn't you play at the weekend, Frank? Was it all right?' When I told him about the five goals Ross shot out of the dressing room to get the manager. I think he must have rung up the shipyard to confirm my story and at the end of training I was invited to play in an official Shawfield Juniors trial the next week.

Early on in that game the ball came to me and I cushioned it on my head, brought it down and laid off a pass – a series of moves which gave me an enormous sense of reassurance that I was comfortable enough at this level. I found it easier to play with good players because they were always in the right position and they seemed to read my game much better than any other team I'd played for.

After the game Wattie Johnson and a couple of the Shawfield committee men approached me in the dressing room and asked me to sign semi-professional forms at once but I still wasn't sure: 'I can't play for you,' I said, 'I'm only a wee fella and they're all men.'

'Well, you didn't do too badly out there,' Wattie replied. But, still, I felt it was too great a leap for me and I refused. Then they offered to buy me any pair of boots I wanted as a signing-on fee – irresistible inducement for a fifteen-year-old. If I'd known that Hamilton Academicals were also waiting with an offer things could have turned out differently. However, the prospect of a pair of lightweight 'Stanley Matthews' boots was all the persuasion I needed to race home and get my parents' consent. I would have signed my life away for a new pair of boots though, ironically, I had to settle for a pair endorsed by Walley Barnes, the Wales and Arsenal full back, since no self-respecting Glasgow shop stocked the ones designed by the Sassenach scourge of Scotland.

It took me a further two months to make my debut and after six months I had become used to seeing my name every week in the Monday newspaper match reports. Sitting on the bus to work one Monday morning, however, I looked over the shoulder of the passenger in front of me at the back page of his news-paper and was surprised to see my name in the headline. There was a photograph of me alongside bold lettering that I read as, 'Liechester City go in for junior find McLintock'. I tapped on the passenger's shoulder and asked him: 'Where's Liechester?'

'London, son,' he replied, and when I told him that the kid in the photo was me, he immediately told the whole bus. Almost everyone up on the top deck came over and patted me on the back. As I was soon to learn, the man's grasp of geography was a bit faulty but I didn't really care where Leicester was. If it had been near Timbuktu I would still have been thrilled. I was on my way.

2

NO MEAN CITY

It transpired that Leicester's Scotland scout, Walter McLean – who had spotted Billy Steel and taken him to Derby County – had been watching me for three months. I knew that Celtic, Hearts, Clyde and the still-interested Hamilton had all made inquiries about me but nothing had so far come of any of them. I wasn't particularly enamoured about the prospect of signing for a Scottish team as I knew that they would simply farm me out to another junior club for a couple of years. If I was going to improve I needed a proper football education. I needed to be a professional, albeit at third or fourth team level, rather than face another two years at semi-pro. England could offer this: Scottish teams could not.

Within a few days of the newspaper headline appearing, I was eating my first ever steak in a Glasgow restaurant alongside Davie

Halliday, the dour Aberdonian who had recently been appointed as Leicester's manager. He must have thought McLean had gone mad in recommending this five-foot squirt to him. I later found out that he was a typically stern Highlander and his long silences meant nothing but that he hardly spoke a word to me was unnerving. Fortunately, he trusted McLean and when we had finished having dinner he offered me a week's trial starting the following month.

My family and I were invited to spend the Christmas holiday of 1956 in a Leicester hotel at the club's expense. In Scotland, then, Hogmanay was a far bigger celebration than Christmas so my dad was especially pleased that he was going to participate in both England and Scotland's best parties that year. It was with my father in the highest spirits, eagerly anticipating a massive sing-song, with food and drink on a scale he'd only dreamed about, that we set off on the nine-hour train journey to Leicester on Christmas Eve.

The Leicester trip was a wonderful opportunity and I am thankful that my employers had finally agreed to let me take the time off to go south. I'd had part-time work from the age of thirteen; at first delivering milk before school until I graduated to an early morning paper round. Neither job was much fun, and both were worse in winter when it was too dark to see what, or who, might be around the corner as you climbed a tenement staircase. Sometimes I'd almost wet myself as I encountered a courting couple, still out from the night before, necking or having a 'lumber' in some dingy stairwell that always seemed to reek of cats' piss.

At least the paper round kicked off with a cup of tea and an egg roll in Willie Scorgie's newsagent's shop, but the dogs that would fly at the letter boxes as I posted the morning paper through frightened me half to death. My great friend, Joe Kelly, did the papers, too. He had only one arm and I was amazed that he managed to carry cumbersome piles of heavy newspapers morning after morning. Mind you, he did get capfuls of tips at Christmas, while I was lucky to get the odd shilling.

Once I left school my mother was adamant that I should become a skilled tradesman. They were still seen as a cut above and, though my school record would have left me to join the ranks of the unskilled alongside my dad, I was fortunate to benefit from a bit of nepotism when a distant relative persuaded Bullock Brothers to take me on as an apprentice painter and decorator. The company was based across town in Anniesland and it took me an hour-and-a-half on three buses to get there each morning.

On my first day I was asked the classic 'What school did you go to?' question, an indirect but accurate way of pinpointing your religion. The man I was working with took an instant dislike to me because my school, named after an obscure saint, was obviously Catholic. I had to put up with the usual 'Fenian bastard' crap for a while but when he tried to get me to cart his brushes home every night, clean them and return them to him every morning I snapped. Being told to get stuffed wasn't advice he'd heard before from a fifteen-year-old and all his nonsense stopped when I said I was willing to back up my words with my fists.

Someone once told me I was way too upbeat all the time and that I suffered from infectious enthusiasm. I don't know if they meant it to be a compliment or a slur but it was accurate; I can't see the point of doing something if you don't enjoy it. Learning a trade was like a badge of honour to me so I threw everything I had into learning all I could and went to evening classes on graining, finishes and sign-writing. The craft was more difficult when I first started as we still used paint as opposed to emulsion. That old-fashioned, oil-based gloss was very hard to work, like applying glue, and it really built up a formidable forearm strength which came in useful later when shielding the ball or holding off a player when marking at set-pieces. Some of the paint had prodigious quantities of lead in it, so our employers used to make us drink milk, which was supposed to protect your organs from over-exposure to the lead's toxicity. It sounded like an old-wives' remedy to me as the majority of my older colleagues had severe breathing difficulties and spent most of the day spluttering.

As the youngest member of the team, my main responsibility was making the tea. Everyone would have a billy-can and a small canister with their own supplies of sugar and tea. I would spend hours every day fetching water, mixing tea and boiling up the cans on a brazier. Once, when we were painting the interior of a new Littlewoods store, I couldn't find any water because the plumbers hadn't yet been in. I couldn't face the boys and their anger if they had to go without tea so, after a long search, I was overjoyed to find that the newly installed toilets were working. Having filled up the cans by flushing the toilet I proceeded to serve what our foreman described as 'the best cup of tea he'd ever tasted'. Half an hour later I was being chased around the shop, running for my life; he had been sick at least three times. Of course, I hadn't touched the stuff myself.

As the youngest apprentice, I had a lot of leeway and was always doing dopey things. There was one old guy – he looked like Ben Turpin, the silent film star – who gave me a deserved clout for messing around all the time. Once, when he was carrying an eighteen-foot ladder, I couldn't resist the temptation to sneak up and tickle him. He turned round quickly and put the ladder straight through a plate-glass window.

I got a great deal of running practice on that job, never more so than the day they 'initiated' me. I had heard all sorts of terrible rumours about what the experienced guys did to young apprentices, so as soon as they made a move for me I was away on my toes and for half an hour they couldn't catch me. Then the foreman bollocked us and sent us back to work. But I didn't realise he was in on it and just as I was beginning to start painting again, they all grabbed me. Five minutes later I was starkers – they'd painted my arse and covered my willy in putty. It was the most embarrassing moment of my life, far worse even than anything Father Gilmartin had put me through.

I loved the laughs we had while working together but the abiding image of myself I have back then is of being up a ladder, shivering, painting the exteriors of houses on a new council scheme. We'd spend the morning scraping ice off the metalwork, then painting over the bits of ice we couldn't chip off and trying, somehow, to make the best job of various other sodden parts. At lunchtime we'd all huddle together, sitting on our casks of brushes, drinking tea and eating slices of bread before having a quick game of football to try to get the circulation going. Just as we'd warm ourselves up, it would be time to climb back up the ladder. Needless to say, we didn't have any thermal gear; we'd be frozen to our bones in our white overalls until the dark ended the day at about four o'clock. Even if I hadn't had that overwhelming yearning to play professional football, it's small wonder that I leapt at Leicester's offer.

Obviously, my parents and I had expected to be met at Leicester station but when we arrived late in the afternoon on

Christmas Eve the place was deserted. Tom Bromilow, the club's chief scout, was supposed to be looking after us but after waiting by the entrance for two-and-a-half hours in the snow, we were beginning to think there had been some mistake. There was only one place open – an Indian café – and we decided, finally, to go in, have a cup of tea and think things through. I remember the café crowd in there looking at us three tiny Scots as though we had just landed from Mars.

We didn't know then that Leicester, quite unlike the Gorbals, had a flourishing Asian community. As Glaswegians, and especially with our accents, we were as exotic to them as they were to us. We were back on the concourse twenty minutes later when I remembered that Leicester's letter had indicated that the hotel we were booked into began with the letter 'C'. After getting, eventually, a passer-by to understand me, we were directed to the Cravenhurst in the city centre where our hosts were waiting for us.

Tom Bromilow came running into the hotel about an hour later. He was full of apologies – he'd forgotten about us and had been busy with his Christmas shopping. Now he was panicking that we would tell Halliday that we'd been abandoned in a strange city for four hours and that he would get the sack. We assured him that we wouldn't let on and he left us to make the most of the evening's festivities, which turned out to be a severe disappointment.

We had imagined that the hotel would be up-market with a fancy restaurant and a Christmas Eve dance. Instead it was a sort of retirement home full of old folks who just wanted a quiet night. My father had thought we'd have a nice booze-up followed by traditional Glasgow entertainment – spin the bottle to find a singer and everyone doing their party piece.

The nearest we got to any excitement was when one old boy dropped his pipe into his lap and set himself on fire. We shuffled off to bed quite early that night. Merry Christmas 1956.

I was looking forward to the prospect of my Boxing Day trial but I couldn't help thinking of my pals back in Glasgow and the fun I was missing out on. They, at least, would be having the quintessential Glasgow night-out: get pissed out of your mind, go to the dance, get a bird, get a carry-out, spark up a fag, fill your face with a fish supper and have a sing-song on your way home.

Glasgow in the mid fifties was said to be 'dancing daft'. There were still almost 100 dance halls, most of which completely ignored rock 'n' roll and employed big bands to play the music of an older generation; that's probably why I'm into Sinatra, Ella Fitzgerald and Billy Eckstine rather than Elvis and the Beatles. The swinging soundtrack to the city would be played out in our haunts like the Locarno on Sauchiehall Street, the Dennistoun Palais and the Plaza at Eglinton Toll but I knew that on that night, Christmas Eve, my pals would be in our favourite place of all, the Barrowlands.

While 'Teds' were causing havoc in England, the Glasgow craze among boys was the Moon man look. We wore suits with three-button jackets and drainpipes, tweed overcoats, ox-blood crepe shoes and we all had our hair in the classic Tony Curtis style. I don't know where the Moon man name came from; possibly from a dance we were all into where you held the girl close and did a little dip every third step. We all tried to look tough by chewing gum, affecting a swagger and having this ridiculous snarl plastered over our faces but we were as nervous as kittens when it came to asking a woman to dance. That was because you had to pluck up the courage to saunter across the dance floor, go up to them and find the right words, usually the ultra-romantic 'You getting up, then, hen?' At first, more often than not, you would be turned away and would have to pretend to your pals that this crushing blow was like water off a duck's back.

The women were far more intimidating than the men. Rude, or 'scruffy' as we used to call it, they could come out with the most ego-deflating stuff. Imagine walking across a packed ball-room, in front of all your friends, to a girl you'd had your eye on all evening, only to be told: 'You're kidding aren't you? Go away.' Then there were the Ladies' choice dances when they were supposed to come and ask you. You were haunted by the fear of not being asked. It would be a total humiliation. No wonder we needed to be blootered before we went near the place.

Being blootered was an easy enough state to reach. The allegation that Scots are tight certainly doesn't hold true for Glaswegians. The men would get their pay packets on a Thursday night and would head straight to the pub where, after a few drinks – a whisky chaser that would be necked but the dregs saved to pour into the accompanying pint of heavy – their hospitality would be boundless. In fact, you could get into an argument for refusing a free drink. Then they'd go home, almost skint – having maybe only four pounds left out of their fourteen pounds' wages – and that's when the trouble would start up. You would hear the wives' accusing, angry: 'Where's the money for the weans?' It happened in our tenement block most weeks and I remember feeling physically sick as a child as the rows invariably escalated into a drunken brawl with the women often receiving a horrific beating.

The Saracen's Head, a pub opposite the Barrowlands known throughout Glasgow as The Sarrie Heid, was the best venue for a pre-dance tanking-up session. Now it's mainly alcoholics who drink stuff as strong as Buckfast Tonic, but in the fifties most places had their own versions of that potent brew. Pubs in the Gorbals had this lethal 'red biddy', made of red wine and God knows what, while the Sarrie served cheap wine and sherry by the half pint and cider so rough it seemed to rip out your stomach muscles. The Sarrie was such a vibrant place and, seeing that 'having a quiet drink' was an alien concept to most Glaswegians, it was always packed full of people aiming to get wrecked quickly, and economically. A couple of hours in there would give you all the courage you needed.

And bravery was always a requirement on a night out. Fuel-driven fights would break out all the time. The bouncers in the Barrowlands were just as bad as some of the punters. In fact they were worse; they soon let you know that they didn't give a fuck about anything and they were always piling into brawls. They'd get a few quid to stand on the door but it was the opportunity for regular violence that seemed to attract these scar-faced nutters to their trade. I've seen them throw drunks down flights of concrete stairs, stick the boot into someone who argued with their decision not to let him in and kick the living crap out of anyone they took a dislike to.

The police, the famous Glasgow 'dicks', at least seemed to be in control of their conduct but they had learned that physical intimidation was the only way to stand up to the city's hard men. They were fearlessly aggressive. If they saw someone messing about they would just chin him. That element of danger on a night out gave me a thrill at sixteen but once I recognised that the violence I witnessed had such a random quality, I realised how easy it was to become a victim rather than a bystander.

Despite the police's tactics, crime was still rampant in the city. There were plenty of bona fide gangsters about but the ones you came into contact with most were the 'Neds', the wannabe Mr Bigs and petty 'gas-meter bandit' criminals. They were easily identifiable by their demeanour and it wasn't too hard to steer clear of them. To us, the really frightening members of their fraternity were the 'bampots'. They tended to be normal people most of the time but, pissed-up, became lunatics with an alarming propensity for mayhem. They saw themselves as defenders of their community and took on the ludicrous responsibility for keeping out trespassers from other areas of town. Their moronic turf wars soon escalated into a razor-slashing epidemic throughout the city.

These territorial arguments often broke out on Thursday, Friday and Saturday nights and their vivid results could be seen on the faces of young men disfigured with gruesome scars. The safety-razor blade was the weapon of choice; split in two it could be hidden in the lapel of a jacket or the peak of a cap. You had to be wary of anyone approaching you and taking off their cap because, with their modified bonnets, they could slit your throat from ear to ear. It was only when the judge, Lord Carmont, still a resonant figure for most people of my generation, handed down a sixteen-year sentence, then another of fourteen years, to two Neds who had been convicted of malicious wounding, that the plague started to abate.

But any evening out could still end in a terrifyingly violent altercation. One night, me and my friend, Tommy Paton, were on our way home from the Barrowlands when the local gang from Glasgow Cross started on us. One of them deliberately barged me off the pavement and I was naïve enough to say, 'Watch it!' It was a dumb error and I should have known they were only looking for an excuse to have a go at any non-local. We didn't hang around and started to run for a trolley bus to escape from them but they kept pelting us with bottles as we scarpered down the street. As I got to the bus-stop, they broke their stride and tried to mingle in with the queue but the bus conductress only let the first five people on board, put out her arm to block me and said, 'No more.'

I couldn't help but notice that one of the guys chasing me had been running with a stiff leg and I could hear a distinctive chink-chink noise as he ran which indicated to me that he had a bayonet or a machete concealed in his trousers. I knew that he was willing to wait for the bus to go to 'do' me so there wouldn't be any witnesses so I grabbed the pole at the back of the bus, barged under the clippy's arm and forced my way upstairs, quickly followed by Tommy. It was terrifying enough that bottles were flung at the bus as it roared away from the bus-stop. I was only fifteen and I have no doubt that I would have been murdered if I hadn't managed to get on that bus. I'd read so many newspaper accounts of lads just being caught in the wrong part of town, getting smashed over the head with a bottle and stabbed with the broken neck, that I knew I couldn't take the risk. I was never part of the Gorbals gangs but you sometimes had to think like a gang member to evade injury. Being vigilant and suspicious helped me to become a little street-wise but since fights could flare up from nowhere that alone couldn't always protect me. Luckily, my ability to run fast kept me out of the casualty ward. The most macabre experience of my life began with me sat eating chips with my pals on a wall in Elmfoot Street, near where I lived. A man and his wife came out of the chip shop and became embroiled in an argument with a pair of drunks. In seconds the drunks had knocked the man to the ground, and were smashing his head repeatedly against the wall we were sitting on, then one of the men took out what appeared to be a hatchet. We were aged about fourteen at the time and wouldn't have been able to help the man fight them off. Something was said that made them stop but it only ended up with the drunks turning on me. One of them came over to me holding out this axe and swearing profusely. I have never run as fast, or as far, in my life.

It was only when I reached Rutherglen that I thought it might be safe to turn back but even so I took a circuitous detour through Polmadie in case they were still following me. Just as I crept back into our street, this guy, covered in blood, lurched out of the shadows and brushed up against me. I almost died of fright. Thankfully it wasn't one of the drunks but their victim but it scared me witless nonetheless.

When you're not much older than a child and you witness that sort of stuff, it doesn't take too much imagination to recognise the dangers of the place you live in. It was exciting too, I'll admit. As city kids we thought ourselves as head and shoulders above the 'teuchters' – the Scots from outside Glasgow – and carried ourselves with New York-style bravado but, in reality, we were petrified a lot of the time.

I can't emphasise too much that I loved growing up in Glasgow. It was a very warm-hearted place despite the grimness of some of my experiences. It's only with the benefit of hindsight, and the income that allowed me to give my own kids every comfort, that I can appreciate now how harsh it was at times. Glasgow has changed so much since I left that some of the defining features of my childhood have disappeared.

During the sixties and seventies, I used to travel back on the sleeper from London and, on raising the compartment's shutter in the morning, the sight of all the black, soot-encrusted monuments would tell me that I was back in my home town; the thick chimney-smoke and its effect was, to me, the city's trademark. Now, I walk around and see all those newly cleaned Alexander 'Greek' Thompson and Charles Rennie Mackintosh buildings and sometimes I can't believe that they haven't just sprung up since I left. The soot must have rendered them invisible to me because I had never noticed how beautiful the city was.

It was an altogether different story almost half a century ago and back in 1956 I wasn't too disappointed to be leaving. The thought of starting my football career at the age of seventeen, utterly alone in a foreign country and 200 miles away from my family, was daunting, yet I couldn't wait to seize the opportunity that Leicester had offered me.

But my first trial for the club, on Boxing Day, didn't go that well. Although I was now playing with footballers from my own age group, I found the constant shouts for the ball confusing and a terrible distraction and I couldn't settle into the match. I was so determined to impress that I was too hyped up to relax and I had played a stinker. But the next game, on 28 December, my birthday, was much better. This time I was ready for the calls from my team mates and for the barrage of instructions from the touchline, and I gave the type of performance that had first impressed Walter McLean. Immediately after the match, Davie Halliday asked me to sign a part-time contract at seven pounds and ten shillings a week. Needless to say, it was the best birthday present I have ever been given.

3

'I'M DEFINITELY GOING TO MAKE IT'

The media likes to use labels to define people, and the convenient tag it attached to me portrays me as a contender for the sacrosanct title of 'Mr Arsenal'. It is very flattering to be remembered for my contribution at Highbury but the analogy used sometimes to describe me, that if you cut me in two like a stick of Blackpool rock then I would have the Gunners' name running through me, is far too simplistic for my taste. Having left Glasgow at the age of seventeen, and my deep affection for my home town notwithstanding, I could never claim, in the words of the pissed-up Auld Da's favourite song, that *I Belong to Glasgow.*

Indeed, my life has been a tale of three cities, and in some ways Leicester, the middle city, was the most influential in my education both as a player and, more importantly, as a man.

Although I spent the worst year of my life there when I returned to manage City in 1977, that bloody awful experience has not tainted my fondness for a place where I made many lifelong friends, met my wife, where two of my four sons were born and where I achieved my fervent ambition to become a professional footballer.

Immediately after my second trial game, Leicester offered Shawfield £400 for me, a sum which they accepted happily. These days, it doesn't sound like much but it kept the club solvent for a number of years. I followed the money back to Glasgow – to pick up some belongings and see in the New Year – before moving down to Leicester and into digs on Groby Road.

It was January 1957 and if ever I was going to succumb to homesickness and scuttle back north – as my mother had confidently predicted I would – it would have been in those first few weeks. My mother had been shocked when I accepted Leicester's offer: she had always hoped I would hold out for an approach from a Scottish team. Her belief that I wouldn't be able to stick it out in England, so far away from my family and pals, was underlined by her only stipulation when she agreed to let me sign; namely, that I should continue my painting and decorating apprenticeship and play football only part-time. The club duly sorted out a job for me with Pitcher Brothers and I began a routine of working for them five days a week, training two evenings a week and playing on Saturdays. This situation continued for the next five years; long after I had become a first-team regular and had played in my first FA Cup final.

At Groby Road I got on very well with my French landlady, Mrs Knight – though I kept out of the way of her husband, who fancied himself as middle-class, was a stuffy snob and treated me like dirt. And, fortunately for me, my new club was a Scottish enclave packed as it was with fellow countrymen: the manager, Davie Halliday; his assistant, Matt Gillies; the trainer, Alex Dowdells, and twenty-seven other Scottish players and trainees, so I didn't have to adapt too much to feel at home.

This Scottish influx was a mixed blessing for the locals: when results weren't good, the club would be derided as Leicester Thistle but, in general, they took great pride in their Caledonian contingent. Moreover, for a time during the fifties, City would run out to the skirl of bagpipes and *Scotland the Brave* until this anthem was jettisoned in favour of hunting horns to herald the 'Foxes'. One happy side effect of maturing alongside all those Scots is that my Glaswegian accent remains undiluted; I had to tame some of the Gorbals excesses, particularly the speed at which I spoke, but otherwise it is demonstrably unaffected.

My childhood memories are, literally, clouded with the industrial smoke that pervaded Glasgow throughout my youth. Likewise, my early memories of Leicester are imbued with the fog that pervaded the city throughout my first few months at the club. I remember particularly my morning cycle journey to work, alongside the canal that ran down one side of Filbert Street. There were always dozens of people there at seven o'clock in the morning, dressed in oilskins and sou'westers, fishing from the towpaths. It had struck me as odd that so many were out so early, and in the thick mist that habitually enveloped the canal in winter, until one of my team mates helpfully explained that they were inmates from the local asylum. I took this as the truth and only years later realised that they were, in fact, genuine anglers happy to fish that desolate stretch in the seemingly forlorn hope of catching something. However streetwise I thought I'd been in Glasgow, I was to remain somewhat green to the eccentric ways of the English for quite a while longer.

Cycling everywhere improved my fitness no end. I used to rampage along the canal banks on my racing bike every morning. Usually I was late for work and would ride far too fast, which was OK along the flat bits but when I crossed the bridges, which were cobbled, my high-pressure tyres would catch in a rut and unseat me. I must have fallen off at least sixty times in those five years, and I'm amazed I haven't had to have plastic hips so often did I bruise them as I flew, sprawling onto the cobble stones. I have a vivid recollection of cycling on to work with a heavily bruised arse, shifting each aching cheek in turn, on then off the saddle, in an effort to ease the throbbing torment.

All that cycling helped me to develop incredibly strong, muscled legs in a very short period of time. By the time I made my first return visit to Glasgow, in the summer of 1957, I had grown six inches in six months. The club had prescribed a daily tonic consisting of sherry, a raw egg and pepper but I doubt that rancid cocktail had much impact on what turned out to be my rapid, albeit belated, growth spurt. That was down to my age and all the training I was putting in. Football was like a burning light to me and given that I was rationed to just two training sessions a week, unlike most of the other youngsters on Leicester's books, I threw myself into it with a vigour that bordered on insanity.

I cannot describe adequately how much becoming a professional meant to me. I can say only that my desire for the professional game was palpable to the extent it was like having an ever-present, internal evangelist constantly spurring me on. I've never been as focused on anything as I was then. If the trainer demanded six laps, I would do twelve. I used to hang on late into the night just doing sprints, usually twice the number I'd been told to do. I had so much energy. I loved running myself to a standstill; dizzy with fatigue, gasping for breath, I often used to flop over a crush barrier on the old Spion Kop at Filbert Street, long after everyone else had retired to the bath. Then, having by now lost my bashfulness about bathing in front of the others, I would strip and wash, then cycle back to my digs for around half past ten, just in time for a massive dinner before bed, sleep and up again at six each morning for work. In the course of my apprenticeship I was up and down ladders all day, I cycled miles all over town as a matter of course and, twice a week, I was running my knackers off in training; small wonder I was soon to become a phenomenally wiry and athletic specimen.

Early on, however, Halliday still wasn't convinced that I was going to have the physique to make it as a professional footballer and he was keen to terminate my contract. As the manager, he trained with the first team during the day and so wasn't around in the evenings to witness how much work I was putting in. Gillies and Dowdells, on the other hand, had seen me belting around the track, skipping in the gym like a kangaroo on speed and they knew I could take care of myself in the boxing ring – still part of our fitness programme in those days. Gillies told me, later, that it was seeing me stand up in an argument as well as training like a Trojan that had convinced him I had enough bottle to merit a chance; and it was he, thankfully, who persuaded Halliday to keep me on.

In the summer I used to go training on my own. It's amazing how alert you feel – almost tingling with energy – when you're super fit and I was keen to hold onto that buzz, even in the off-season. Part of the coach's mantra in the fifties was that if you wanted respect as a professional footballer you had to be two-footed, and so, every evening after work I worked to address my over-reliance on my right foot. I took a borrowed Thompson laced ball – which was extremely heavy – down to the local park, put a football boot on my left foot and a plimsoll on my right and practised, hour after hour, kicking the ball in the long grass with my left. Catching the weight, or worse the lace, of that ball on your flimsily clad, plimsolled foot soon ensured increased use of your other foot; if you practise long enough, it can become instinctive. Perseverance was the key to improvement, and the benefits of being two-footed quickly outweighed the initial discomfort from my alternately smarting and numb right foot.

The contrast between training and playing with Shawfield Juniors and turning professional, albeit part-time, proved sharp and I had a lot to learn. At Shawfield I'd had more in common with Alf Tupper, Tough of the Track, running around in smelly old kit on shale pitches, and with my belly full of chips. At Leicester, training was more refined and – though the kind of functional coaching I enjoyed under Dave Sexton and Don Howe at Arsenal was still a pipe dream – we did an awful lot of proper conditioning work. Mostly, George Dewis took the sessions, though David Jones, Gillies and Dowdells were often present, too.

Dewis had been a centre forward with Leicester and was a bit like Andy Gray in that he much preferred to head the ball than kick it. Accordingly, every evening began with head tennis in the gym. We used to play it a lot in the narrow closes back in the Gorbals so I had something of a head start over the other trainees. Head tennis is a great teaching method; it instructs you how to develop all the variations and perfect the angles – cushioning the ball, power forehead headers from the back of the court, precise side-headers and snide little 'glancers' up by the net.

Dewis also taught me a valuable lesson when he noticed that I was always shouting for the ball in matches. 'That wee fella, he doesn't half go on,' he said, and told me that before I shouted for possession I should 'view the field'. That piece of advice encompasses so much because it asks you to assess all your options: look at which players are available, decide whether you've got time to take a first touch, and get into position on the half-turn so that you can play it in any direction without having to make too big an adjustment and open yourself up to a challenge. Thinking in such terms was a key difference from the semi-pro level; you have to take responsibility for your words as well as your actions on the field at all times. In short, viewing the field makes you think like a professional footballer, something that you can't learn if you're running around like a scalded cat.

After the head tennis, Dowdells might take charge and have us performing fifteen minutes or so of intricate skipping manoeuvres building up to the rapid crossovers that boxers use. Then we'd go outside to run double-laps of the pitch, do some sprints and, finally, we'd get the ball out. Leicester must be one of the smallest places in the UK to have three elite sports' teams – City, the county cricket team and the rugby club – and we would often find ourselves training with the cricketers in the winter. I hadn't had much experience of cricket in Glasgow, obviously, and I used to think that it must be a funny game if these guys, some with markedly d-shaped guts, could make a living as athletes.

We'd play for about forty-five minutes before going back to the gym for more physical jerks and boxing; that's when I used to stay outside and carry on running. Charlie George once said to me at Arsenal in the early seventies, when I was thirty-three, that he couldn't understand why I was still punishing myself on the track after the official session was over. It was simple. Not only did I have to get the energy totally out of my system before I felt satisfied, but I also felt that fitness gave me an edge. It provided the foundations for whatever talent I had to express itself properly.

I enjoyed everything about my early days in Leicester apart from the digs and this one problem was solved when the club moved me to Jarom Street where I became a surrogate son to the Smith family. I stayed there for a year-and-a-half and Mr and Mrs Smith and their son, John, opened their home and hearts to me. Mrs Smith couldn't have made a penny profit out of her lodger, though, as I had a colossal appetite. She used to send me off to work in the morning with a flask of soup and sixteen slices of bread and when I got home from training there would always be a plateful with an enormous Alp-sized mountain of potatoes waiting for me. I've always been a hungry Horace and the boys at Sky TV still make rude comments about the amount of food I can put away – thankfully my metabolism just seems to burn it off.

At the age of seventeen I was earning about nineteen pounds a week – seven pounds from football and twelve pounds from the painting and decorating. Given that the maximum football wage was pegged at twenty pounds, I was earning just less than the few who played the game for a living, without another job to supplement their income. However, after tax and board I had only about five pounds left and my mother insisted that I send home three pounds and ten shillings of that every week. This left me with about thirty bob a week for myself, which my mother thought was a bit indulgent and she would badger me to send home more. I don't know whether she thought it would keep me out of trouble or whether I was some sort of golden goose, but it seemed scant reward for all the hours I was putting in.

My painting and decorating apprenticeship continued in much the same way as it had in Glasgow but I had to write off one of the two years' qualification I had already done since, in England, apprentices only started training at sixteen. My foreman, Eric Sleith, was an ex-RAF sergeant-major and he treated us as if we were conscripts, in a kindly but rigorously disciplined fashion. He used to give us an allotted time for each task – twenty minutes to black a drainpipe, fifteen minutes to gloss a door – and he'd go loopy if we didn't meet his targets. I'd get thirty minutes for lunch, no more, and he'd be there, putting me back to work, even if I had to stuff chunks of bread in my mouth as I went back up the ladder. He brought me up, as he had been brought up himself, in a very strict manner and it has made me a stickler for punctuality and not messing about when there's work to be done. I always sang while I worked and Mr Sleith would say: 'Keep singing, Frank, but no ballads mind. Sing a fast song,' so that I would match my painting tempo to the song's and get finished on time.

It can be a hazardous occupation for us brothers of the brush. Once, I was painting the upstairs windows of a house in Coalville and I was burning off the old paint with my blister gun. To get access to the full sill I propped the window open but the wind blew and I incinerated the net curtains. I ripped them down, still burning, with my bare hands and threw them twenty feet down onto the ground. My hands were charred like two pork chops on a barbecue but I was basking in the relief of not setting the house on fire . . . until I noticed that the flaming curtains had landed on top of my acetylene tank. I slid down that ladder six rungs at a time and extinguished the blaze by beating it with my smouldering coat. If I had dallied for a few seconds more I would have been blown to bits.

The company I worked for had the maintenance contract for Filbert Street. My job was to paint the crush barriers, the steel girders in the stands and the floodlight pylons. One afternoon, a colleague and I were 120 feet up a pylon, sitting on our rope cradle, happily painting away, when the knot I'd secured us with gave way and we went hurtling towards the ground. My mate, thank God, was strong enough to grip the rope even though it tore into his hands, and he managed to stop our fall and re-tie our harness with a non-slip knot thirty feet from death. I could hardly complain when he turned the air blue and semi-paralysed my eardrums as we swung precariously above the old Popular Side of the ground.

From then on I was always strapped securely, high in the heavens above Filbert Street – a good platform from which to josh the professionals training on the pitch below. As they were doing their laps I provided a commentary and encouraged Alex Dowdells to 'give the lazy sods more work to do. I'm sweating more than them up here.' I'd get all sorts of interesting hand gestures in response. My best trick, as they lapped the pitch in their immaculate royal blue shirts, was to splash paint on them. It would take about five seconds to drop from my perch and if I timed it right, just as they were reaching my corner, I could flick my brush, hit them and be looking away innocently by the time they looked up. One of the players, Joe Baillie, thought he'd teach this comedian a lesson and said he'd get me, but as soon as I came down I charged him, brush in hand, chased him into the dressing room and painted his bare chest before he could do anything about it. I reckon he thought I must have been a maniac; not a bad reputation to have if you're keen to avoid a deserved smack.

I know it sounds a bit glib to say that the established professionals already at Leicester were from another era, but they were markedly different in terms of attitude – and even shape – to the footballers who followed ten years later. With their magnificently out of proportion upper bodies, the majority of older players had more in common with Mr Incredible or Desperate Dan than with the relatively lean and scrawny tyros that dominated the game from the mid sixties onwards.

Arthur Rowley was the undisputed star of the team and scored a frankly ridiculous 265 goals in 321 appearances in the eight years he was at Leicester. He was huge and would often come back to pre-season training a couple of stones overweight only to punish himself by wearing three heavy polo-neck sweaters in training to help sweat off his excess lard in the summer heat.

I don't think I've ever seen a player with Rowley's power. He was built like a battleship with a left foot like Ferenc Puskas's. He would often shoot from thirty-five yards, and used to strike the ball with such violence that it seemed to gain momentum as it sped towards the back of the net. On several occasions he struck the ball with so much ferocity that when it hit the back of the goal the iron stays fixing the net to the pitch were uprooted.

Jack Froggatt, the centre half, was another who would appear ponderous to the modern eye but he was a formidable player.

He always had his sleeves rolled up and the top of his shorts rolled down to show off his gleaming, Vaselined muscles. He had the dimensions of Bluto from *Popeye* but was a great footballer, a magnificent passer of the ball, and had won back-to-back championships with Portsmouth in 1949 and 1950. Together with Derek Hogg – a tremendous winger who used to 'tear the arses' off full backs and 'thwack' in early crosses for the centre forward, Rowley – Johnny Morris and Froggatt were the stand-out players of the Leicester side that I started to watch as a trainee.

Back in Glasgow, I had been too busy playing to see many games, though I would go along to Clyde or Celtic Park occasionally if I could afford it. The experience of watching football at Filbert Street was certainly more palatable than in the Jungle at Parkhead where I used to go to see my heroes, Bobby Evans and Bertie Peacock. If you got there early enough you could get so close to the pitch that you could actually smell the liniment smeared on the players' thighs but you had to be very careful to avoid the torrents of piss that would cascade down the terraces and saturate your shoes, leaving its distinctive and unshiftable aroma with you for weeks.

Those four Englishmen – Hogg, Rowley, Morris and Froggatt – made a strong impression on me with their talents on the field but it was the Scots, with their patter, who made me feel that Glasgow was never far away. As trainees we looked up to the full-time professionals and would always defer to them if they turned up at the snooker hall and we were monopolising a table; we would stack our cues, stand aside and let them play. Nonetheless, they would always make me feel welcome in their company. Totally unpretentious, they ignored the age gap as though it was obvious to them that we were all the same, just working men doing our job.

Big Ian MacFarlane was noisy and had a great guffaw of a laugh that used to get a regular airing. He'd come to our house in Jarom Street and pat our Boxer, Brandy, with his shovel-like hands and be so loud and jovial that the poor dog's ears were permanently pricked. John Ogilvie, 'Big Ogie', was the king of the dressing room or, more accurately, its court jester. He had more stories than Rudyard Kipling. A fantastic raconteur, he was like a character out of *Guys and Dolls* as he kept all of us enthralled with his tales. You could always hear Ogie before you saw him and he'd have us in fits of laughter as he recounted the latest gossip, fixed up parties to take us to or when he wagged a sardonic tongue over the antics of our Scottish goalkeeper, Johnny Anderson, who was obsessed with cowboys.

It must have been a generational craze for post-war Scots because I, too, have always loved Westerns, and long before John Wayne purloined my name for his comedy turn with Maureen O'Hara in *McLintock*. McLintock's a good name for a cowboy, or a Chicago cop; I've always thought it would suit a snub-nosed character in a black and white film but it lost some of its hard-boiled grandeur and sounded a bit daft when John Wayne kept pronouncing it 'McLinnerk'.

Anyway, if I dabbled in Westerns, Anderson was a nut for them. He would try to make us laugh by painting on a moustache with soft soap and sticking two lengths of cotton wool down his legs as improvised chaps. He would parade around the dressing room naked – save for his props – a cigarette dangling from one corner of his mouth, and draw his imaginary six-shooter. I am afraid dressing room humour doesn't translate all that well. It can sound rather innocent in retrospect, but it was hilarious to us.

Footballers, especially the Scots it seemed, just got so much pleasure out of making you laugh. They'd be impersonating gangsters and doing affected walks and I, as a wide-eyed seventeen-year-old, would not be excluded from all the banter. All workplaces, I suppose, have their comedians and their long running in-jokes that mean little to outsiders, but it was so much fun to be part of that gang of down-to-earth people who revelled in the privilege of being lucky enough to be footballers. They wanted to take as much enjoyment as possible out of their careers before the inevitable proper job ended their extended adolescence.

At Leicester City, I went straight into the youth team and was made captain at the beginning of my first full season there. We tended to play the cream of local amateur teams – like Anstey Nomads – in the Leicester leagues. Some of the players alongside me had impressive pedigrees as schoolboy internationals – Brian Wright, David Cartlidge, Oliver Beeby and Roy Thomas among them – but none of them made much impact as professionals at Leicester.

Why some lads shine at the age of fifteen but never progress is an old football conundrum – but it's not that difficult to work out why it happens. Of course, some of it can be put down to dedication, or rather the lack of it, at such an exciting time of life. Largely, however, it's to do with the natural erosion of the physical advantage that allows some kids to prosper earlier in their development. By the time they've reached eighteen and had proper training for a year or two, the distinction in size and fitness between most trainees is all but obliterated. I was just five feet and two inches tall when I signed for Leicester and the runt of my age group by an embarrassing margin. But by the following Christmas

I had grown to five feet ten inches – leapfrogging most of my contemporaries in the youth team – and was playing for the reserves.

In fact, my last season as a fully fledged reserve was capped when we won the Football Combination title by beating Spurs 2-1 at Tottenham. Our team had ten Scots in it that day and we all had a pop at the only English lad in the team for ruining what could have been a perfect day for Scotland.

At the beginning of that 1958-59 campaign, David Halliday had resigned as manager and been replaced, initially as care-taker, by Matt Gillies. He had captained Bolton Wanderers just after the war and joined the Leicester coaching staff in 1956 at the age of thirty-five. A lot of us had had quite rough upbringings; we were toe-rags to a certain extent. Gillies, though, was an educated, Edinburgh-born man and spoke with a forceful elegance that commanded respect. We held him in esteem because he behaved like a gentleman but he was as tough as they come. His charm, intelligence and tenacity trans-formed Leicester City from an archetypal yo-yo club into a consistent contender for domestic trophies throughout his ten-year reign. He was the perfect guy to have as a mentor and his constant encouragement, from the day I got there, made a significant contribution to my burgeoning confidence.

He was such a shrewd man and had the enviable ability to dish out a reprimand without being too heavy handed about it. No one ever resented Matt Gillies. It's quite common when you leave a football club to chat with an ex-colleague who will, belatedly, reveal his uncensored thoughts about a manager. 'Oh, do you remember what that old bastard had us doing?' Or, 'What a twat, he was.' These conversations occur quite regu-larly but, in the forty years since I left Leicester, I have never heard anyone say anything derogatory about Gillies.

When I was still in the reserves I got involved in a Saturday night fight outside the Palais in Leicester. My friend, Jimmy Mee, had taken a beating from some big lump for dancing with his girlfriend. Once we were outside, I approached the 'big lump' and asked him why he'd thumped my pal. He said it was a case of mistaken identity and pointed over to the supposed perpetrator but as I turned to look, he sucker-punched me. Within seconds his mate had joined him and it turned into a free-for-all. I waded in, fists flailing, pinned the guy who had belted me up against a hot-dog stall and hammered him. The stall went flying and I remember seeing my assailant lying in the gutter surrounded by sausages and onions while the vendor scrabbled around trying to pick them up. There was a policeman only a few yards away but he let me get on with it and didn't say anything even once the guys had scarpered. He'd seen everything and must have thought they had deserved it.

On the following Tuesday night at training, I was shadow boxing in the gym with David Cartlidge. I was easily slipping his punches, bobbing around and clipping him because his guard was open. Matt Gillies came over and said to David: 'Ach, you'll never beat the Glasgow boy. He'll turn you over like a hot-dog stand.' He had such a good way of letting you know that he knew, keeping you on tenterhooks but without any nastiness.

When we got out of the ring, he pulled me into a corner of the gym and said: 'I don't want to hear of you fighting in the street again, but I am glad you stood up and looked after your friend.' He had that uncanny knack of marking my card in the most appropriate fashion for my character and it made me hyper-sensitive to the fear of letting him down.

His astuteness was very similar to Lawrie McMenemy's and they shared a gift for being endearing to footballers without being perceived as soft. Years after that fight, my great friend, Davie Gibson, and I decided to play golf one Thursday afternoon, even though we were supposed to be resting up for Saturday's trip to Anfield; this was about as big a break of the disciplinary code as we ever made. After some persuasion Davie agreed to have a quick nine holes. I had assured him that there was no chance of us getting caught if we went to a course a few miles away, so we drove over to Rothley Park.

We had played the first four holes when Davie went as white as a sheet and said: 'Guess who's playing the hole behind us?' It was Matt Gillies. We were shitting ourselves and hid in some bushes for at least forty-five minutes – giggling hysterically, like children frightened of being caught, bollocked and fined – until he'd played through and gone a few holes past. We then finished our nine holes and felt very relieved at our luck. On Saturday we beat Liverpool 2-0 in a great game and I have, immodestly, to admit that I played exceptionally well, and Davie scored one of the goals. The two of us were sitting together in the dressing room, just blathering away over a cup of tea, when the manager came in and knelt between us. He put a hand on one each of our knees and said: 'You two can play a game of golf whenever you like so long as you beat Liverpool 2-0.' He'd known all along. He didn't embarrass us on the golf course and hadn't mentioned it to wind us up before the game. It gave us a lovely chuckle, and a nice warm feeling towards him as well. He'd let it go. I suppose he might have gone potty if we had lost but he knew just how to handle us.

Gillies had another side to him, too, but, apart from his exasperation with Gordon Banks and me when wage controls were abolished, he used it on me only once – and that had nothing to do with football. It was New Year's Eve 1958 and Pitcher Brothers had refused my request for an extended Christmas break so that I could celebrate Hogmanay in Glasgow with my pals. I had returned to Leicester after Christmas and on 31 December I was crouched in the pouring rain wearily painting park railings in the city centre. I was freezing, and seething about missing my first Hogmanay at home, and I just thought: 'Stuff this.' I downed tools, stuck my brush in the pot, ran back to my digs in my painting overalls, got changed and caught the afternoon train to Glasgow.

I knew I was in trouble when I returned to my lodgings and found a note from Matt Gillies asking me to report to him immediately. He suspended me from football for two weeks and fined me a fortnight's wages. I was fuming but he just said: 'It's your own fault, son. You will have to put up with it.' He knew me well. The suspension was worse than the fine. And he smoothed the way with Pitcher Brothers; I apologised and they took me back.

While we were winning the reserves' league, the first team had struggled throughout Matt Gillies's first truncated season in charge. In fact, as late as Easter that year they'd been marooned in twenty-first place but had fought their way out of trouble by winning four and drawing three of their last nine games. It must have been that summer when I auto-matically came out with a statement that shocked me with its vehement confidence.

We were queuing up to go into the swimming baths when Alan Gammie, a colleague in the reserves, said to me: 'I am worried about the future. You do realise that only one in a hundred apprentices ever make the grade.' Without thinking

I just came out with: 'No fear. I'm definitely going to make it.' It sounds arrogant but it wasn't meant to be. It was a spontaneous declaration of something I'd felt for months. As a player, I was getting better all the time and was holding my own in the reserves where other youth-team graduates had struggled. I was sure that with Halliday gone and my champion, Gillies, running the club, it could only be a matter of time before my development was recognised with a first-team berth.

It came a bit quicker than even I had anticipated. Leicester had begun the 1959-60 season with our usual patchy start, winning two of the opening seven games. In early September, aged nineteen, I was picked for the team for the eighth game. It was a Monday trip to Blackpool and Gillies had to negotiate with my employers to give me the day off. On the morning train to the seaside, Ian MacFarlane, an experienced pro and a stalwart of our successful reserve team, said to me: 'We think you're going to be a good player, Frank. But it's too early for you. You're not ready yet.' I shrugged non-committally while thinking, but not in a malicious way, 'I'll fucking show you who's ready.'

I didn't feel nervous, though I did have diarrhoea – perhaps a sign of nerves after all – but I didn't have that horrible, stomach-jangling feeling of apprehension. I was just in the bog a lot. Blackpool had quite a few famous players – Bill Perry, Harry Johnston, Jackie Mudie, Jimmy Armfield and Stan Matthews – and were still a comfortably established mid-table side.

I got into my stride quickly and after fifteen minutes Tony Knapp, our centre half, who had overheard MacFarlane's comment to me, shouted: 'I don't know about "not ready". You'll play for Scotland, son, before the season's out, never mind Leicester City.' We took a 3-1 lead and were set for our first away win of the season when Blackpool went down to ten men through injury. It completely threw us and we struggled to cope with their new formation. Their inside left dropped back and I found myself strolling around the right-half position with no one to mark. We weren't tactically aware enough to adapt. Our rhythm just went, Matthews started to turn it on and Blackpool equalised with minutes to spare. It was a disappointing result but I felt I had done justice to Matt Gillies's faith in me.

He must have thought so, too; he put his arm around me in the dressing room and told the local press that picking me had not been a gamble. Because of the demands of my job I hadn't been in the pre-season squad photograph and was, therefore, unknown to the Leicester public at large. Even though I'd been at the club for two-and-a-half years, the *Mercury* played on this asking: 'Where did this McLintock prodigy come from?' After the next five games when, according to the newspapers, I gave two 'man-of-the-match performances' and was 'going from strength to strength', they stopped asking.

In the seventh game of my debut run in the team disaster struck, ironically enough, against Arsenal. I went to tackle Jackie Henderson, over-reached with my right leg and found that I couldn't get up again. Alex Dowdells, the physio, strapped up my knee and I hobbled about at outside right as a nuisance value for a further twenty minutes or so and I was such a naïve bugger that I kept shouting for the ball, which was the last thing I needed at the time. I could run in a straight line but every time I tried to change direction my leg gave way. They finally persuaded me to come off when I collapsed for the third time.

Shortly after I had been taken to the dressing room, the

directors came to see me and were all looking very gloomy. I was in some pain but their expressions bothered me more. They obviously felt that they had a blossoming new star in the team and he was lying there crocked after half-a-dozen games. The salutary lesson to all of us at Leicester had been provided by the misfortune of Gordon Fincham. A player who's all but forgotten now, but in the mid fifties Fincham's exceptional qualities at centre half had generated talk of how he would dominate the international scene for years to come. He was the club's golden boy, the finest prospect City had groomed since the war. He was six feet four inches tall and he looked a bit like Rock Hudson, he was brilliant in the air, a class act with the ball at his feet and, it was said, would be better than Neil Franklin and Billy Wright combined. And then came his injury. He eventually recovered to play for Plymouth, but his livid surgical scar was a constant reminder to us all of the severity of any knee operation.

Almost at once it had been decided that I had either one of the two worst injuries; a ruptured cruciate ligament or extensive cartilage damage. The doctor performed the test by grabbing my heel and checking for abnormal movement in my knee. There was enough evidence for him, after a brief consultation with the directors (but none with me), to propose immediate surgery. The first drastic thought that occurred to me was 'knee surgery equals career over'. Before keyhole surgery, any procedure that involved cutting into your knee spelt danger to a footballer. I was petrified but Alex Dowdells had the guts to save me.

As a lowly employee it would have been difficult to speak up in front of all these important-looking people in their tweed suits and homburg hats. Dowdells chose to tackle the problem in a roundabout way, creeping up to my side while the directors and doctors were distracted in conference and whispering: 'Ask for a second opinion.' When I followed his advice, the directors looked at me as though I'd gone mad and the club doctor spluttered apoplectically. Dowdells, however, knew that one Professor McLeary – knee-specialist and Leicester fan – was sitting up in the stands. He was summoned and, after prodding and stretching my knee for a few seconds, announced that he did not agree with the earlier diagnosis; neither my cartilage nor my cruciate were traumatised. He thought that six weeks of immobility with my whole leg encased in plaster should settle the strain I had inflicted on my medial ligaments. I was so relieved I would have hopped for joy on my other leg but by then the pain, which presumably had been held in abeyance by the shock, had started to kick in.

I was actually out for sixteen weeks in total. When they took off the plaster there was still some lateral movement in my knee and I spent the next ten weeks gradually building up the strength in my thigh, to cope with the discomfort and regain confidence in its stability. During this time out, I went back to visit my parents in Glasgow and met Alex Ferguson for the first time, at the Plaza in Eglinton Toll. We were just two young professionals, fanatical about football, and we spent the whole night talking about the game. That evening made a huge impression on me and we still talk about it more than forty years later.

It was great to have a few weeks to convalesce at home because my mother treated me like the original blue-eyed boy. She was obviously worried for me and was very solicitous – I'd wake up in the morning and there'd be a glass of boiled water waiting for me, and I would gorge on orange juice, ham and eggs. My poor sister Jean was never indulged in that way and I'm so pleased that she's got a new lease of life since my mother died, and sorry that I was blind for so long to the way she had to bear the brunt of my mother's old-fashioned expectations of her.

My return to the first team came in late February 1960. I scored my first goal that day in a 3-1 victory over Manchester United at Filbert Street. Controversially, I kept my place for our FA Cup quarter-final against Wolves the following week. Ian White, who had been signed from Celtic in 1958 and was one of the ten Scots in our reserve triumph, had taken over from me in the team and done very well. There was a big outcry when I retained my place for that cup tie; White was thought to be the steadier player but Gillies evidently thought that my box-to-box power was a bigger asset. It didn't pay off for the manager, but it turned out to be a cracking game in front of our biggest attendance for a couple of years. We held the eventual winners of the competition at 1-1 with minutes to go before the eternally unlucky Len Chalmers deflected a cross past Gordon Banks for Wolves to win.

My leg felt fine during that game but I had found it hard to get back into the swing of things. I was slightly off the pace and my timing had gone to cock. It was only when the new season started that I felt as good as I had before the injury. And it was only then that I established myself as a regular in the first team, belatedly proving Tony Knapp's prediction of international honours to be accurate whilst poor Len Chalmers began to wonder whether the FA Cup and he were jinxed.

4

BICYCLE CLIPS, SHARP SUITS AND WEMBLEY

As Leicester City entered the sixties, by far the club's most successful decade to date, we felt very optimistic about our prospects for silverware. The league was far more open than it eventually became and no team, apart from Manchester United and, fleetingly, Tottenham, had the dubious prestige of being thought more fashionable than any of the others.

International players were sprinkled throughout the First Division and clubs like Burnley, Sheffield Wednesday, Preston North End and, indeed, ourselves were plausible contenders for honours. The only benefit of the maximum wage from a player's point of view was its levelling effect on the aspirations of all clubs. No one club could ever get overblown since they all, at least officially, paid the same wages and, without freedom of contract, players would not be sold provided the clubs that held their registrations were solvent enough not to cash in. The downside of the latter, for managers, was that it was very difficult to strengthen a team through the transfer market and, unless they had a prodigious nursery system in place, clubs could quickly stagnate. At Leicester, thankfully, we were on the upward curve of our team's development.

Earlier that year I had moved into new digs on Wyngate Drive with two other young professionals, Jackie Lornie from Aberdeen and Davie Agnew from Kilwinning in Ayrshire. We quickly became inseparable. The club had changed its policy with regard to players' lodgings and, instead of having us all spread around the city, had bought some houses. Mrs Cartwright and her husband were installed in the house on Wyngate Drive to look after us. She had actually been working in the Cravenhurst Hotel on the day my family had arrived in the city in 1956 so our bonds were strong. She was like Mrs Smith but even more so.

Mrs Cartwright worked ridiculously hard for us; she got up regularly at six o'clock in the morning to make sure we had a proper breakfast before work, gave us a massive dinner every night and encouraged us to keep in touch with our families, insisting we wrote home at least once a week. God only knows what brought her together with her second husband, whom she met while working at the hotel. They couldn't have been more contrasting characters – she loved life and was full of warmth and energy while he was a remote and fussy, sour-faced old so-and-so.

Jackie and Davie were trade apprentices too; one a joiner, the other an electrician. We could have gone into business together. We started to meet girls, go dancing and go out to pubs on a Saturday night. We were all sports mad and would get the bus over to Nottingham to watch Forest or County if they had a midweek game, or we might play a bit of golf, or go to the boxing which had a fanatical following in the city. The three of us bought a car together – a dilapidated 1937 Rover for thirty-five pounds – but it kept conking out in embarrassing places. Any eagle-eyed City fan out and about on a Saturday night could often see two furious professionals pushing, one steering, this old jalopy away from Leicester's Clock Tower.

I never had much luck with cars in the early days. That Rover had an infuriating semaphore indicator that was designed to lift itself out of the wing to signal. It lifted all right but it wouldn't go back in or, much worse, it would drop right off. Trying to act cool when giving a lift to a girl is a futile exercise if every time you indicate right you have to stop to cram the errant part back in its slot.

Later, George Meek, a winger we had signed from Leeds United, persuaded me that a friend of his in Yorkshire would do me a bargain on a car. So Jackie and I drove up to Leeds and I bought this beautiful black Wolseley that was like a majestic old police car. About halfway back down the road to Leicester, Jackie asked to drive – neither of us had ever driven a nice car before so we were excited. He took the wheel and I went to sleep in the back. The next thing I knew I was upside down resting on my head with my legs upright. Jackie had hit a kerb and flipped the car onto its roof. Some pedestrians had to smash the windows to drag us out. I had saved up for months to buy that car and it had been written off in less than three hours. No wonder then that until 1980 my motor insurance still stipulated: 'Exceptions to the above: Mr J Lornie is excluded from this policy and prohibited from driving Mr F McLintock's vehicle.'

The chap in Leeds was quite a crook and I was dumb enough to continue to patronise his establishment. The last car I bought there was a Sunbeam Rapier convertible. Rashly, I bought it at night and when I got up the following morning was shocked to see that it was a ropy old rust bucket; it died when I accidentally reversed it into a grass bank, drove off and left the exhaust embedded in the soil.

My misfortunes with cars aside, life could not have been better. City had lived pretty dangerously in the First Division in the three years since promotion in 1957, toiling arduously to maintain our top flight status. But in 1960–61 season our floundering ended and we began to make headway. This was largely due to three factors: the growing maturity of some of our young players who had been elevated from the reserves – Richie Norman, Ian King and myself; the full-time return of a couple of national service recruits, Howard Riley and Colin Appleton, and two judicious Gillies signings, Albert Cheesebrough and Gordon Banks.

The introduction of Bert Johnson as first-team coach was also pivotal to our improvement. He was a lovely guy, full of encouragement and he brought greater tactical awareness to the team than we had enjoyed hitherto. The relationship between him and Matt Gillies was ideal – they complemented each other so well, Johnson was very approachable while Gillies liked to keep his distance. Their real strengths, however, lay not in tactical or strategic coaching but in getting a fairly smart group of players together and keeping everything else pretty simple.

Of course we used to practise set-pieces quite a bit but we didn't endlessly discuss formations or run through ingenious new routines. The art of management that Gillies perfected was of its time in British football, as everyone essentially still played the same system. Back then, being shrewd enough to spot and recruit a group of players who understood each other was the most impressive skill a manager could display. Getting them to play in a coherent way was important, too, but assembling a cohesive team was rather more than half the job.

Throughout the late fifties and early sixties most teams still played the WM formation with only minor variations. It was set in tablets of stone, despite the humiliating experiences of England's twin thrashings by Hungary. Remember, too, that players tended to be typecast for the position they played according to sheer size alone which meant that football could, at times, seem a simple battle between two teams on a level playing field and devoid of anything as suspiciously un-British or ungentlemanly as tactical skulduggery. There was so much space on the pitch that there were bound to be plenty of goals. Indeed, in my five full league seasons in the first team we scored 365 goals and only won or lost 1-0 on a handful of occasions each season.

The easiest way to un-pick the WM formation was for us wing halves to hit plenty of cross-field passes. If the ball was on our right wing, their left back would be out to deal with it on the touchline, and his colleague at right back would edge in towards his centre half. If our right winger could play the ball back to me in this position – instead of trying to thread it through for our inside right – it was far more productive for me to hit a quick forty-yard pass out to the left wing. The winger would then have more space to run into with their right back infield and on the back foot.

That's why so many goals were scored because with only three defenders it's a difficult tactic to stymie. If you can get the ball to the feet of your winger with fifteen or twenty yards to run at a full back (who had been covering the centre) he could create plenty of chances. Space means goals in football and that's why the fifties was dominated by plenty of 4-3 results. Yes, teams were more attack-minded but it was also to do with the defensive frailties inherent in the system. Certain games became formulaic as each team tried to exploit the oppositions' full backs. The addition of a fourth defender by Brazil in the 1958 World Cup final – and its eventual adoption in league football by the mid sixties – eventually put a stop to the goal fests.

Our greatest asset in those free-scoring years was our one truly world-class player – Gordon Banks. Though he famously looked like the now-forgotten French actor Fernandel, we all called him 'Sugar'. Gordon's party-piece was his impression of Freddie Frinton in that sketch *Dinner for One*, which, bizarrely, is still played on German television every New Year's Eve. Banksie took off the drunken butler played by the end-of-the-pier comic to a tee – right down to the broken cigarette stuck out of the corner of his mouth. He would top this off by slurring his way through the butler's song: 'Sugar in the morning, sugar in the evening, sugar at suppertime . . .' To this day whenever anyone mentions Gordon to me, I smile, thinking of him doing his little routine.

As a goalkeeper Banks was simply magnificent; not just the best I ever played with but the best I've ever seen. His intelligence really shone through in his positioning. It amuses me when people say about a goalkeeper: 'He's a good shot-stopper.' They're all bloody good shot-stoppers. That's their job. What separates the great from the adequate is their judgement, and Gordon's was unparalleled. Bob Wilson had persistence and will power; a good mixture of craft and graft. He was so dogged he flogged himself until he became a top-class keeper but Gordon was even better.

In the early sixties Gordon, Davie Gibson and I used to go down to Filbert Street every Sunday morning for an impromptu training session. Even though we'd run ourselves ragged the previous day, we three *amigos* had an arrangement with the ground staff to open up and let us in. We were that fanatical about football.

If Gordon was a masochist for training, Davie and I were happy to play the role of Sunday-morning sadists. We'd have the run of a wonderful stadium to ourselves for a few hours – an enormous privilege – and would pepper him with shots and crosses. He was understated and, it's strange to say given the regard he is held in, remains underrated. Goalkeepers as a breed were enormously undervalued, I think, until Cloughie signed Peter Shilton and proved the worth of having an outstanding goalie by saving Forest fifteen points a season in their glory years.

Gordon was unlucky that he never got to a big club that could regularly show him off on the European stage but that was symptomatic of the times. In transfers even the best went for peanuts, as most managers thought that the difference between having an exceptional keeper as opposed to a reliable one was negligible. Fortunes would be spent on forwards of dubious worth to the team but even the best goalkeeper in the world commanded the absurdly modest fee of £50,000 when Matt Gillies sold him just a year after England's World Cup win.

With 'Sugar' in goal we shouldn't really have shipped as many goals as we did but, as I've said, everything was more free-wheeling then. Like most of our rivals, City were set up to be a dynamic, attacking team and that left Gordon rather exposed at times. At the start of the 1960-61 season I was still recovering from the knee injury that – after my brief reappearance at the back end of the previous season – had left me bereft of my usual verve. I was out of the team until the beginning of September and I think we had shipped ten goals in three games by the time I made my comeback. Our revival was not solely down to me as Howard Riley, Ian King and Ken Leek were all introduced at roughly the same time, but something did begin to click in the autumn.

If we were still conceding far too many goals this was at least mitigated by the ease with which we were able to outscore opposing teams. I don't want to claim that football was unsophisticated back then but it *was*, demonstrably, less sophisticated. In some ways the clichéd view of the game in the late fifties and early sixties – that it was unpretentious and dominated by the 'it's not important how many you let in as long as you score more than them' ethos – misrepresents the attitude of players and staff who remained extremely concerned about defensive weaknesses inherent in the WM system. Nevertheless, it is an efficient way of describing the essential simplicity – and I mean simplicity in a good way – of how we felt when we were actually out there, playing in a game. It encouraged us not to brood too much on mistakes and always to play with our heads held up.

Whenever I'm asked about that season, it's always about our FA Cup run. However, our league form was more than decent and our sixth-placed finish was the club's highest since the late-twenties. The two inside forwards, Cheesey and Jimmy Walsh, and the centre forward, Ken Leek, scored fifty goals between them and we had some great results: we massacred Manchester United 6-0 at Filbert Street, we beat Arsenal home and away and we scored five against both West Ham and Newcastle. Our most notable performance, however, came against a team that had controlled the season and were eventually to make history at our expense.

In early February we went to White Hart Lane and scored three times to hand Spurs their first home defeat of a double-winning season. Colin Appleton and I played brilliantly in tandem that day; he hung back at left half for the majority of the game while I foraged forward a lot and set up Jimmy Walsh through the inside-right channel to score two of our goals. Ken Leek, against whom Tottenham's centre half, Maurice Norman, openly admitted his discomfort in playing, got our third.

Hammering Manchester United just ten days previously had been our best result to date but that game in North London against Blanchflower, Mackay, White and the other eight immortals boosted our profile no end. From then on we were seen as credible contenders and consequently expectations, both from our fans and ourselves, began to soar.

Our inconsistency in the league and Tottenham's opening sally that season – when they won their first eleven matches – meant we were never going to catch them in that competition; they eventually finished as champions by an eight-point margin over Sheffield Wednesday and clear of us by twenty-one points. The FA Cup, however, was a different story. It was one of the most ridiculously prolonged campaigns I've ever played in. Normally we would have had five games to progress from the third round to Wembley. That year we played nine in total, with replays in the fifth and sixth rounds and two replays in the semis.

The first of these epic ties was against Birmingham City and I got the worst concussion I've ever experienced. I went up to head the ball and was clipped flush on the side of the head by Jimmy Singer. We were both unconscious for over a minute and, while he took the sensible precaution of going off, I rashly insisted on staying put. Looking back, I think I expected cartoon-esque side effects – like seeing stars or tweeting birds – but the effect was even more disorientating than that. It was my hearing that was most affected, every ten seconds or so it just cut out so I'd be deaf for a few seconds and then the sound of the crowd would build up to a frightening crescendo – a sensation which persisted for the rest of that drawn match. It wasn't until the following morning, when I was sent home from training with pupils dilated up to the size of saucers, that I understood how seriously bashed up I had been.

I still played the replay on the Wednesday after only two days' bed rest. Now, I shudder to think what would have happened if I'd taken another blow to the head so soon after the first, but at the time it seemed entirely normal to volunteer to play – and just as normal for the medical staff to allow it. Two fine goals from Ken Leek sealed the game for us in front of a home crowd of almost 42,000, by far the biggest at Filbert Street for years. That the attendance figure was up by an astonishing 14,000 (fifty per cent) from the previous round was a sure sign of the impact, at least in the cup, that we were starting to make in the city.

We beat Barnsley in the quarter-finals in a Wednesday afternoon replay at Oakwell, remarkable largely, if I remember correctly, for the huge crowd of miners that were at the game, some still with the discernible signs of coal dust from the early shift on their faces. Like the first tie it was a pretty dour match and we struggled to show the two-division difference in class between us since they never let us settle. Ken Leek again won the tie for us, in extra time, to set up a return trip to Yorkshire to play Sheffield United at Elland Road in the semi-final.

The first two games, both 0–0 draws in Leeds and Nottingham, were very tedious to play in. They must have been excruciating to watch as both sides nervously neutralised the other in gruelling displays that featured almost no skilful play whatsoever. By the third game at St Andrews, we knew each other's players and tactics so well that it was surprising we didn't just bore each other to death. In fact, at long last, a game of football did break out, but it wasn't one for the annals. Indeed, both sides missed penalties but we got the upper hand through Jimmy Walsh – and kept it, thanks to Ken Leek – to finish 2–0 victors after five hours of the most ball-achingly dull football I've ever played. But we didn't give a monkey's for the lack of entertainment. We were in the FA Cup final.

My first experience of Wembley was, I think, unique. I actually worked the Friday morning shift white-washing a cellar in Leicester before cycling back to my digs, showering and putting on my Italian suit. I was very dress-conscious in those days, insisting on well-tailored jackets with thin lapels and I always demanded narrow pants. Suitably attired in my charcoal suit, white Van Heusen shirt with its crisp, high-cut collar and a dark, slim tie, I got back on the saddle and headed to Filbert Street where I parked my bike in the garage and jumped on the bus which deposited us four hours later on Park Lane.

We stayed that night at the Dorchester and got the thrill of our lives when we spotted Richard Burton and Elizabeth Taylor in the foyer. They were very kind and wished us good luck for the match. Elizabeth Taylor looked absolutely stunning, and she seemed to be staring at me with an amused look on her face; could it be possible, I wondered, that the most desirable woman in the world had taken a shine to the Gorbals kid? I thought I looked pretty sharp but this was a really unexpected development. All became clear when she came over to me, as my heart leapt through the roof of my mouth, and whispered seductively into my ear: 'You've still got your bicycle clips on.'

The match itself was a similar example of dashed hopes. We were hobbled before we got there by Matt Gillies's decision to drop Ken Leek, who had scored twenty-five times for us that season including goals in every round of the Cup. Gillies announced it at the Thursday training session when Ken was called over to see the manager on the touchline; Ken returned to the group with a face as pale as a white pudding supper. They thought he was kidding them on when he said he'd been dropped but his tears quickly convinced everyone that he was telling the truth. When I heard, I was just as shocked. It was a very strange feeling to have such a blow to team morale when training that week had been characterised by a palpably euphoric spirit.

Why the manager chose to do it has long been shrouded in mystery. I've heard countless rumours, mostly slanderous, but none dafter than the official explanation; that Ken's replacement by twenty-year-old Hugh McIlmoyle was a choice made on form alone. It made no sense to me. Of course, Hugh was a good enough player and had shown significant promise, but you don't stick a lad with seven career first-team appearances into an FA Cup final against the league champions unless you can't help it. Moreover, McIlmoyle was more in the Teddy Sheringham mould than an out-and-out centre forward while

Leek, more suited to the spearhead role, had terrorised Maurice Norman in our previous meeting with Spurs.

Gillies never elaborated beyond his pat response, which failed to quash the speculation. When I became manager of Leicester I tried to look at the board minutes dealing with the issue but found them to have been destroyed, so we'll probably never know whether it was a case of a broken mid-week curfew – as some of my former colleagues maintain – or something else. All I can say is that it has always seemed strange to me because needlessly handicapping his team was anathema to Matt Gillies's professional conduct, while being so cruelly insensitive was wholly uncharacteristic of his calibre as a man.

Sympathy for Ken Leek aside, however, I was determined to make the most of the day at Wembley and had arranged tickets and transport for my parents, sister and brother-in-law, Andy Henderson. It was marvellous to have them at the game but it added to the pressure, because without any television exposure for football, it was almost the first time they had seen me play. It made me so desperate to do well and make them proud of me, for the simple but foolish reason that they might not believe that I was any good unless they actually saw the evidence themselves.

The weeks building up to the game had the distinctive aroma of one of those pompous but charming newsreels from the late-forties. The whole city got behind us; shops were decked out with blue and white balloons and bunting, banners slung around the city read 'Good luck, Foxes' and average towns-people – not just regular Filbert Street attendees – sported scarves and rosettes during cup final week itself.

It's so easy to be blasé about the cup now, and I recognise that modern fans don't like old farts banging on about how important the competition used to be, but you'll have to forgive me here. It was an enormous event for the players and people of Leicester and dominated the life of the city for weeks before the game. We almost felt like the army in that Peter Sellers film *The Mouse that Roared*; like a tiny expeditionary force representing a small city against a monolithic power.

We got to Wembley just after noon on Saturday morning and as our coach approached the stadium I spotted my brother-in-law among the throng by the players' entrance. They should have christened Andy 'Nae Bother', because he takes everything in his stride and is kindness personified. Jean could not have had a better husband and I could not have wished for a nicer chap as a brother-in-law. He was typically unfazed when I got off the bus and managed – despite the stewards' protestations – to drag him through the main gates, lead him up the tunnel and join us as we spent a good forty-five minutes walking around the pitch. As we paraded, waving at the cheering fans, Andy – who was a Tarmacadam foreman making roads in Strathclyde – was with us every step of the way. He took the salute from 40,000 fans in the Leicester end and shook the Spurs' legends' hands. He's dined out on that story for forty-five years and I'm sure that Jean and their three lovely children, Cathy, Frank and Drew, must have heard it more than a few times.

The game, too, was a surreal experience. It was a blustery day and the pitch was extremely difficult to play on. The grass was so dark green and pristine that you would think no one had ever played on it. For years there was too much topsoil on the Wembley pitch, which gave it that verdant finish but made it spongy underfoot in the rain. The dual effect of a slow ball and quickly knackered legs made the game far less of a spectacle than anyone had anticipated.

The other disconcerting thing was the substantial grass apron outside the pitch markings which totally screwed up your perspective when hitting a longer pass. The springy pitch, the fact that your timing goes awry because you have to wait longer than you would instinctively assume to receive a pass, and the difficulty in measuring longer passes on that vast, flat area were not, however, the main contributing factors to the dearth of classic cup finals in the fifties and sixties; that was down to the so-called Wembley injury hoodoo and the absence of substitutes.

For the opening fifteen minutes or so I felt comfortable enough and had a couple of shots blocked on the edge of the Tottenham area. We seemed to have more fizz about us than our opponents, and we were playing pretty simply; our inside forwards, Keyworth and Walsh, were playing tight up against Blanchflower and Mackay, with McIlmoyle dropping off deep to try to pull Maurice Norman out of position. My instructions in those early minutes were to support the attack, thread a few passes down the inside-right channel, or switch the play out to Albert Cheesebrough on the left wing to have a run at Peter Baker, who was steady but not the quickest full back. I was enjoying myself, and quickly grasped that I had to under-hit my cross-field passes to adjust for the distorted view I had of the pitch. But when I slotted a ball back to our right back, Lenny Chalmers, he overcompensated for the heavy pitch, waited a second too long, and gave Les Allen the opportunity to tackle him.

Les went in with his studs up and caught Lenny on the ankle. I've seen it a couple of times since on DVD and I have no doubt that it was a reckless challenge. I'm not saying it was a deliberate foul, or that Les Allen was a dirty player, but it was viciously mistimed and Chalmers was crocked by it. Around that time, so many cup finals had been ruined by injuries putting one side at a numerical disadvantage that we did not feel uniquely cursed. However, the farcical sight of Lenny Chalmers gamely limping around on the right wing, me playing right back for the first time since 1955, and Howard Riley slotting in at right half, did mean that our attacking strength was both severely weakened and lopsided. It didn't even take someone with the unusual intelligence of Blanchflower to work out that we wouldn't be all that penetrative down the right for the last seventy minutes of the game.

We held our own for the next fifty minutes by constantly harassing the Spurs players – balking them, as the jargon of the late fifties had it. Playing with ten men at Wembley is not easy but by sheer endeavour we prevented Tottenham from unleashing a whirlwind. Indeed, John Arlott wrote that I 'raced through the work of two men like some pale, controlled fury'. I wasn't alone: Colin Appleton and Kenny Keyworth were also relentless in trying to bridge the gap, but it must have made for a poor game from the neutral's point of view. There was little doubt, though, that Spurs didn't like playing us. As Danny Blanchflower admitted afterwards: 'We never have a good game with Leicester. It's as though the chemistry of the teams doesn't mix.'

We continued to create a few half-chances that fell to McIlmoyle, but by the time Bobby Smith scored their opener on sixty-nine minutes we were dead on our feet. When Terry Dyson made it 2–0 seven minutes later all that was left for us on the day was to form a guard of honour to applaud the winners of the first double that century as they came down the tunnel after the presentations. We may well have lost the game even if Leek had been selected, but we certainly couldn't cope with the twin blows of his absence and the injury to Chalmers.

All sorts of people tell you they are sore losers, as if the obvious corollary of that statement is that they are winners. Well, for many years I was a pretty petulant loser, and won nothing either. My reaction to defeat was like a petrol-fuelled explosion. The feeling of rage went quite quickly but, that afternoon at Wembley, I still hurled my medal across the dressing room as though it were a turd. Thankfully, one of my colleagues slipped it back into my pocket while I was in the tub and I was extremely grateful for it – once my anger had subsided.

I could see that we had played well in spite of the difficulties, and that Spurs hadn't achieved any sort of dominance over us. In some ways it was seen as a 'glory loss', or perhaps a 'glory, glory loss' given the opposition, but it took me a good twenty-four hours to come to terms with it. I was gutted on the coach back to the Dorchester, had calmed down a lot at the banquet and was over it by the time I picked up my bike at Filbert Street the following evening and enjoyed a few hours of hung-over kip before I was back up a bloody ladder on Monday morning.

Later that month, I finally qualified as a painter and decorator. Just weeks after the cup final I had become a fully fledged skilled tradesman and I hung up my bicycle clips for good to focus on football full time. Even now, though, I can still gloss a double garage door in thirty minutes, an invaluable trick if tedious chores threaten to delay my departure for the golf course. Giving up the day job left me free to go on our post-season trip to Rhodesia and South Africa. It had been set up to reward us for reaching the FA Cup final, and for my first

ever trip abroad – disgusting discriminatory politics notwithstanding – it was a devilishly exciting prospect. We won matches
in Salisbury, Bulawayo, Durban, Pietermaritzburg and drew in
Johannesburg, but the games themselves were of the instantly
forgettable 'jolly' variety. The scenery – the red soil especially
– climate and wildlife, however, made an indelible impression
on me. If it had not been for the despicable Afrikaner attitude
towards non-whites, who the generous treated like lackeys and
the average Afrikaner treated like slaves, it would have been
my favourite ever trip.

You could have got your head turned quite easily if you
weren't careful because our hosts lived like kings, but there was
a strange stench of decadence about some of the people we
met. In some places the married women were quite openly
after us. We were told that shagging around, and please
remember this is 1961, was commonplace because a lot of
whites had nothing else to do. Bored witless, they'd wait for
sundowner hour, go to their colonial clubs, get wrecked, then
bed-hop. The Barrowlands never seemed further away.

My most vivid memory of the trip was a day spent on the
beach in Durban. We had been reading the newspapers on the
train and they all led on the story of a mammoth shark that
had somehow swum up from saltwater to freshwater and was
attacking people. We sat there spooking each other out with
tales of dismembered bodies and gnashers the size of elephant
tusks.

When we got to the beach we were all clearly anxious but,
typical footballers, we refused to admit it. Most of us spread
out to sunbathe but Albert Cheesebrough, showing the most
bravado, grabbed one of the little half-surfboards and went into
the ocean. He was lying on his board, paddling around, when

he suddenly caught a huge wave that launched him about six feet in the air and dumped him fifteen feet back up the beach. He was covered in sand, and a bit of blood. We had no sympathy at all and were in hysterics for about half an hour.

Eventually, the lifeguards convinced us that the shark nets made it safe for us to go into the sea. Though tentative at first, I began enjoying it and was standing chest-deep in the water, chatting away. Suddenly, I felt this enormous set of choppers digging into my thigh and I don't know how I didn't have a heart attack. I scooted out of the sea like a cartoon character with his feet skipping across the surface. I had been almost murdered by a machete-wielding lunatic, fallen more than 100 feet from a floodlight pylon and nearly exploded an acetylene tank but I have never been more petrified than I was at that moment; I thought a great white had got me and was going to drag me under. I was twitching with fear when I made the beach but everyone else was doubled up, weeping with laughter. The shark's name turned out to be Gordon Banks. He had swum underwater and grabbed my thigh with his vice-like goalkeeper's hands, digging all ten nails into my flesh. It must have been a hilarious sight and once my heart rate got back to normal I could see the funny side, too. The whole holiday was spent in a similar vein, two weeks of constant piss-taking. It was the perfect way to boost our morale after Wembley. But for me to exorcise the ghost completely, I had to go back to Wembley and win.

5

SECOND THAT EMOTION

The key to progress as a football team without an unlimited transfer budget lies in gradual development by increments. In retrospect, jumping from twelfth to sixth in a season and reaching the FA Cup final does not look too much of a leap, but we were definitely caught out in the 1961-62 season by an inability to keep the previous year's momentum going. It often happens with young sides that it's a case of two steps forward, one step back. In our case it looked at times as though we had already reached our pinnacle and that the flash in the pan could not be kindled into a blaze.

The problem we faced was similar to that of every other club in our predicament. The manager had substantial profits from the cup run to invest but he could not buy without offering over the odds if clubs did not want to sell. This was anathema to Gillies who, in common with most managers of his era, was so stingy with the club's money you'd think it was his own. In fact, we embarked on our first European campaign in the Cup Winners' Cup (thanks to Spurs' double) having sold Tony Knapp and, less surprisingly, poor Ken Leek, with no additions to replace them.

When I saw Matt Gillies's stated transfer targets – Paddy Crerand, David Herd and Alan Gilzean – as identified by his friends on the *Leicester Mercury*, go to clubs like Manchester United and Tottenham I was disappointed but could accept that it was reasonable. But when we were unable to outbid Second Division Leeds for Jim Storrie, or offer enough to tempt Rochdale to part with George Jones, I started to think that we'd never be able to close the gap. Of course, talk of dressing-room discord at the club's failure to bolster the squad would have been premature at this point but the first signs of disaffection began to seep in that summer.

Because of injury I played in only one European game. I was ruled out of our comfortable 7–2 aggregate victory over Glenavon but returned for the home leg with Atletico Madrid on a Wednesday night in late October. Funnily enough, Filbert Street's floodlights were much better than Wembley's before that stadium's upgrade for 1966, which meant that England's 1962 World Cup qualifier scheduled for that same Wednesday took place in the afternoon. This enabled Gordon Banks to be in the England squad for the England game then tank it up the motorway just in time to play the Spaniards at Filbert Road that evening. We whooped with delight when he threw open the dressing-room door with half an hour to spare and, showing no sign of his long, frantic drive, 'Sugar' gave his usual, impeccable performance.

Atletico were streets ahead of us in terms of tactics. For example, if they were attacking on the left, our left back would have to pay attention to what the right winger was up to because – much like Freddie Ljungberg now – he was always looking to spin his marker and bomb into the box. In a domestic game, ninety per cent of those playing wide in defence when the ball was on the opposite flank would be gazing across the field at the ball. On the continent, the winger would wait for the player to take his eye off him and then make a diagonal burst, either behind him into space or directly into the penalty area.

Moreover, even if they were paying attention, the wingers tended to jockey the full backs a lot and get them scuttling about like spooked crabs. Our continental cousins' other aim was to pin the full backs to the by-line and, therefore, as a wing half, I would not only find myself constantly having to drop off to prevent the winger getting in the box but also trying to take care of the inside forward. If you're playing in midfield or at the back, you always want your opponent in front of you. The last place you want him is lurking about parallel to you – on your shoulder as we call it – because you would never be able to catch him if you were going back-wards.

The continental defenders were an education, too. They had perfected a technique of marking the inside of your shirt; I suppose that's why they were not as tall as their British coun-terparts. Having mastered the black arts of their trade, they didn't have to rely on height to gain an advantage – they defended by making a physical nuisance of themselves. Although we had heard horror stories about the lengths some defenders would go to – twisting your knackers or jabbing a finger up your arse were the two most eye-watering – I only ever witnessed niggling stuff like pinching, hair-pulling, the occasional bite and the ubiquitous bumping.

Bumping, seemingly the most innocuous, was by far the most annoying. I can only give you a flavour of what it was like if you imagine yourself in a similar scenario: say you're down the pub; you've just bought your pint but every time you try to lift it to your mouth a guy nudges your arm, spilling the drink. Now imagine this happening several times. You're getting thirstier by the minute but you can't slake your thirst with laughing boy nudging you. Pretty soon you'd want to belt him, wouldn't you? But you can't. That's how frustrating it can be –and it gets worse when he throws the odd, sly gob in your face.

Off the pitch the continental defenders were urbane and charming; on the pitch they would do anything to stop you scoring. I think they must have learned from the Argentinian defenders – by far the best I played against. The Argentine game in general was becoming increasingly influential, and their defenders – also very civilised off the pitch – had learned the hard way that you can't give a continental striker space in the box because they're almost invariably lethal.

Look at Rio Ferdinand in 2005. For the difference in national attitudes, even after all these years, there was no better example than the Englishman's performance for Manchester United in Milan. He's a super player but when the ball's up the pitch he tends to mark space. When Milan shifted the ball into the box with such speed on to the head of Crespo, he was totally compromised. No Argentinian defender, or his continental disciples, would have been so lax. Even in 1961 they would be right up beside you all the time; pulling, pushing and clipping you. They were absolute bastards to play against.

As I found to my cost in Austria a couple of years later, the culture shock of facing what one newspaper called 'continental defensive skulduggery' had a more sinister side. In my defence I must say that I had still only ever played one proper European tie up to this point so I was incredibly naïve about the level of cynicism exhibited. In one of my last matches for Leicester, a post-season friendly in Innsbruck, I was playing at inside forward. I had just scored my second goal before half time and I was enjoying the game. I had been enraptured by that beautiful city; it was one of the most gorgeous venues I've ever visited and I would love to go back. But if I do, I would hope that they haven't got long memories.

We were comfortably ahead and playing for half time when the first incident occurred. I was ushering a ball out for a throw-in when the guy who was challenging me fell forwards over the touchline and brought his left leg up, catching me flush in the face and splintering my nose. I was bleeding profusely and felt a bit dazed, but I felt better when it had been re-set – with that sickening crack that sounds much worse than it feels – in the dressing room. All my colleagues were of the opinion that it was a deliberate assault but I was having none of it; I just didn't think that anyone would purposely do that, especially in a friendly.

Five minutes into the second half I was waiting for Banksie's goal kick in the inside-left position, quite near the touchline, waiting to fight for the header if it came my way. My assailant from before was marking me, and when the ball came it bounced just in front of us and skipped over our heads. As we turned to chase it, I collided with him and we both ended up sprawled on the ground. I got up first to pick him up and as he was rising he lashed out and kicked me in the chest. It wasn't the wisest thing he could have done because of all the eleven Leicester players out there I was the only one who had given him the benefit of the doubt when he had kicked me earlier.

I'm not normally violent but, as I've said before, when I lose my temper I really lose it. I caught him with a delicious upper-cut, knocking out his front teeth and sending them floating slowly over the touchline. It was surreal, and part of me wanted to laugh at how comic it looked. Unfortunately, his team mates were no fans of slapstick humour and four of them surrounded me. I had my hands up as if to say 'game over' − to let them know that, although he'd done me twice, honour was now satisfied − when their brawny right half nutted me squarely on the nose, breaking it for the second time in less than half an hour. Davie Gibson says that I was like John Wayne that after-noon. Reeling backwards from the head butt but still on my feet, I threw a right-hander at the midfielder, hitting him on the point of the chin and knocking him spark out.

It went a bit mental from then on. Five of them piled in on me. I managed to throw a few punches but I was taking a severe pummelling. Incidentally, the Leicester lads, who had all gone out of their way to convince me that there was some-thing fishy about the first foul, hung back. They had wound me up and just stood there enjoying the consequences. After about two minutes the referee broke up the fight and sent me off; I was led from the pitch, quite literally, by the men in white coats − two medical orderlies escorted me towards the dressing rooms. I was off my rocker at this point and responded to the crowd's booing by adopting that old schoolboy trick of flicking V signs back at them. It was like a scene from *One Flew Over the Cuckoo's Nest*; the white-coats escorting a disturbingly deranged man off to be sedated. My team mates found the whole thing hilarious. I must stress that I am not normally like that, but when provoked I did have a tendency to go berserk. Knowing this, my fellow players just stood back and lapped up my performance. And, somehow, the Leicester chairman managed to get the sending off rescinded, so I got away with it.

Back at Filbert Street on that October night, we drew 1-1 with Atletico, Adelardo equalising Ken Keyworth's opener in the ninetieth minute. I couldn't shake off a thigh injury in time to play in the return leg but I did travel with the team. The thing I remember most was the vibrant atmosphere within the Vicente Calderon stadium. It was absolutely electrifying, with none of the restraint displayed by our domestic crowds back then. For ninety minutes Atletico's 50,000 fans screamed like banshees, creating a fervent atmosphere that only became commonplace on our shores towards the end of my career.

Although we lost 2-0, we put on a good show but the Spaniards were too clever for us. They were obviously delighted with their victory and, deservedly, went on to win the competition that year. After the match, their club's president took us out to a night club he owned and we all got shredded on champagne. When you lose a match, alcohol can be a useful way of obliterating the immediate pain – but, in reality, it only defers it to the following morning when your dire physical state matches your mental one. The next day on the flight home, I felt physically and mentally desperate, in equal measures, but I was absolutely resolved to make sure that European football should become a regular feature of my career.

That season, City never looked like getting high enough up the league to qualify, but by the following year our revitalised team was on course to follow Tottenham's lead and snatch the most improbable of doubles. Our transformation was due to two signings – Davie Gibson and Mike Stringfellow – who changed the way we played dramatically. As an inside/outside left combination those two players were the best in the league. When Gillies put Gibson and Stringfellow together someone once said it was a marriage made in heaven but, like a lot of other events in football, it was not actually planned. Stringy had been a target for a couple of years but Matt had originally intended to partner him with Pat Quinn of Motherwell. But it was only because Bert Johnson had raved so much about Hibernian's Davie Gibson that Gillies eventually relented and put in an offer for him.

Physically, the two players had nothing whatsoever in common but they had an uncanny understanding between them. Stringy was a brave, tall, angular winger who, unusually for someone who played wide, neither complained nor struggled if he didn't receive a perfectly weighted pass to feet every time. He liked to come short and pull the full back in, allowing Davie to subtly flip one over the top, with a hint of backspin, into space for him to run onto. You rarely got the ball back from Mike but we didn't care; he had a tremendous shot and the sort of running power that torments defenders. He scored buckets of goals from wide positions, was good in the air when the ball came from the other side and, paradoxically, was both selfless enough to run all day in the service of the team and selfish enough to bombard the goal at almost every opportunity.

I was twenty-two and Davie Gibson twenty-three when he breezed into my life in January 1962. We hit it off from the start. He'd just finished his national service with the Kosbies

(King's Own Scottish Borderers) and, like the other conscripted professionals, had lived the life of Riley in the army. In common with most Scottish footballers, he had an impeccable touch and was such a bright-minded, fizzy little player that he gave our team great impetus.

Davie and I got on brilliantly as men and as players. He's a football fanatic and still talks tactics and players non-stop. If you have a drink with him he'll pepper you with trivia questions all bloody night. As soon as he arrived at the club he was off, telling stories about his idol Gordon Smith of Hibernian, and forty years on he's still at it; the way Davie went on about Smith you'd think he was the first James Bond. Davie could go on all day about Gordon Smith's skill as much as he could about his silk shirts, Italian moccasins, his MG and how he was better looking than Cary Grant. He's equally keen on Heart of Midlothian's Willie Bauld, and seems to know every detail of that great forward's career.

Davie's been my friend for forty-three years and I love him to bits, even though, like a lot of wee men, he could be argumentative when he'd had a few and expect muggins here to bail him out. We've argued all over the world and we still go on holiday together. I love winding him up and it made my year when his wife, Mavis, told me this story. Davie and Mavis run this retirement home in Leicester, and have done for many years. When a guy from the council came round for a routine inspection a few years back he spotted Davie at an upstairs window and informed Mavis, when she opened the door, that he'd just been greeted by one of her patients, 'a kindly old gentleman'. Davie was fifty-five at the time.

Lacking the physique to outmuscle the opposition, Davie – five feet six inches, and a touch bow-legged – had to out-think them. That famous ball over the top to Stringy was just one move in his repertoire. He could rifle a ball between the full back and the centre half and he was the best exponent of the short-angled killer pass into the box that I ever played with. His impish stature belied his shooting power and he scored stacks of goals himself, as well as being our best goal creator and the man who regulated the tempo at which we played.

If he had a fault it was his tendency to be too theoretical – 'you're too bloody clever by half', we used to tell him. In the army, he had played alongside Jim Baxter whose love of intricate dead-ball routines had rubbed off on him. Davie was always up to something and one of his major successes was this thing he came up with for throw-ins: to knock the defenders off guard, I'd sprint over to get the ball, shape to throw, then just bounce the ball a couple of yards back for him to take it. It sounds simple but it worked. At Burnden Park he devised this routine where three of us stood over the ball, but he and I would run over it and Bobby Roberts would play the ball in. When it came to it, Bobby and I got a tad confused and all three of us dummied it and burst into the box leaving no one to take the kick. Roy Hartle, Bolton's bull-like full back, just stared at us and said, in that inimitable Lancashire brogue: 'Too many fookin' cooks spoil t'broth, lads.'

That mishap didn't deflate Davie and he continued to come up with his schemes. Whenever we had a free kick, he would be full of: 'You run over and go wide, he'll pass it to me, then I'll back heel it to you and you shoot.' In the end, if a shot on goal was on, it was best to just push him out of the way and get on with it. In one game, against Wolves, instead of fannying about when we had an indirect free kick from about eight yards, I just got someone to nudge the ball to me and I'd shot and scored while Davie was only halfway through explaining his plan. He'd wanted a four-man move to dupe the opposition and he was genuinely mortified that I'd resorted to something so crude.

Long before I got into the first team, and for five years after I left, the Leicester style was rather gung-ho. Davie's introduction – along with that of his left-flank partner – only enhanced our options for going forward and we continued to score quite freely. At about the same time as Davie and Stringy were signed, Graham Cross, a very good cricketer for Leicestershire and a magnificent player for us, also came into the team. Initially, he played at inside right instead of the injured Jimmy Walsh, though he eventually ended up in his natural position at centre half.

As a teenager, Graham still had a bit of puppy fat on him and he didn't have the stamina that I had developed. I've read many times of Gillies's tactical ingenuity in compensating for this by getting Graham and me to swap positions. Some have gone so far as to say that this move combined with Gibson's surgical passing – 'the switch' and 'the whirl' as the press christened them – laid the foundations for what became known as 'total football' and, furthermore, illustrated the tactical nous of our manager and coach. I, in no way, wish to denigrate Matt Gillies, but this simply wasn't true.

Of course, we used to switch positions all the time but it wasn't something that came from the chalkboard. It just happened instinctively. When he dropped back the left half would follow him, leaving a nice big gap for me to bomb into. It surprised a lot of teams and we got a lot of praise for it, but it was down to the fact that Graham got a bit puffed at times and I had energy to burn. We were encouraged to continue doing it, but it had started as a happy accident and was not the metaphorical ripping up of the coaching textbook that some pundits claimed.

We used our set-pieces to great effect in the 1962-63 season, tricking flummoxed teams into yielding space around the penalty area. It was all about the little teams within the team. Our captain, Colin Appleton, an excellent footballer whose ears made him resemble the Scottish Cup trophy, orchestrated the left-hand side of the park from his position at left half, patiently winning and calmly offloading the ball to the Gibson/Stringfellow axis. On the right, Riley, Cross and I thrived on our triangular interplay, constantly moving, passing and probing until we could exploit an opportunity to get the ball to Kenny Keyworth in the box.

Obviously, the integration of the two new signings took time to gel and though the beginning of that season saw a marked improvement in results there was still the occasional lapse. By November we had the hang of how best to use our resources and – apart from a thumping at White Hart Lane, largely due to Jimmy Greaves and his ruthlessness – we felt entitled to consider ourselves as title contenders.

A decent run throughout November and December got us to third in the league before extraordinary circumstances intervened and we did not play another league match for forty-five days. The weather that winter was horrendous and in late January we had ten days of constant blizzards. Football everywhere went into hibernation and the only training we did was indoors, except for one trip to run on Brighton beach at the end of January. I was incredibly relieved that I wasn't still painting and decorating – I'm sure my fingers would have frozen right off – but, despite being ensconced inside most of the time, living through that freeze was still a rotten experience. No matter how

amily holidays in Largs with sister
ean, dad Archie and mum Catherine.
'm desperate to get into that icy cold
cottish water.

On holiday again. Isle of Man this
time. Aged 16 with my first girlfriend.

Vhen not holidaying, I played football. Still 16 at Shawfield Juniors.
. misnomer if ever I heard one. The team was full of grizzled ex-pros
5 years my senior. But they gave me great confidence. Back row, 3rd right.

Leicester mentors. 1st left, Bert Johnson, played a pivotal role in our improvement; 3rd left, George Dewis, taught me how to 'view the field'; 4th left, Alex Dowdells, saved my career with a quiet word; 3rd right, Matt Gillies transformed us into trophy contenders. Others, from left, trainer David Jones and team mates Appleton, Gibson and Cross.

Leicester's famous half-back line. Me with Ian King and Colin Appleton.

WEMBLEY HOODOO

FA Cup final 1961. Against Spurs. My first final, but I still remembered to wave to mum and dad (and take off my bicycle clips).

COLORSPORT

But it wasn't to be. Tens of thousands of City fans watched us trudge dejected off the pitch. The mouse didn't roar loud enough that day.

And having made it back, no refuge. Following tradition Spurs manager Bill Nicholson offers us a sip from the victory trophy. It didn't agree with me.

DAILY HERALD

COLORSPORT

Victorious against Liverpool in the '63 FA Cup semi. Left is Davie Gibson, my best friend over the past 43 years; Ian King, who came through the reserves with me; Gordon Banks, our one truly world-class player.

Defeat again. The 'Lawman' strikes for United in the '63 final.

'68 League Cup final. Mugs and tankards. Leeds mugged us and we walked away with Hardaker's tankards. Jim Furnell and myself are not amused.

EMPICS

'69 League Cup final. Wellies should have been required for the inspection before the game. The Horse of the Year Show was to blame for the pitch but we couldn't give the same excuse for our performance.

DAILY MIRROR

Still reeling from the shock of our '63 Cup final defeat, a few days later I walked up the aisle with Barbara. This more than made up for any disappointment.

My favourite photograph of Barbara.

McLintock boys. Don't think I could do this now. From left, Jamie, Scott and Iain, Neil on ground.

First day's training at Arsenal. £80,000 of expectation and full of hope. Left to right: fellow Scot Ian Ure with whom I shared digs; the phenomenal Joe Baker, one of the reasons I joined the club; and manager Billy Wright.

Hope and expectation slowly fading. Second game. Second defeat. The start of two years of torment. But at least I wrong-footed Greavsie. Or did he just slip?

Groundbreaking innovation. To break our downward spiral I pushed for an all-red shirt. It didn't seem to work. Funny that. Here against Fulham in '66. Many years later Rodney was still giving me an earful.

Hanging on Dave Sexton's every word. His arrival in '66 had a far more positive impact than my red shirts. My great friend Jon Sammels is on the right.

Dave left and Don Howe became first team coach. Barbara and I moved in a couple of doors down from him and his family. His skills proved the foundation for our later success.

Tokyo, May '68. 'Ronnie and Reggie' aka myself and my great pal George Graham. Arsenalmania was evident throughout the trip. No screaming girls mind you.

much coal we threw on the fire, no matter how many steaming piles of mashed potato we shovelled down our throats, we endured weeks of never really being warm.

By the time I became manager of Leicester in the late seventies, the pitch was protected from frost by an innovative, if slightly absurd, giant balloon. We didn't have that in the early sixties and under-soil heating, too, was still a pipe dream but, still, we restricted our postponements to January only, while other clubs went up to ten weeks without playing. And we were fortunate to have a groundsman who was prepared to clear the pitch of snow, layer it with a coating of topsoil and hay, and sit up all night feeding coke into a dozen braziers scattered across the field. So, in the 1962-63 season we were able to get playing earlier than most, and our run of six straight wins put us up to second place while most other teams were still kicking their heels.

We changed the way we played slightly as the pitch, despite all the attention lavished upon it, was still frozen in places. As the only team braving the conditions, we became known as the 'Icemen' but we had to adopt a long ball game, not quite Wimbledon-style, but one which made the most of our fast-flowing wingers.

In early April we found ourselves top with five games to play after beating Manchester United 4-3 at Filbert Street. Points in the bag are always better than having games in hand, but we couldn't sustain our push after injuries to Banks, Gibson and Keyworth disrupted our rhythm. We drew one, and lost four of our five remaining games, giving up nine points to finish fourth – the exact margin that the eventual champions, Everton, held over us at the end of the season.

Throwing away that lead knocked our confidence but we

took great consolation from a discernible sense that we were on the brink of real achievement – and we still had the small matter of the FA Cup final before us to make amends to our fans. Getting to the semi-final that year was straightforward compared to 1961 but we all felt that Liverpool, the team standing between us and a return to Wembley, were going to be bloody awkward to get past.

We had done the double over Liverpool in the league but we recognised how relentless they could be. Playing them when they were performing at the top of their game was like plastering your face with marmalade then kicking over a wasps' nest. If you couldn't establish control early on, the attacks just came at you in waves. There was nothing particularly sophisticated about their approach so early in Bill Shankly's tenure, but they embodied his furious work rate to such an extent that at times they threatened to overwhelm you. Their main weakness in this their first season back in the top flight was that they also shared their manager's exuberance – this made it vital to slow them to your pace, and to take advantage of their impatience in order to hoodwink their markers out of position. If you had the nerve to do that then you had a chance.

All our good intentions, and the days of meticulous practice, were no help in Sheffield as the Hillsborough semi-final turned into a master-class in how not to play Liverpool. They absolutely battered us for ninety minutes, and for most of the second-half ran us to a standstill; we simply could not compete with their attacking vigour. This was long before matches were analysed statistically but if someone told me that we had more than ten per cent of possession I would call them a liar.

We sucker-punched them on the break after eighteen minutes through Mike Stringfellow but if it had not been for

Gordon, who made something like forty saves – five of which were world class – they would have annihilated us. The way Roger Hunt and Ian St John combined that afternoon meant that Colin Appleton and I never got forward. We were constantly dropping back to bolster our defence which was run ragged. I made as many tackles in that game as I would expect to make in a month of matches, but somehow we survived and Gordon made a flying save from Ian St John in injury time that was the equal of anything he ever did – the Pele save included. It was the most one-sided game I ever played in and our win was the biggest travesty of justice I witnessed during twenty-one years as a professional.

Something equally unfair happened as we came off the pitch. When you steal a game, your relief at such flagrant larceny often manifests itself in hysteria and we just couldn't stop laughing at our luck. Banksie, however, was stitched up by a photographer. He, Richie Norman and I were embracing in the middle of the pitch, all of us grinning maniacally, when the photographer clicked his shutter. He caught us in the midst of our elation but something in the background of his shot must have set the cash register ringing in his ears. Ten yards from us an inconsolable Ian St John, quite visibly in tears, was trudging off the park. Cropping Richie and me out of the photograph and foreshortening the distance between Gordon and Ian to make it look like Banksie was taunting him, the newspaper stirred up a torrent of abuse from Liverpool and, for the next couple of months, Banksie received reams of vile hate mail from Merseyside.

I felt so sorry for him. No one, let alone Banksie, would have goaded an opponent so crassly in those days and it took years for him to live it down. Those sacks of poisonous letters and scores of obscene phone calls, some issuing death threats, were the only stains on our joy at getting back to Wembley so quickly. This time, we vowed, there'd be no heartache.

Funny as it may seem to younger readers, we were odds-on favourites to beat Manchester United in the 1963 cup final. Our opponents had endured a woeful season and only evaded relegation by three points. I remember arriving at Wembley and feeling almost serenely confident as we went through the cup final ritual of reading the good-luck telegrams and thumbing through the programme before going onto the pitch to greet our fans. We'd had such a good season and had not lost to United. We all assumed that we would definitely win if we played at our peak.

Unhappily, we were absolutely atrocious. Something I've recognised through writing this book is that a great many foot-ballers suffer from a selective memory. I've wiped out so much of that game that when I tried to piece it together only a few random thoughts remain. And speaking to some of my colleagues who were there that day I have discovered that it's the same for them. I suppose that's how players are able to recover from such disappointments, a sort of protective instinct kicks in and buries all the traumatic details so deep in some dark place that you can never retrieve them. Most of the salient facts have been obliterated and, instead, you are able to tap into only that sense of raw dejection.

Alan Hoby in the *Sunday Express* wrote that we were like 'actors with stage-fright on the big day', but it wasn't as simple as that. I have always felt that it was indicative of that old saying about cream rising to the top. Manchester United had a mouth-watering team – including Denis Law, Bobby Charlton, Paddy Crerand, Johnny Giles, Albert Quixall and Noel Cantwell – and they tore us to shreds. We never got going. Our strength was our teamwork but as soon as that went out of the window we were like sitting ducks. All the players we relied upon to spark us into life – myself, Davie and big Stringy – gave pedestrian performances. We had shockers that day and it led to panic. Davie, our engine, could not cope with Crerand's anticipation and distribution. We had no direction and United snuffed out the link between our defence and attack so easily that we might as well have gone home at half-time.

It was a demolition job. We couldn't live with Law and Crerand and though we rallied to get the game back to 2-1 – through Ken Keyworth – we gave a shabby impression of our true selves and – thanks to an uncharacteristic fumble from Gordon Banks – eventually lost another goal. When you win at Wembley you remember so many details, but my most resonant and abiding memory of our defeat that day is the sound our studs made on the long, concrete tunnel that leads downhill back to the dressing room. After a win there was that rat-a-tat-tat of jubilant players almost skipping their way back. When you lose there's a slow clack-clack – it sounds like the death march and it haunts you for years afterwards.

Davie Gibson says he woke up the following morning knowing that the game had passed him by and wanting desperately to play it again. I know exactly what he means. That sense of missed opportunity and anti-climax transcends everything else. I felt humiliated and couldn't shake that embarrassment for weeks. We went back to the Dorchester Hotel and sat through the banquet, attempting to null the pain with copious bottles of Skol. We had been on for the double and ended up with nothing. It had been the greatest season in the club's history but at the time that was no consolation. I've always been fairly bubbly and, eventually, the passage of time snaps me out of depression, but the sense of loss and sorrow can only really be masked by winning something. That summer, for the first time, I started to wonder whether that was going to be possible at Leicester.

6

GUNNING FOR CAPS AND HONOURS

Sometimes I like to kid on that I must have been still reeling from the shock a few days after our diabolical performance against Manchester United at Wembley when I walked up the aisle to marry Barbara. Thankfully, I can get away with the odd quip like that after more than forty years together and Barbara knows I'm only joking. I have mellowed in a remarkable manner and have discarded the chauvinistic attitudes I grew up with, but a part of me still prefers to be flippant about anything we used to call lovey-dovey.

I expect it's pretty much the same today in football. In the dressing room, if you were daft enough to talk about emotions you wouldn't last five minutes – everyone would be mincing around and blowing kisses at you. It's a bit odd when you think about it; admitting to your mates that you loved a woman would provoke accusations that you were a poof. And for me, and many men of my generation, the reticence that reaction instilled will never go away entirely. It's foolish, I know, but the thought of showy public displays of affection still make me cringe a little.

As I wrote earlier, I met Barbara on a Saturday night out at the Palais in Leicester. And at that first meeting I made a date to see her again at Brucianni's coffee shop in the city centre the following week. We just took it from there, really, and were together for the next two years before we got married. It was fantastic to meet someone who understood the life – long before she became a footballer's wife Barbara had had long experience of the game as a footballer's sister so she was well steeped in the game. Her brother, Reg Warner, had played briefly for Leicester before a bad cartilage injury effectively ended his career – though, later, he did manage a few games for Mansfield Town – while her father ran the Anstey Nomads team.

It was inevitable that we met in the Palais because it was the only place in the city where you could successfully meet girls and going there was my only big night out of the week. The great thing about Leicester's location – bang in the middle of England – was that it was relatively easy to travel to and from away games. We would come back on the train on a Saturday evening, even from London, and still have time to get in to the Palais.

Mind you, if we got back before closing time we used to go straight to the pub for a drink with the lads and arrange to meet our girlfriends later in the night club. We didn't think we were being selfish, it was just the way we behaved back then. Our celebrity status in the city was pretty low-key but we were treated well wherever we went. There were few privileges and no hero-worshipping, except that people were unusually courteous and complimentary, which made us feel special. The one perk we made regular use of was free entrance to the Palais. It made for quite a cheap night out, particularly if you weren't with your girlfriend when she had to pay to get in.

Seriously, though, we weren't that tight. It was the custom: the men went one way, the women the other before meeting up towards the end of the night. That was the mindset back then, but I shudder when I recall what happened the first time I took Barbara to Glasgow. As I've said before, Glaswegians are very keen to get you pissed so you'll enjoy yourself. They can be overpoweringly persuasive about the merits of getting arse-holed. Well, Barbara is not a big drinker but on our night out with Jean's husband, Andy, and his father, they kept buying her these snowballs and urging her to drink them quickly so we could move on to the next venue. Barbara must have drunk seven in forty-five minutes and she'd begun to feel unwell. It shows you just what the male mentality was, or the extent of my bloody cheek if you want to be less forgiving, that I put her in a taxi to my mother's and stayed out with the others for the rest of the night.

Despite my shortcomings, Barbara still consented to marry me. Our presiding priest was Father Russo from Albuquerque. The week before the wedding, I took him to Les Ambassadeurs, a supper club, in Leicester where he smoked twenty Capstan full strength cigarettes and drank at least ten whiskies in a couple of hours. I was pie-eyed, but this was just a 'quiet night' for him, he explained. Apparently, he rationed himself when he went out midweek.

My team mate Jimmy Walsh was my best man and his two

children were bridesmaid and page-boy. It was a lovely day with my family and all my team mates present. Barbara and I would spend our honeymoon in Jersey – the City lads had hidden kippers in our car's manifold, so were feeling pretty queasy by the time we'd driven to Birmingham airport to catch our flight. And there was more; when we arrived at our hotel in Jersey we found they had stuffed our suitcases ten inches deep with confetti.

Our honeymoon did not get off to the best start. Barbara got sunburned on the first day: 'Great,' I thought, 'some honeymoon this, I can hardly get near her.' That evening, leaving my new wife in bed, I went down to the bar to meet a couple of Glaswegians I knew who lived in Jersey then. We had a few drinks before they went off to a club for the night. I'd turned down their invitation to join them but, because they couldn't get a taxi I had lent them the car I'd hired.

Barbara had heard their Scottish accents as they left the hotel, and she'd got up, looked out of the window and seen two men – one tallish with dark hair – get into our car, with a couple of birds in tow. I spent another hour or so in the bar then went up to bed, only to find a hysterical wife. Evidently, as I learned later, she thought I had pulled some girl on only the second night of our marriage. But she wouldn't speak to me, refused to tell me what was wrong. I thought she'd gone mad and I said: 'My mother told me that, "You'll never know her properly until you're married and then you'll see the real her." Well, she's right!' Eventually, it all came out and my mother's cynical advice proved not to be true. Thank God the last five days of our honeymoon recovered from that inauspicious start.

Having married a local girl and, that summer, bought our first house, just outside Leicester, you would have thought that leaving the club would have been the furthest thought from my mind. But I had become sceptical about the club's ability to recruit the two or three extra quality players that would make us genuine contenders year in, year out. For me to claim now that the increasingly rancorous pay dispute that Gordon Banks and I became embroiled in with the club had its foundations in our ambition for the club would make most Leicester fans burst out laughing. Nevertheless, it was partly to do with that. We felt that the club's policy of pegging wages so low precluded any chance of buying the type of player that could strengthen the team. The type of players we believed we needed would turn up their noses at the thirty quid ceiling imposed by Matt Gillies in the aftermath of the abolition of the twenty pound maximum wage.

The club very much held the upper hand when it came to wages and the extremely hierarchical football culture at the time just served to reinforce City's 'upstairs downstairs' attitude towards employees. Directors were more interested in the kudos their position at the club gave them in the community than in taking money out of the club for themselves, but it didn't stop them defending every penny of income from consistently high gates. The club secretary, Charlie Maley, used to hand out the weekly wages. We had to line up in the canteen at Filbert Street and he would hand over a three-inch-square brown envelope with cash inside. He couldn't restrain himself from making pointed little comments as he doled them out: 'You should pay us this week', or 'You don't deserve this'. It made you feel like Oliver Twist.

It pained Gillies even to discuss money. He had a silver tongue and could tie you up in such knots that you'd feel ashamed for wanting higher wages. Yet he still managed to leave the impression that he was trying so hard to be fair to you – 'despite all the club's overheads . . .' You'd leave his office feeling that you were trying to rip him off as you went home to consider an offer he thought extortionate while it was less than half the sum you'd asked for. Gordon and I were the first to hold out in 1962 and, courtesy of Matt's great pal at the *Leicester Mercury*, Harry Brown, we suffered a summer of vilification in the local press.

Harry wrote about us every other day for two months. First, he was 'sick and tired of these greedy footballers', but he soon moved on to describe our 'continued attempts to get blood out of a stone', condemning us as 'all pay and no play footballers' who, the final straw, 'put bank balance above everything'. All Gordon and I had asked for was an increase from twenty to thirty pounds per week, but Harry Brown's sarcasm had made me feel like a criminal. It finally stopped when I burst into the *Mercury's* building one afternoon and chased Harry round the office.

I went potty with him for writing lies, for inventing the inflated figures he was claiming we'd asked for and for publishing them for over 100,000 readers who must have thought me a right mercenary bastard. I had no specific plan in mind when I decided to pay Harry a visit but I was angry. My anger led to a comic scene featuring me going one way round the desk to grab him, him bolting round the other way until we finally stopped and stood, face-to-face, on opposite sides of the desk.

Of course I didn't hit him but I obviously struck a nerve. He apologised and listened to my side of the story. From then on, he was a bit more understanding of our plight. Harry was a good guy and, ultimately, we became friends but like some other regional journalists he identified himself too strongly with the club's board and manager and operated like a propaganda machine for them. My argument seemed to persuade him and later in the dispute he wrote: '[Banks and McLintock] are fine examples of the new deal footballer with a mind of his own. Good luck to 'em.'

After signing three consecutive monthly contracts at the stipulated dispute level of fifteen pounds a week, Gillies, Gordon and I compromised and Banksie and I signed for twenty-eight. In the three months of our hold out, we had each forfeited sixty quid, compared to our colleagues who had re-signed at twenty. It doesn't sound like much today, but it was not an easy sacrifice to make in 1962. Imagine how we felt when, weeks after we had settled, Matt Gillies called a meeting to announce that he was putting the entire first team squad up to the pay level Gordon and I had won.

We weren't pissed off because we wanted to defend the principle of a differential. We were furious because for three months the two of us had put our necks on the line, lost income and faced bitterness from press and public, yet those who had done nothing to help our cause were to benefit equally. I fully understand that the manager had to have the last word in matters like that; he had to be seen as the winner. But the way in which it was done, almost as a deliberate snub to Gordon and I, meant that we would be even more reluctant to compromise next time.

Of course, the supporters are entitled to their opinions and I could see why they would not be impressed with our holdout; I had no problem with that. I was mortified, however, when I received a letter concerning Neil, my new, firstborn son. Neil had been born prematurely weighing only a worrying 4lb 11oz.

There were some stories in the press at the time, and when he was strong enough to come out of the incubator there were photographs of us, the proud parents and the wee fella. Shortly after this I received a letter from someone saying that he was fed-up reading about me and my sick son who looked 'like a skinned rabbit'.

It wasn't the nicest thing a father has ever had to read. If that warped individual is still alive today I would like to tell him that Neil, in his work with the BBC, has had Bafta nominations for his camerawork, worked on World Cups and is now a senior camera co-ordinator who was in charge of the pictures for the Live8 broadcast in the summer of 2005. Not bad for a 'skinned rabbit'.

Anyway, we played the same game of pay chess over the next two summers until I was finally allowed to leave. It wasn't that I felt Leicester intrinsically inferior to one of the elite clubs but I got sick of waiting for the sort of reinforcements that could have enabled us to win the league. I was so ambitious, and not for cash, but to win something. I regret that Matt Gillies and I fell out ostensibly over money and I wish now that I had been able to stay close to him, maybe to play golf with him, and soak up all that wisdom, but it wasn't to be. At the age of twenty-four I simply wasn't mature enough.

I knew that it was Matt's job to keep the pay down and never suspected that he was trying to do me over. He saw himself as a custodian of the club's traditions and of its money; I recognised that and never tried to go over his head to the board. Tortuous wage negotiations aside, we must nevertheless have been a great group of players for him to manage.

We were such a bright lot, football fanatics to a man and full of old-fashioned fun. There weren't any rascals at Filbert

Street, no petulant shits and none of us earned a fortune. We weren't badge-kissing hypocrites trying to suck up to the fans while ripping off the club. When you're young, ambition can blind you but I sincerely believed that what was right for Leicester wasn't necessarily right for me. When I eventually left, I did so with many happy memories of the club. I only hope that Matt realised how grateful I was for everything he'd done for me, and how much he meant to me. I certainly wish I had taken the time to tell both him, and Bert Johnson – a wonderful influence on my career who is still living in Leicester today – how much my future success was a result of their skill and intelligence.

However, even though my mind had been made up for several months, it was still extremely difficult to get a transfer in the early sixties before the George Eastham case went to court. Even if you were in dispute with the club and out of contract, you had to sign three consecutive monthly contracts before you were entitled to appeal to the Football League. But if the league's management committee deemed the contract offered to you 'fair and reasonable', you were stuck. I can't remember anyone successfully forcing a transfer by this method and, in the summer of 1964, my case was duly rejected. My only hope, then, was to refuse to sign anything other than a monthly deal, relying on this to persuade the chairman to release me, and trust that a buying club would put together a fee so large that the board had to accept it.

Officially, I was left in the dark to wait and see if another club would come in for me but the system in place to agree transfers – a secret and honourable dialogue between clubs at board level – was routinely abused. It hadn't quite got to the point of regular newspaper briefings – designed to unsettle a player – or of arranging a shadowy assignation in a Greek restaurant with representatives of another club. Tapping up was not so subtle then as players didn't have agents to conduct the wooing process and keep us from getting our hands dirty. Managers just came straight out and tested the water with you, direct, to see if it was worth their while making a bid.

The first time it happened to me was at the Dorchester in London, during the dance after our cup final banquet in 1961. I was on the dance floor with Barbara when I got a tap on the shoulder from Bill Shankly: 'Hello, son,' he said. 'How would you like to play for a good team?' If you bear in mind that Liverpool were in the Second Division at the time, you will recognise how impertinently, yet amusingly, self-confident Shankly could be. 'You know Ian [St John]?' he continued. 'He'll do a great job for me and I've just signed Ronnie Yeats at centre half. He's a bloody colossus of a man. Him and Ian will be great together but I want you to be the third Scotsman in the team. With three Scotsmen in the team we'll win bloody everything. Mind you, if there's any more than three, there'll be fucking trouble!'

He was as brazen as you like in front of the Leicester directors and his pal, Matt Gillies. And, proudly wearing his bright red Liverpool club tie, he made no attempt to be discreet or disguise who he was. It was typical Shankly. I gave him a non-committal reply but I later learned he'd made a bid that our board had turned down. Subsequently, I never got to know him as well as I would have liked but I had enormous respect and affection for him. If ever I was up in Liverpool he would always seek me out for a chat and be full of encouragement. The last time I saw him he still lamented: 'Ah son, you should have played here. You'd have been a great player in red.' Some people might say I did all right in that colour anyway but Bill always had a tendency to discount anything achieved by what he termed 'those Cockneys' that he may have failed to notice.

While Shankly made a characteristically shameless approach, the next manager to sound me out took the cloak and dagger option. At home one evening, I heard a knock at the door and when I opened it saw an indistinct figure looming in the mist outside. It was like that scene in *The Elephant Man*. I didn't know what to expect when it stepped forward and standing in front of me was a guy in a Crombie, collar turned up, a thick muffler obscuring his mouth and chin and a cap pulled low over his forehead. I thought it was a tinker hoping for a mug of tea but there was something about his eyes that stopped me from telling him to piss off. It took me a few seconds of awkward silence to recognise who it was. Five minutes later – his disguise discarded – Don Revie was sitting by our fire making me a wonderful, if illegal, offer to join Leeds United. Knowing the mutual affection Scottish players had for each other he did a terrific selling job on the club, telling me all about Billy Bremner, Bobby Collins, Eddie Gray, Willie Bell and Peter Lorimer. His package was for eighty quid a week plus a signing on fee of £8,000. It was a jaw-dropping offer – particularly when you think the house we had our discussion in had cost us £2,500. I would have accepted it readily but, once again, Leicester rebuffed Leeds' formal transfer bid and, like the Liverpool deal, never even told me about it.

Throughout 1964 I received regular telephone calls from Billy Wright, manager of Arsenal, and several visits at Barbara's parents' home from Paddy Ryan, chief scout of West Bromwich Albion. Both men spent months laying the groundwork for a transfer, selling me the merits of their respective clubs. Arsenal held the stronger attraction, not only because of their two star players – George Eastham and Joe Baker – but also because Wright insisted I was to be the pivot of a new team that would also include Don Howe, Ray Wilson and Gordon Banks. And there was the added appeal of London. I had been impressed by Dave Mackay's description of life in the capital and I really fancied living there.

Incidentally, on a Scotland trip Mackay told me he had recommended me to Eddie Baily, Bill Nicholson's assistant at Tottenham, and that he was considering me as a replacement for Danny Blanchflower. For more than a year I waited in vain for the rumoured Tottenham offer; given the prevailing secrecy I've never found out even if one was made. Shortly before I left Leicester, Nicholson's £72,500 offer for Alan Mullery was accepted, and he, not me, put on the number four shirt at White Hart Lane. My life could have turned out very differently indeed if I'd gone to Spurs.

Still at Leicester City, I began the 1964–65 season still on a monthly contract and in our eighth game we played Arsenal at Filbert Street. I scored twice and then hit the post, but my imminent employers came back and stole the game 3-2 with George Eastham grabbing the winner at the death. I must confess I was a bit scared that Arsenal's win might persuade Billy Wright that the Gunners were getting along fine without me and discourage him from pursuing his interest. Fortunately, he rang me the next day to tell me how good he thought I'd been. I decided, then, that things had come to a head and I had to stop mucking about by trying to provoke Leicester into releasing me. I went to see Matt Gillies and handed in a formal transfer request.

The manager was, understandably, exasperated but he briefed

the board that I was now adamant about leaving. Mr Needham, the chairman, and an exceptionally nice man, agreed to see me later that week. Looking a bit like Wilfrid Hyde-White in full Colonel Pickering mode, he had an easy charm and was always very solicitous towards me and my family. All those dispiriting months parrying over wages were cast aside when he asked: 'What do you want, Frank? Seventy a week. Eighty? We need you here.' It had never really been about money and my resolve did not slacken when he generously upped the ante; the board, he revealed, had also informally agreed to buy me a sweetshop or newsagent's as an additional financial incentive to stay with the club.

Sums like that must have given Matt Gillies kittens and he would have been very uncomfortable if I had agreed to stay while pocketing twice as much as the club's next highest paid player. To be fair to the board, though, I do think it was a sincere offer but I couldn't be persuaded. I told Needham that I wanted to go to a club that would ultimately help me win 'cups and caps' and he reluctantly accepted my reasoning. A couple of days later he telephoned Highbury and named his price.

A few days after that discussion I played in Leicester's midweek 4-2 victory against West Bromwich Albion at Filbert Street, scoring my sixth goal in only my tenth game of the season, before heading for Porthcawl to join up with the Scotland squad for that Saturday's home international in Cardiff. And it was in the Welsh capital that I took the last of many clandestine telephone calls from Billy Wright, though the fact that I was summoned from the hotel's lounge to take a 'trans-continental call for Mr McLintock' meant it didn't stay secret for long. Wright was calling from Odense, in Denmark, where

Arsenal were playing a friendly; the club had agreed to meet Leicester's quoted £80,000 fee with no haggling, and that we should link up after the weekend when the deal would be completed.

The official press photographs show me signing for that record domestic transfer fee in Arsenal secretary Bob Wall's office at Highbury on the evening of Monday 5 October 1964. But that was just a re-staging with the appropriate props. In fact, Billy Wright and Bob Wall had driven up the M1 that morning to ward off a late bid from Wolves and, thus, I signed my first contract for Arsenal in the boardroom at Filbert Street before heading for London in the back of Wright's car for the photocall. It's common to smile on such occasions, but the genuine glee I felt wasn't just relief at ending my dispute with Leicester — I was so proud to be joining Arsenal, so hopeful of doing well, that the pictures show me grinning more broadly than Liberace after a fistful of happy pills. It would be more than two years until I smiled with such confidence and sincerity again.

7

ALL RED BUT NOT ALL RIGHT

Of all the clubs in England, no one needed to do much of a selling job to convince players to sign for Arsenal. I'd played at Highbury many times before and had been tremendously impressed by the facilities and the sheer air of class about the place. I was aware, too, of the team's stature within the game's history, but I had never had the behind-the-scenes grand tour that I was given that Monday evening. The whole set-up lent itself to grandeur, not only its famous marble halls, but also in the astonishing attention to detail throughout.

On the first floor of the East Stand, Bob Wall's large, imposing office was panelled in walnut, giving it the air of an Edwardian bank. The other offices, though smaller, still whispered the club's aristocratic pedigree. Both dressing rooms were luxuriously palatial with heated floors and beautifully tiled walls, while the treatment room housed its own X-ray machine and was equipped with all the state-of-the-art machinery needed to conduct minor surgical procedures on the spot.

The prestige of the club was so great that I had no hesitation in signing a contract for fifty-five pounds a week, significantly less than I would have received elsewhere. Little did I know that I had been impressed by a façade. Had a gossip grapevine existed in the mid sixties, tales of disharmony may have reached my ears and made me more cautious, but the glamour and the calibre of players like Joe Baker and George Eastham, already on the books, ruled out all doubt. It took me less than a week to realise that the club I thought I'd signed for was an illusion. The serenity on the surface hid chaos beneath. I have only myself to blame as I was aware that Arsenal had been in the doldrums for eleven years since their last League Championship but I had been swayed by Billy Wright's grand talk about his shopping list of stars and I was big-headed enough to think I could make a huge difference if joined by the likes of Wilson and Banks.

Meanwhile, life in digs beckoned once more – Barbara was in the late stages of her second pregnancy so that she had been unable to come with me at first to London. I became a part-time husband and father for a few months, often spending as much time on the train or motorway as I did with my family. I joined a fellow Scot, Ian Ure, in Maisie Mather's house in Southgate, an area I've lived in ever since. Sharing digs was so much better than being stuck in a hotel and eating those bland meals, alone. Both Mrs Mather and Ian were excellent company and prepared me perfectly for living in London. Indeed, everything off the field went well. My primary reason for being there, unfortunately, was an entirely different matter.

My first game was not the happiest of omens. In fact, it accurately foreshadowed almost two years of hell. The night before the game, I stayed with Alec Forbes – the legendary Joe Mercer's wing-half partner in the last relatively successful Arsenal side, the team that won the league in Coronation year – and he praised Arsenal, as a club, to the skies. The next evening, as I got ready to play Nottingham Forest at Highbury, Alec's eulogy to the club doubled the excitement I felt at putting on that famous shirt for the first time, and my excitement rose still further on hearing my name applauded by the North Bank when the team was read out.

My euphoria, however, lasted less than fifteen minutes into the match. I was absolutely useless and felt like a harassed Italian traffic policeman, unable to gain any control as everything accelerated all around me. The worst of my many dire moments involved John Barnwell, the man I was supposed to be marking and who had recently been sold by Arsenal. It would have been bad enough just to mis-hit a back pass and gift Forest an easy goal but to play in Barnwell, the man whose transfer had financed part of my fee, and in so doing to have embarrassed Billy Wright in front of the Highbury crowd who adored him, put the tin hat firmly on a worryingly wretched debut.

I don't think either Forbes or Ian Ure knew what to say to me that night as we sat in mortified silence, staring at the wall in Alec's front room. Perhaps they thought that Arsenal had signed a pup. I couldn't blame them. I'd played crap. But that was not my major concern. I was experienced enough to realise that I'd played poorly before and would doubtless do so again. I also recognised that one training session was scant preparation to grasp the intricacies of Arsenal's game. Similarly, that gnawing feeling of unfamiliarity on the pitch was only to be expected. At Leicester, I'd played for years with Davie Gibson, Howard Riley and Colin Appleton; of course, they had anticipated my moves, and I theirs, far better than George Eastham, Alan Skirton and Terry Neill possibly could after just twenty-four hours. No, what had genuinely scared me was the absence of an identifiable system of play. For all Billy Wright's fine words in his team talk, Arsenal shuffled through a hotchpotch of styles. There was no positional discipline; everything was off the cuff, a cornucopia of incoherence. After agitating so long for the move, I lay in bed that night with one haunting question rattling around my head: 'What the fuck have I done?'

My only hope was that first impressions can often be misleading. Stop panicking, I thought, this is a top club, last night must have been an aberration. But our 3-1 defeat at White Hart Lane the following Saturday and our 4-0 loss at Bramall Lane a fortnight later proved that my initial fears were not an over-reaction. I felt that I'd left Leicester to come to Arsenal and win things and found myself in a worse predicament. To my mind, Leicester City were twice the team Arsenal were. There was no consolation from any department. It wasn't as if we were well-organised but couldn't score, or that we had a leaky defence but were great going forward. The whole manner in which we played was plainly awful.

There was nothing at all to hang your hat on and conclude that if we worked on one failing then the rest would come right. There's no point trying to kid you and claim that I was merely disappointed at the team's inadequacy. That wouldn't come close to representing the vehemence of my anger. After just four games I thought, and forgive the vernacular, 'I can't stand this. This is the biggest load of shit I've ever seen in my life.' That sense of frustration inhibited me for two years.

Moreover, the team, like me, bereft of structure, discipline and confidence, deteriorated at a rapid pace.

If one is being scrupulously honest, when looking to allocate blame for Arsenal's shambolic state, it is difficult to look much beyond the manager. The problem one faces is that his status as a player and gentleman makes you reluctant to stick the boot in. No one wants to traduce a legend and, for all his faults as a manger, being critical of Billy Wright still makes me feel a little grimy.

Furthermore, I'm not immune to understanding how difficult it must have been for him. Football must have seemed so easy to Wright at one point. He had 105 England caps and was the darling of the media. His spell coaching the England youth squad immediately after he retired from playing for Wolves had been successful, and though, given his inexperience, his appointment by the Arsenal directors in 1962 was peculiar, you could see why they did it.

The board obviously got carried away with his iconic status as a player. He had the look of a comic book hero: bright blond hair, charming smile and that white England shirt with the eye-catching, outsize crest – exactly the sort of image that appealed to directors. He was, after all, in the immortal words of chairman Denis Hill-Wood, a 'jolly fine chap'. The only flaw in their recruitment policy was the sobering fact that he was completely out of his depth with a team that had as many shortcomings as Arsenal.

In retrospect one can appreciate that inexperience can have fatal consequences for a manager's career. I should know. On his appointment, the clever thing for Wright to have done would have been to hire an established and hardened coach. A veteran with a bit of streetwise savvy who could share the manager's burden, and relieve him of the anxiety that caused him to vomit before every match, might have given Billy a chance. Instead, he appointed Les Shannon, a trusted FA staff colleague from Lilleshall. Les was a decent enough coach but it seemed to me that their partnership had been put together solely because of their friendship and their pleasure at working together. Beyond that they had identical strengths and weaknesses, with neither man compensating for the other's defects.

Paramount among these was their inability to put on a proper coaching session. It takes time, trial and error to get these things right but for all the theoretical brilliance derived from their work with the FA, Wright and Shannon too often resorted to murdering us with endless, uninspired fitness work. The best coaches know how to communicate with players. They tell you how they want you to play and 'groove' you through the constant repetition in practice of the basic principles of their system. Hard work and the drip, drip, drip of doing the same things day in day out are how habits are formed.

The Wright/Shannon approach was flashier. We'd try a new routine for fifteen minutes and then it was a case of, 'Well done, now try this one'. That lack of continuity, their failure to build sound tactical foundations, meant that we never had anything to fall back on when our flair players – Baker, Eastham and Skirton in particular – couldn't conjure up a bit of improvised magic to turn a game.

Note that I did not count myself among the flair players, even though I would have put myself in that category at Leicester only a few months previously. My friends and former colleagues, Davie Gibson and Bobby Roberts, came to watch me play quite early in my Arsenal career and both said afterwards: 'You look a different player, Frank.' It was kind of them to try to spare my feelings by polishing up their criticism in that neutral phrase but I could easily decipher their meaning. In three months I'd gone from a free-wheeling wing half whose game was all about bombing forward, pinging shots at goal, throwing myself at crosses, tearing back and getting tackles in, to become a crabbed and intense spoiler and scrapper.

I know everyone still views me predominantly as a centre half but my reputation and record transfer fee had been built on my attributes in midfield. Yet only a few weeks at Arsenal had turned me from a clear-headed, precise passer – as dangerous in general play as at set-pieces – into a run-of-the-mill, battling mud-lark. It came from trying too hard. People say it's a good fault to have but it isn't ideal for a footballer, especially when you're striving to justify a large transfer fee to thousands of new and increasingly sceptical fans and, more importantly, trying to persuade yourself that you haven't made a terrible mistake and potentially ruined your career.

I was far too uptight and, for those first two years, I played with my fists metaphorically clenched all the time. Nothing felt right. My muscles were never properly relaxed during a game and my mind was never far from being clogged with a jumble of doubt and trepidation. I was just grinding through matches, putting in tackles that I should have left for someone else if all my trust had not expired, chasing all over the bloody place trying to put out fires. I was full of good intentions but there was no quality to my game; I wasn't picking my runs accurately, my passing was sound but excessively cautious and I rarely felt comfortable enough to shoot.

I was ashamed of the way I was playing, even though I ran my tail off. No one could ever have had a go at me for lack of effort but it was all method and no imagination. I felt crippled by the responsibility and my constant sense of anxiety. Most of all, I needed to calm down but I got myself into such a state of disillusionment that I over-compensated by running myself to a standstill – as if to demonstrate that I, at least, could be exonerated from guilt for Arsenal's appalling form.

My house-mate, Ian Ure, suffered in a similar way. Something of a paradox for a centre half, he was brilliant at ball-skills and could play keepy-uppy better than any teenage show pony. He could also kick you from here to the end of my garden. Ure was a very clever lad, but the most distinguishing thing about him was his build; he was one of those awkward, angular players with that Scottish raw-bonedness that could hurt you even if he didn't necessarily mean to.

An accomplished international, he had had some great games and could hit top level at times but he shared the team's maddening inconsistency. He didn't have a specific, consistent weakness, but he'd make mistakes – all sorts of different ones. Such mistakes came from concentration lapses, I suppose, but he must also have felt that the team's overall lack of organisation affected him; when things aren't quite working out in your game, a structure can give you something to fall back on, but it was so higgledy-piggledy at Arsenal that it must have hurt him. Many good careers were stunted during Arsenal's two years of tactical famine.

We finished the 1964–65 season in thirteenth place in the First Division and suffered the humiliation of being knocked out of the FA Cup in the fourth round by Third Division Peterborough United. It was correctly seen as a disgraceful result for us and, though the press continued to support Billy Wright's efforts to turn the team around, the fans were not so forgiving. We were just so hit and miss.

I would be in the depths of despair after back-to-back defeats and then we'd win two on the trot. This upswing would, inevitably, be followed by three further losses. The frustration this caused was difficult to overcome because neither did we really understand why we lost so many games, nor did we really understand how we managed to win games. In a way, it's easier to accept that you're just not good enough and are regularly trounced, but the tantalising hope offered by inexplicable victories can send you loopy trying to figure out the best course of action.

It can be very difficult for a team to perform when the crowd is prone to long bouts of indifference interspersed with short bursts of blistering anger, but one could sympathise with the fans' irritation as we did have enough decent players to be in a better league position. The promised Gordon Banks and Ray Wilson never materialised, of course, but in Joe Baker, George Eastham, Alan Skirton, Ian Ure, Terry Neill, Don Howe and myself we had enough quality and experience to complement the three tyros of genuine promise – George Armstrong, Jon Sammels and John Radford – that had emerged from the youth team.

Joe Baker, in particular, was a phenomenal player. He was all you could want in a goalscorer – equally adept with both feet and with the sort of pace that Ian Rush later used to such advantage. I love players like Joe, with the economical grace of Jimmy Greaves, the short back-lift when they shot and the bravery that distinguishes the great from the merely good. Joe once knocked out Ronnie Yeats with a punch, which, of course, I can't condone. But there's part of me that admired his courage in even trying it on with someone as intimidating as Liverpool's tough-as-teak centre half.

Eastham, like me, had fought hard to get to Arsenal. His apparent physical frailty was an illusion as he had stamina in abundance. I've said before that the best players are bright-minded, and George was a perfect example of a player with Teddy Sheringham-esque shrewdness and a very cunning intelligence. A great judge of a pass, he had nice, delicate control and was a good athlete – despite his funny, loping shuffle when he ran at full tilt. Like Baker and me, he must have thought that these were wasted years and yearned for a better team. Baker and Eastham galvanised the fans, gave them a bit of hope in that dreadful period, and I wish they had been around later. I bet that they wished that, too.

Later parts of this book may read like a glowing testimonial to Don Howe's skill as a coach but I also played alongside him for eighteen months before a gruesome compound fracture – sustained in a dour match against Blackpool – effectively ended his career. Signed a few months before me, he, too, found it difficult to settle. He was a very astute, attacking full back, which was relatively rare in the early sixties. We became good friends when Barbara and I moved into a house just two doors away from him, his wife Pauline and their four boys. Don remains a smashing man, the kind you would trust with your life, and although he has always seemed pretty strait-laced – never a drinker or a carouser – he's lightened up considerably in recent years and become quite the joker. Ever the model professional, he must have been appalled by Arsenal's lax discipline and bungled attempts at coaching. His maturity and loyalty in those early days gave him a stoical disposition towards the anarchy around him. It was something that I, ever the hot-head, could not share.

If any one player embodied what was wrong at Arsenal it

was Alan Skirton. He was a colossal outside right, six feet one inch tall and weighed fourteen stones. Fond of a drink, he brought some levity to our desperate plight with his constant wise-cracking, delivered in an engaging Somerset burr.

Our physiotherapist, Bertie Mee, got hold of him when he was injured and in just two weeks sweated at least a stone off him by working him flat out. Bertie would perch on his back like a jockey and force him to run up and down the terraces screaming: 'Come on, Alan. Drive yourself. My God, you're supposed to be a professional footballer.' As Bertie thrashed him towards fitness, we'd be lapping the Highbury pitch witnessing the comedy. When Alan came back, at the right weight, he played in a friendly match against a Brazil XI that was chock full of internationals yet he was easily the best player on show. He was unstoppable when he wasn't carrying all that excess timber, his power enabled him to shoulder-charge brutish full backs out of the way and his crosses were belted in like guided missiles.

This world-class form would last for about five games after his sessions with Bertie but then he'd be back up the snooker halls and his weight would creep up again. Billy Wright should have made Bertie flog him three days a week, even when he wasn't injured, and had him train with us only on Thursdays and Fridays. I'm convinced Alan Skirton would have been an Arsenal legend if he'd been handled with greater discretion. Even at his self-indulgent best he still scored more than fifty goals in 150 appearances – a freakishly good record for a winger. But the environment at Arsenal failed to provide the motivation Skirton needed to make the most of his enormous talent.

For most of that first season I was so wrapped up in trying to overcome my own poor form that I was uncharacteristically non-confrontational about everything else that was wrong with the team. On our post-season trip to Italy I finally exploded – at half-time, in a friendly against Lazio, when we were 2–0 up. Les Shannon had given firm instructions before the game that both central midfielders, Jon Sammels and I, should sit in front of the back four and not support the attack at all. However, it soon became patently obvious that Lazio weren't all that up for the game – and, anyway, they were rubbish – so I started to nip forward, set up one of the goals and almost scored myself. Les went crazy with me at half time and all those months of frustration that I'd bottled up came flying out in a bitter argument.

'I've told you to play defensively, and you've completely disobeyed me.' he shouted. 'You have to watch their midfielders breaking. They're going to score if you don't do what you're told.'

What really got me was that we'd been devoid of confidence all season and here we were, looking relatively comfortable for once, and all he could do was undermine our rare sense of optimism. 'Play defensively?' I ranted. 'Watch their midfielders? They're fucking piss poor.' I'm not proud of that outburst, but what we needed then was a boost, and the encouragement to go on and tear the opposition apart. Our altercation escalated as Les, quite rightly given the slur on his authority, had to have the last word. 'You're nothing but £80,000 worth of trouble, McLintock,' he yelled. I should have left it there but I couldn't. 'And you,' I blurted out, 'you couldn't fucking coach white mice.'

I should never have said it, and certainly not to him – he was by no means the only culprit for the team's malaise – but, at that moment, expressing the rage I'd felt for so long was almost cathartic. That feeling didn't last, but I had got my anger out in the open. However, in that era it just wasn't the Arsenal culture to sanction that sort of dialogue. I have always felt that it's better to discuss the pros and cons, though not always with so much rancour, and come to a judgement about who's right and who's wrong. Then it is possible to make some progress. But in this case the issue, along with our mutual antagonism born of frustration, were smoothed over quickly with apologies that neither of us felt justified in making. It was an unhealthy solution and typical of the club's ethos at that time.

When I signed for Arsenal it had never dawned on me how heavily the club was labouring under the burden of its glorious past. And it didn't take long for me to become as intimidated as everyone else. The marble halls were a daily reminder of our current inadequacy, and the fans' constant references to the vast pantheon of legends often made me feel like an impostor. There was a time when if someone trotted out any name from the list of heroes – Charlie Buchan, Alex James, George Male, Eddie Hapgood, Cliff Bastin, Ted Drake, Joe Mercer – I would literally cringe. Such was the club's illustrious history that the list could probably have had sixty names on it but those seven were the most popular choices when people wanted to lament the way we were sullying the club's heritage.

The pressure was intolerable and it led to one of my more outlandish ideas – one that I'm slightly ashamed of now, even though I had the best of intentions. I thought that one way to snap everyone out of dwelling on the past was to change our kit. I believed that the red shirt with white sleeves had become too identified with a gluttonously successful record that we could not possibly hope to emulate. We could barely breathe under the weight of expectation those legends of the past had generated. If we did what Don Revie had done at Leeds – but for the opposite reason – and ditched our trademark colours, it might signal to the fans that this was a new beginning. Only then might we be rid of the stigma and all those unfavourable comparisons.

For weeks, I pestered Billy Wright with this dramatic suggestion until he finally relented and we made the switch to an all red shirt for the following season. Thankfully, it was only a one-year experiment because it proved to be a wholly frivolous gesture. But it just goes to show that, long before kit manufacturers and commercial sponsors routinely interfered in kit designs – with scant regard for a club's history – one nagging player could succeed in dumping Arsenal's emblematic shirt.

If, fifteen years on, I had not struggled through my ill-fated first year of management with Leicester City I doubt if I would have eventually come to sympathise with Billy Wright's dismal predicament. But at Leicester I, too, had to face the problems that scuppered his ambition and I found them just as impossible to conquer. You need a grounding to tackle such a big job: you need the experience to be realistic about what is achievable, the single-mindedness to dismantle a team and take a step back before you proceed and you need the tactical know-how to accept that what was right in your day as a player is not necessarily suitable several years down the line.

When he was sacked at the end of the season, Billy Wright did at least leave us with a glittering legacy in the club's youth policy, even though his habit of enforcing discipline in a haphazard fashion – occasionally jumping on young players in a very heavy-handed way while letting established pros, me included, get away with murder – meant that he almost squandered that happy bequest. Overall, though, both Billy and

Les were on hidings to nothing and I'm sorry that they suffered such a terribly torrid time because of the pressure of the crowd and their frustrations at not being able to revitalise the club. But, in the mid sixties, what Arsenal needed was a skilled surgeon, not a pair of dashing and well-meaning but inexperienced junior doctors.

Of all the young players at the club given their debuts in the dying months of Billy Wright's tenure, Jon Sammels seemed to me to have the brightest future. Although there was only a couple of years' age difference between us, we almost immediately struck up a father and son type of relationship. Jon had all the attributes of a top player: he could run all day like Colin Bell, he had an exquisite right foot and a more than adequate left, he could hit a powerful bending shot and he was a very crisp and accurate passer. All in all he was an absolutely tremendous, dedicated guy but was quite shy for a footballer and suffered intermittent spells when he lost all confidence. This, sadly, prevented Jon from achieving all that his talent promised.

Great players need the swagger of a Mackay or a Cantona, the certain knowledge of how good they are. Cockiness and self-assurance – as long as they don't lead to conceit – are fine attributes for footballers. I have never seen a player so affected by the crowd as Jon. He wasn't a boo-boy as such, rather the crowd's impatience led to jeers, which sometimes made him think too long and dither more on the ball. He was the last person they should have jeered because he was sensitive and it shook him. I tried all the time to cajole him, but it wasn't enough; sessions with a proper sports psychologist, unfortunately unheard of in the mid sixties, would have propelled him into the top echelon of professionals.

I had a different approach entirely to the crowd's criticism. With the club in the doldrums, we started to get the bird quite regularly and, as attendance figures had dwindled alarmingly, you could easily hear a lot of the barbed comments. After a pre-season friendly with Rangers, I was walking towards the tunnel when I heard a voice shouting: 'You're a fucking disgrace, McLintock.' I snapped and shouted back: 'Meet me outside and say that again.' Having stripped and got changed I forgot all about it until the following morning when I read about the exchange in Desmond Hackett's report of the game.

Hackett was usually a fair journalist but he was also a bit of a mischief maker and had added the fan's idle boast in the final paragraph of his piece: 'McLintock didn't turn up as promised.' However angry this made me, it was nothing compared to my father's ire when he telephoned me and said: 'What's all this about you not turning up when someone's had a go at you? This is a spit in the face. What are you going to do?' Looking back, to be reminded of the Gorbals' code of honour was probably the last thing I needed but it was pretty clear that I had to do something about it not only to save my face but also my family's standing in their own community.

I put out a few feelers to discover who the man was and was more than a little disconcerted at reports that he was a vicious bugger with a reputation as a hood. Everyone I spoke to warned me to be careful, but I had to do something or I feared I wouldn't be able to hold my head up in Glasgow ever again. After training on Monday morning I grabbed Jon Sammels, told him the situation and asked him to mind my back when I went to confront my tormentor. Poor Jon, who is one of the kindest and gentlest guys you could ever wish to meet, had been brought up in Suffolk, far from the badlands of Glasgow and dodgy North London boozers. He must have thought that I was insane – but it shows you just what sort of man he is, that he came to support his friend without quibbling, even after I told him that rumour had it the man might be carrying a gun.

I strutted through the doors of the gangster's local with a sense of foreboding that I tried to conceal with an affected toughness. I marched over to a group of shady characters at the bar and demanded to know the whereabouts of the man who'd told the press I was a coward. One of them went ashen-faced and I knew immediately that it was him. As I grabbed him he protested: 'Frank, it wasn't me. That lying press guy made it all up.' There was some scuffling and bawling for a few moments as I tried to push him out of the door – I didn't want to upset the landlord by walloping him in the pub – but he clung to the bar with both hands and I couldn't pull him out.

After playing tug of war with his horizontal body for a while and screaming threats at him, I was calmed down by the gushing apologies offered by him and his cronies. It was settled in a pretty unsatisfactory way to my mind but as long as he and my father knew I would never back down when confronted, I felt that the slur on my character had been removed. When I think about it now, it was bloody madness that I could have been shot for something so absurdly petty. This Glaswegian notion of self-respect can be a very dangerous streak to live with.

My professional pride, however, continued to take a real beating throughout the next torrid season. Our pre-season in the West Indies was farcical and a match in Jamaica had to be abandoned when we were pelted with bottles after a twenty-two-man brawl following an eye-watering kick to Ian Ure's groin. During another match – mirroring my spat with Les Shannon in Italy just weeks earlier – Joe Baker got so fed up with Billy Wright's hectoring, half-time team talk that he flung his boots at the manager and refused to go out for the second half.

Strangely, given all the ructions, things had looked up at the beginning of the season. We lost only two of our opening thirteen games, but we soon slipped back into our familiar pattern, the sort of inconsistency that saw us losing 3-5 one week and winning 6-2 three weeks later. From the turn of 1966, we won only three of our remaining twenty games, finishing in fourteenth place; just four points off relegation. All these matches were played out against a backdrop of bickering and a rotten atmosphere in the dressing room.

Whenever we lost, a very frequent occurrence, Wright and Shannon would ladle the blame on the likes of Armstrong, Peter Storey, Sammels and Radford. I know the lads thought they made convenient scapegoats as they were youth team products and were unlikely to answer back with the same confidence as Baker, Eastham and myself. It was a ridiculous way to deal with young players and I started to stand up for them, but this just made for more hostility between me and the management team. Barely eighteen months after getting what I'd thought of as a dream ticket – my move to Arsenal – I could take no more and handed in an official transfer request. It was turned down but I remained determined to get away at the end of the season, and I'm pretty sure I would have done had fate not intervened.

On 5 April 1966, for a midweek match against West Bromwich Albion, our home attendance fell below 10,000 for the first time since 1914. It was a depressing and eerie evening. In a ground that could hold well over 50,000, that tiny, maudlin crowd meant that you could actually hear the traffic outside. Exactly one month later, against Leeds United at Highbury, that pathetic and embarrassing attendance figure was halved to 4554, a pitiful crowd even if the game had been strangely moved to a Thursday night. The demonstration outside the East Stand entrance after our sorry 3-0 defeat was louder than anything those few faithful fans had conjured up all night. 'We want a manager!' they demanded. And 'Wright must go!' In my experience of the club, Arsenal will always try to do the decent thing, and do it with some style. For all the board's breeding, they are no mugs. Hit them in the pocket and they react just like anyone else. That fans' boycott was Billy Wright's death knell.

At the end of the season the chairman, Denis Hill-Wood, came to the same conclusion as the supporters and players and Billy was sacked. I had been dissatisfied with his management all along but I did feel very sorry for him on a personal level because I respected him as a player and, despite our dressing-room spats, he had always behaved with the utmost kindness towards me. I wish I hadn't been so awkward, but you can't put an old head on young shoulders and I didn't have the maturity or the patience to sit there silently as my career went hurtling down the dip. I had always adored playing the game, whatever problems I had, but those first years at Arsenal were hateful. I appreciate now that Billy Wright's shortcomings as a coach were not the main reason for our poor form. The truth was we didn't have an outstanding squad for him to work with – merely a few good players but no depth, and inexperience left him ill-equipped to cope with the team's deficiencies when his charisma proved an insufficient tool. The pressure of four seasons of failure had taken a huge toll on him and he admitted, almost immediately, that he was relieved to be out of it.

As for me, I was prepared to put aside any grievances with the club and write off the beginning of my Arsenal career as a false start. Moreover, if the rumours about Arsenal's determination to bring in the best possible candidate to replace Wright proved accurate, I was sure that I was in with a real chance to salvage my dream. By the time I left for my summer holiday my old enthusiasm was renewed in eager anticipation of pre-season training under one of the two rival favourites for the job – convinced Arsenal were about to embark with a new regime under which we could not fail to prosper I would have been happy with either man. It only remained to be seen whether it was to be the Revie or the Ramsey era.

8

MANNA FROM HEAVEN

To say that I was thunderstruck when I heard that Arsenal had appointed our physiotherapist, Bertie Mee, as the new manager would be a monstrous understatement. I thought I had been made the butt of a peculiarly cruel joke and responded with disbelief and no little truculence. Although in this narrative he has featured only in a brief cameo, Bertie's skill as a physiotherapist had made a great impression on me, but I couldn't help but feel that the appointment of a mere physiotherapist to tackle the enormous problems at the club smacked too much of unorthodox and possibly irresponsible thinking.

Not one of my colleagues could offer a plausible explanation for our physio's elevation – other than his formidable reputation as a hands-on disciplinarian when supervising an injured player's rehabilitation. Moreover, we were doubtful that his approach –

more martinet than father figure – would improve the existing, poisonous dressing room atmosphere and rid it of the moaning and recriminations that had done for his predecessor. Indeed, later, Bertie's occasional pompous outbursts invited comparison to Captain Mainwaring of *Dad's Army*. Bertie, too, must have shared our doubts because it was common knowledge around the club that he had negotiated the option to return to his original position after a year should Denis Hill-Wood's gamble not pay off. I refused to be so patient and decided to give him six months to prove himself or I'd force through a transfer, come what may.

I should have seen that Bertie was the only member of staff at the club with the right blend of professional integrity and determination, born out of his respect for Arsenal and its chairman, to take on such a difficult job. After the turmoil of the Billy Wright era the board had clearly felt uneasy about the prospect of another outsider taking the helm. Thus, they had reverted to the blueprint that had served the club so well just after the war, when Tom Whittaker, another insider – and, indeed, another physio – had been given the job. Before joining Arsenal, Mee had been the rehabilitation officer at the famous Camden Road Centre, working with wounded and injured servicemen. He had been approached by the club for his expertise and, at Arsenal, blossomed into the finest sports physiotherapist I have ever worked with.

At Highbury, Bertie created a treatment culture that was the best in football. Some clubs treat injured players indulgently, others – back then, notably Liverpool – treat them like pariahs. The approach favoured by Bill Shankly, when he would waspishly tell his assistant, Reuben Bennett, to fetch a gun whenever he encountered an injured player – as they were no use to Liverpool – was only half in jest. For some years Liverpool's idea of physiotherapy was to send Bob Paisley or Ronnie Moran running onto the pitch to shove a wet sponge on a prostrate player's bollocks and tell him: 'Get up, son. You're all right.'

Mee was far more scientific but he expected a work ethic that was in sharp contrast to the lax approach that had prevailed under Billy Wright. When injured you had to report to Bertie's office at half past eight for the morning workout, there was a forty-five-minute lunch break at half past twelve followed by the afternoon session that finished at five o'clock – leaving you to fight home through the rush-hour traffic, a real pain in the backside even in the mid sixties.

Everything about Bertie's regime was designed to make you strive to get fit as soon as possible. The sessions themselves were purgatory. If you had a thigh strain, he would work on that leg but for the rest of the day would have you doing sit-ups, weight training on the fit leg and a punishing schedule of circuits in the gym. At other clubs they let you read the paper but Bertie's mantra was: 'No newspapers, no tea, and definitely no biscuits. You're here to work.' When the injury had healed he would take you out on the track and have you running until you became delirious through exhaustion. I soon came to see what the board had recognised in this stickler for the highest standards; Mee's vigour and rectitude were the perfect prescriptions to remedy Arsenal's sickness.

Almost at once, we began to see a change as Bertie rigorously enforced a hitherto overlooked disciplinary code. It has become a cliché to talk of football managers having a military approach but the analogy suited Bertie particularly well after his six-year stint as a sergeant in the Royal Army Medical

Corps. We were told that club ties and blazers were now oblig-
atory and that any unpunctuality would be fined. He saw us
as a unit to be trained and moulded, and promised to thrash
the vagabond instinct out of us on the training field. It took
only six to eight weeks under his strict discipline for the vast
majority of the squad to fall into line.

As you can probably tell, the new manager was hardly a
laugh and joke merchant. Some of those who didn't know him
personally but admired him from afar have described him as a
kindly uncle-type – which doesn't fit him at all. Mee was quite
severe and always remained aloof. There was a bit of a debate
over whether he preferred to be known as Bert or Bertie, but
I have no doubt that it was neither. Had he not already been
so familiar to us from his stint in the treatment room we would
have had to address him as Mr Mee.

His smallish stature reinforced that officious air and he was
very sparing in his praise – influenced, perhaps, by the old army
saying that 'a pat on the back and a kick up the arse are only
twenty-four inches apart'. The one real compliment he ever
paid me – that I was a better league player than Bobby Moore
but that Moore was streets ahead of me at international level
– genuinely shocked me. I was surprised more by him saying
it than what he actually said. However, I did not see his cold-
ness as a significant defect, at least not until we fell out all those
years later in Birmingham; you always knew where you stood
with Bertie.

Of course, there were still high jinks in the dressing room
and we continued to have a few drinks from time to time, but
you were always aware that he would pull you up for it if you
went too far. Everything Mee achieved stemmed from creating
the right environment from the start. For four years, he had

observed Billy Wright's travails and had struggled to keep his mouth shut. He let us know from the very beginning that he was not going to make the same mistakes.

To his great credit, Bertie wasn't at all precious about admitting certain of his obvious weaknesses. He had not been gifted with the ingenious tactical understanding to match his superb organisational skills. Similarly, while he knew how to handle footballers and was particularly adept at spotting a bad apple in no time at all, he did not have much of a feel, or love, for the game itself. Fortunately, though – as he had proved by assembling the best physiotherapy and training staff in the country – he had a flair for recruitment. Not that we instantly recognised this at the time.

Given that Arsenal were in need of wholesale reform, we soon became confident that Bertie would provide the framework of order and structure we had lacked hitherto; we also ruefully anticipated the prospect of him making us the fittest team in the country. And when we heard he'd sounded out fellow managers and consequently employed Dave Sexton – to bring the tactical input that we knew he could not provide himself – we began to think that the wee man might just turn out to be a better appointment than we had initially dreaded.

Dave Sexton is a football evangelist. Now in his mid seventies, he is as smitten by the game as any soppy teenager in the throes of their first crush. After his experience as coach to Tommy Docherty at Chelsea he came to us at the optimum time, both for his own professional development and for our education. He had found it very hard to cope with the attitude of some of the young players at Stamford Bridge, where a post-training afternoon session in the pub – which Dave naturally abhorred – was commonplace.

He had retained the fervour of his Jesuit upbringing and hated the insouciant, showbiz posturing that thrived under the Doc. Yet those who thought Dave was a soft touch quickly came unstuck. His father had been a professional boxer and Dave knew how to handle himself. Peter Osgood once told me that Dave got so frustrated with him that he said: 'Right, you and me, outside, now.' Big Ossie, one of the most fearless players in the game, quickly backed down. Yes, Dave was a mild-mannered man but if you crossed him or abused the values he cherished in the game he loved, he'd do you, no danger.

At Arsenal, we were so desperate for someone to lead us out of the maze that Billy Wright had got us lost in that we were never going to give our new coach the problems he'd had from the Kings Road playboys. We were a receptive bunch with a lust for learning. We wanted someone who could offer a practical route to success. No airy-fairy bollocks. We felt like artisans who had the motivation yet lacked the know-how. After his shattering experiences with Chelsea – and pretty lean times with Orient and Fulham – Dave was fortunate to hook up with us, and fortunate, too, to work under a manager like Bertie Mee who happily delegated responsibility for all on-field strategy to his second in command.

Bertie dictated the broader policy, which was that in our present state we couldn't expect to win every game but we did need to stop losing so many; this we would achieve by becoming conspicuously athletic and thus extremely difficult to break down. When it came to applying his policy, Bertie gave Dave totally free rein. Just as importantly, Bertie was prepared to take all the heat from the board and the supporters until Dave turned the team around. For Dave, it was the perfect opportunity to put into practice all that new thinking he had picked up as a disciple of Walter Winterbottom, the ex-England manager turned coaching guru. And he could not have found more willing guinea pigs.

That first vital pre-season under Dave Sexton took place against the backdrop of England's 1966 World Cup triumph. Unlike many fellow Scots – most notoriously Denis Law who shunned the final by playing golf on an almost deserted course – I had been avidly following England's success and took pleasure in their triumph. However, no Arsenal players featured in the victorious team so there was no world champion in our ranks to inspire us.

What we did have, though, was Sexton's analysis of the tournament, and his determination that we should appropriate the best from it. He transported a projector and several spools of film to our training camp at Lilleshall and, having been struck by Hungary's 3-1 win over Brazil at Goodison Park, spent hours, night after night, stopping and starting the film to illustrate points he wanted us to learn from Albert, Bene and Nagy. Their use of the near-post ball to unsettle the Brazilian defence was something we practised for hours. By the end of the week we'd watched that film so often we were clamouring for a bit of Sophia Loren for light relief. Unfortunately, Dave's concept of beauty ran more to tubby Hungarian footballers than buxom Italian starlets.

The main innovations introduced at Arsenal that summer were a man-to-man marking system combined with the adoption of a ten-man pressing game. The former was later dubbed 'mindless' by our new full back, Bob McNab, but I could see its benefit as a quick fix for a defence in disarray. That Bob should detest it was typical, as he had the most sophisticated tactical intelligence of any player I've ever met. But he was also extremely single-minded and dismissively abrupt. Two years on, once we'd grasped the rudiments of containment, man-to-man marking was dropped. The ten-man pressing game, however, became the bedrock of everything we achieved over the next eight years.

At seven o'clock each morning we would leave our spartan dormitories to begin fitness work, then move on to hours of shadow play to develop positional awareness. This would be followed by the rigorous routines that Dave brought back from his busman's holidays spent observing Italian training methods.

First, he had us drilling relentlessly on shutting down players man-to-man; if the player I was marking was in possession, I would have to rush to within five yards of him and jockey him in a half-crouch – aiming to stop him lifting his head and playing a long pass. You would neither hang back and give him space nor would you dive in and commit yourself – this would give him the time to clear the ball – you would stay, hustling him until he offloaded it or you intercepted his pass. You wanted to be a constant irritant to him.

Once we'd got the hang of this, our next lesson was all about anticipation: assess all the options of the man with the ball and, if any involved the player you were marking, cut off that option. Once we gained competence marking man-to-man, we moved to pattern plays – two men versus two, then three versus three – which taught us to play as defensive teams within a team. If the opposition's left back had the ball, for example, me, our outside right and our right-sided centre forward would form a unit against him, their centre half and their left half. If we were not in a position to steal the ball, we'd try to force him to pass to the centre half – usually any team's least reliable distributor.

From working as defensive teams within a team, we

progressed to squeezing up and pressing as a single unit in order to condense the pitch; this allowed us to retain a shape that was difficult to break down. If your team's defence is operating in this manner, there should never be more than forty-five yards between your line of defence and your forwards; the aim of this approach to defence is to obliterate the divide that would have separated your midfielders into attacking and defending units. The midfielders should always be close enough to support the attack and defence equally.

When mistakes were made on the training field – if, for example, someone failed to close off the touchline, or a forward switched off and didn't cut out the full back's pass to his centre half – Dave would blow his whistle, explain what had gone wrong and make the miscreant do ten press-ups. Today, the ten-man pressing game is well established, everyone does it, but it was a revelation to us. Once you've mastered it, the most difficult phase is learning to calm down when you win the ball so that you choose the most effective next option – you can become so focused on pressing that your brain just races. Dave trained us to have two mindsets and, after weeks of practice, to turn them on and off instinctively. Our new game had, of course, lost the purity of old-style attacking football – and from the spectators' point of view the pitch looked pretty congested – but it enabled us to grope towards the light and see an end to our previous tactical confusion. To us it was manna from heaven.

It was principally our industry on the training field that made us a much more competitive team in the 1967-68 season. But Bertie and Dave had also capitalised on the rich inheritance of young players – thanks to Billy Wright – augmented by a couple of judicious signings in Bob McNab and George

Graham, of which the latter had impressed Sexton when he coached him at Chelsea. Significantly, it was with the addition of McNab and Graham, plus Peter Storey, Peter Simpson, George 'Geordie' Armstrong, John Radford and myself, that Arsenal now had the nucleus of the team that, four years later, would win us the double.

It was significant, too, that our young players really began to make their mark under Mee. A well conditioned team with good on- and off-field discipline is, obviously, a perfect foundation from which young players can develop and make an impact and in this regard Highbury's new regime had set down good, clear guidelines which the youngsters followed readily. And it was no coincidence that the team as a whole started to improve from the summer of 1967, once the more jaded, 'seen-it-all-before' old pros had left during the close season.

After each training session we became more adept at executing Dave's game plan. I was striving so hard to regain the status I'd had as a player at Leicester that I wasn't immediately aware of the progress we were making. It built almost imperceptibly but when I look back at it now I realise the strides we made. The evidence was there to see at the end of the season in the number of goals conceded. In our last season under Wright we shipped seventy-five goals, in the first under Mee and Sexton, 1966-67, we got this down to forty-seven.

While I don't think I was ever as good a midfield player for Arsenal as I had been for Leicester, my game saw a dramatic improvement as I scored nine goals to go with Jon Sammels's ten from central midfield. That came directly from our greater confidence in the defence's security. It wasn't quite tight enough yet to establish a sequence of 1-0s that later became our trademark but having overcome the mercurial nature of our former game, we ground out draws and victories that would have been impossible before.

We had trained like lunatics, working on the team ethic and honing our minds and bodies to be sharper and meaner. Morale was up and the team had taken shape, though we were keenly aware that we still had a long way to go to challenge Manchester United, Liverpool, Everton and Leeds in earnest. But at least we could look forward with a dash of optimism.

All this was jeopardised early the following season with the announcement that Dave was going back to Stamford Bridge to manage Chelsea. It came as a hell of a shock, particularly as the first we knew of it was when he didn't turn up on the coach for our away trip to Wolverhampton. As soon as Bertie announced the news, the atmosphere on the bus changed. The banter was replaced with the sort of cursing and muttering that had been absent for the past year. Though we read Dave's sincere good luck telegram in the Molineux dressing room, we could not recover from the huge psychological blow and lost 3-2. We felt that the foundations we'd all struggled so hard to build had been kicked from beneath us.

I took the matter up with Bertie on the Monday morning after the match. I asked him quite aggressively why the hell he'd allowed it to happen: 'Dave wants to paddle his own canoe' was his justification. I couldn't believe it: 'Fuck his canoe. This is bollocks. At last we're getting a team together and you're letting him go.' I can understand the reasons now, both Dave's ambition and Bertie's reluctance to hand over the reins which we felt might have persuaded Dave to stay, but at the time we felt abandoned. Our guide had left us halfway up a bloody steep mountain.

Our greatest misgiving about the future concerned Bertie's

lack of adequate coaching resources. There was no conceivable way that he could fill the gap himself. Once, when Dave's daily commute from his home in Brighton was held up by engineering works, Bertie took the coaching session but after a farcical twenty minutes he packed it in saying: 'As you can see this is not where my expertise lies.' So he took us over to the track and had us running all morning. There he was in his element, with his stop-watch and clipboard at the ready. His background in physical training and his mastery of optimum times for each member of the squad meant that there was no chance of shirking the punishment. He had great presence, too, and even under Sexton we upped the tempo still further when Bertie was in attendance. 'Here comes the wee man,' someone would say and we'd take it up a notch even if we thought we'd been going flat out.

Bertie sometimes came across as half sergeant-major, half headmaster but such zealous people often make very good managers. He identified the same qualities in Don Howe and promoted him from reserve team coach to take over first team affairs. It was an inspired choice but while we were still mourning Dave's departure, I am ashamed to say that we proceeded to give him a rough time as our sulkiness proved difficult to shake off.

Don sympathised with our sense of bereavement and indulged us for a short time, suffering our stroppiness for about a week before exploding in characteristically forthright fashion: 'Right, I have fucking had my fill of you lot. Dave Sexton's gone. I'm the coach now and if you don't do what I tell you, you can get out of here.' He was justifiably furious and hauled us out of the gym and made us do double lap sprints. From that day on he controlled us, dominated us and earned our total respect. He was a wonderful workaholic and functional tactician, an excellent coach who just got better and better every year.

While Dave certainly had more patience with us – and I will always be grateful for the largely unheralded spadework he put in to launch us towards being a good side – I think it's fair to say that Don was probably more attuned to Bertie's ideas about how fitness and discipline are paramount to a team. But for all his intensity and dedication he wasn't as one-dimensional as the boss; Don knew how to be a sounding board for all our gripes and could help us to rationalise disputes when our hotheadedness threatened to find a target in the person of our manager.

By far the best example I can give of the values Bertie and Don shared, and the irreproachably loyal service Don gave to the boss, came on our pre-season trip to Germany a year or so after his appointment. At training camps we generally tended to have three sessions a day. We'd be ready to start at eight o'clock in the morning, do two sessions in the morning and go back at four in the afternoon to work on ball skills and maybe play a five-a-side. We were staying in Hennef, a pictur-esque town on the Rhine between Cologne and Frankfurt, and though we stayed in a classy hotel that served the biggest portions of food – Dover sole the size of tea-trays were their speciality – we hadn't had a drink for a fortnight. Towards the end of the trip, we were excused afternoon training and were taken on a boat trip up the Rhine. When we disembarked to wander around one of the villages, we were told that it would be two hours before the boat came back to pick us up so it was OK for us to have a glass or two of beer.

We all had three or four pints of strong German lager and

it hit us like a torpedo. By the time we got back on the boat and discovered the bar, our concerns about what Bertie might do if we didn't try to hide the fact that we were a bit pissed went straight out of the window. Encouraged by thirsty German day-trippers to join them in ordering jugs of beer, we started a sing-song. At this point Bertie and Don came down off deck to find us absolutely steaming. When we eventually arrived back in Hennef, they knew we were too far gone to train and led us straight to a *bierkeller* and let us carry on drinking. We couldn't believe that they had let us get away with it and there were quite a few toasts to our tremendously generous management team that night.

The following morning most of us were nursing dreadful hangovers and reported to the training ground in a state of acute mental dishevelment. Straight away, Don calmly announced that we were to do the three-mile cross-country run that had become part of our daily schedule. We knew, however, that we had a game the following day against Borussia Mönchengladbach and a cross-country run was out of the question. I protested vehemently: 'Bloody hell, Don. We can't do a cross-country the day before a game. We'll be fucked.' But he replied: 'I don't care who you're playing. We told you how much you could have but you abused our trust. You will never do that to the gaffer or me ever again. You need to get cracking and I want you all to be back here in no less than eighteen minutes.'

So off we went and came sprinting back, huffing and puffing, but ahead of the time. It was like a scene from a battlefield as players lay spread-eagled across the field. 'Well done,' Don conceded. 'Right, catch your breath for half a minute then I want you to do it again the opposite way.' Even though some players were on the verge of puking their guts up, we managed to get round a second time. When we got back he dragged us over to an old ash running track, which was almost ankle-deep in red cinders, and to finish the session had us run an 800 yards, a 440, a 220, two 110s and two 60-yard sprints – all against the clock.

Twelve minutes into our match the next day George Graham got himself sent off for retaliation after a foul. Back then, George was the biggest piss-taker on earth and while we battled on with ten men for almost eighty minutes in sweltering heat – breathing out of our arses as the dressing room term has it – George was sitting on the substitutes' bench with the greasiest smile plastered across his face, exaggerating his pleasure at downing pints of liquid in a display of comic mimicry. We drew 0–0 and absolutely ran our socks off. It was a fantastic performance and a great result considering what we had been through, and privately – though they'd never admit it, given the circumstances – Bertie and Don must have been proud of the way we had responded. Still, for quite some time afterwards we made sure that we never drank their health without a wary eye on the consequences.

For the remainder of his first season, 1967–68, as first-team coach Don only tinkered with the system we had devised under Dave Sexton. His was very much a safety-first approach and that was reflected in our league form, where we drew more games than we lost but we couldn't quite marry our new defensive strength to any real verve going forward. But our emphasis on the defensive arts paid dividends in that bastard child of Alan Hardaker's, the League Cup, where we qualified for the final to face Leeds.

Even then, the competition did not share the kudos of the FA's showpiece but I was thrilled at finally getting the opportunity to slay my Wembley hoodoo. The undoubted Johnny-come-lately nature of a competition apparently devoid of pedigree was no deterrent to the fans of both finalists since Arsenal had gone without a trophy since 1953 and Leeds had yet to break their duck. The Leeds fans were prepared to suffer greatly in pursuit of that elusive success. Good job, too, as even the most ardent among them might have got more than they bargained for on that turgid Saturday afternoon at Wembley.

Playing Leeds was no carnival at the best of times, but with both teams at their introspective worst – scarred by failure both were more obsessed with not losing than actually winning – the final was an awfully dreary game. From the kick-off each team set out to negate the other, strangling space so tightly that at times you could have thrown a lasso around the twenty outfield players. You would have had to be a fan of the two clubs to get even a tiny bit of enjoyment from the match. There were few mistakes and however hard we tried neither side could engineer any opportunities to score from open play.

Leeds' winning goal came from a set-piece, naturally enough, but it was a goal I still dispute almost forty years later. I've said before how unusual it was to come across tall players in my day, but in Jack Charlton Leeds had a player who understood how to exploit ruthlessly the physical advantage he enjoyed. When Leeds had a corner, they would stick Jackie on the goal-line, in front of the keeper, and get either Peter Lorimer or Johnny Giles from the left, or Eddie Gray from the right, to belt in a pace, in-swinging cross with a flat trajectory – the aim being for Charlton to flick the ball on, lay it off or score while the keeper flailed away behind him. I'm happy to salute the ingenuity of the ploy but I still think it was illegal. Given that clearly his intention was to obstruct the goalkeeper, we thought the tactic, though not Charlton's conduct in executing it, was in itself a foul, but referees chose to judge it case-by-case.

Eddie Gray's corner seventeen minutes into the game was as powerful as usual and, though it went over Jackie's head, he and Paul Madeley managed to sandwich our goalie, Jim Furnell, and take him out of the game. As George Graham headed the ball off the line at the far post, it fell to Terry Cooper who volleyed it past the obviously impeded Furnell to take the lead. I sprinted over to the referee, Mr Hamer, and harangued him for a good minute or so as he trotted backwards to the half-way line but he was adamant that the goal was fair.

When we later won a corner I decided to take matters into my own hands; I shoulder-charged Gary Sprake fractionally after he had come to take the ball and he rolled into the back of the net. Charlton, Sprake, Ian Ure and I then had a brief altercation involving some jostling and shoving, but Hamer intervened, gave the foul to Leeds, and that – apart from a late shot from Terry Neill cleared off the line by Billy Bremner – was the sum of our assault on their goal.

Leeds defended staunchly, not risking anything but not really needing to, while we failed to break them down despite dominating possession. Littered with sideways passing and constant retrenchment, it was a forlorn, dull match suitable only for the most masochistic of supporters. In that incarnation Leeds were like us; a promising side, mentally tough but not quite there yet in terms of adventure. We cancelled each other out in the most boring game of tactical chess ever played.

Later that night, as I cradled my loser's tankard – Hardaker must have thought medals old hat – I could grudgingly admire Leeds for the way they mugged us. And that deliberately implies that we were robbed, an assertion that I will never abandon. Could I not take some comfort in the relative youth of our team and the unarguable evidence that we had made progress?

No, not really, at least not immediately. My record at Wembley was played three, lost three. I'm not one for self-pity but that doleful sequence of lost finals coupled with the fact that I was by then twenty-eight did get me down. At bad moments I began to speculate that it might represent the pinnacle of my achievements, that I was destined to be a nearly-man. As ever, after a few days, I managed to dispel my negativity, though I did not know then that it would get much worse, humiliatingly so, before I finally cracked my cup final jinx.

9

BRAVEHEART

My first autobiography, published in 1969, ends with me in a wistful mood. Reading it now I can still get a jolt from the aura of acute disappointment that I seemed to be projecting; the sense of coming to terms with the mortality of my career as a player, and the probability that whatever years I could still eke out would likely remain unfulfilled. If someone had told me then that patience was a virtue in football, too, I would have had to curb the desire to smash his face in.

Of course, I still revelled in training and playing and I successfully managed to banish those doubts that give you the three-in-the-morning tremors during the course of the season. But in the summer you don't have all that work and your team mates to preoccupy you and that's why my natural bubbliness seems to have evaporated by the end of that book.

Given that it was written in the immediate aftermath of a fourth cup final defeat, there's little wonder that my mood sometimes veered towards the bleak. Since our conquerors in the 1969 League Cup final came from the Third Division, it's amazing to me that I wasn't thoroughly disconsolate. Some maintain that the will to win is forged in the crucible of such harrowing setbacks and consequently you appreciate it more when you actually win something. All I could think of that theory back then was that I would bloody relish the chance of testing it out.

Having said that, in the aftermath of our defeat to Leeds I did manage to pick up the Arsenal Player of the Year award from the Supporters' Club but because the four-year contract I had signed back in 1964 was coming to an end, I wasn't sure if I would be around to defend that honour the following season. I set off on our post-season tour to Japan and Malaysia with several misgivings about staying with the club, and secretly hoping that Dave Sexton might intervene to take me to Chelsea. I had intended to make my mind up in the Far East but the distractions were so numerous that I came back still undecided.

On previous tours we had been to Commonwealth or Western European nations. Japan, in contrast, was so unfamiliar that it seemed like we'd stepped into a science fiction film. I remember being struck by the ubiquity of golf on television and by the incredible number of driving ranges in Tokyo, some of them ten storeys high to make best use of limited land. We played three matches, travelled on the bullet train – faster in 1968 than anything in Britain today – and attended countless press conferences. Our hosts had drummed up a lot of interest in the exhibition matches and at times George Graham and I found as many as eight photographers outside our room wanting to take publicity shots. I'd never experienced anything like it for a football team. There were no screaming girls but Arsenalmania of a sort was evident during our short stay.

We had a greatly enjoyable time all round and the only mistake we made was when we were introduced to this one chap, who had struck George and me as a typical hanger-on. He wanted to pal up with us but after half an hour we'd had enough of the small talk and went off on our own. He went out, instead, with Terry Neill and turned out to be the manager of Andy Williams, the singer.

While we were trying to make our daily allowance extend to the extortionately priced beer – five times the price it was at home – Terry had found that solitaire wasn't the only game in town; hanging out with Andy Williams, he'd had the run of the city, its best restaurants and met Charles Aznavour and a host of other stars at a party after a concert.

All in all, it was a great bonding trip and we rounded it off perfectly with three victories and a celebration banquet, attended by Sumo wrestlers and karate stars, at which we spent half the evening on our feet either making or responding to toasts. Later that night I discovered to my cost that drinking sake is not the most efficient way of re-hydrating oneself before a long flight.

Terry Neill, the prime beneficiary of our Japanese hosts' hospitality, had relinquished the team captaincy to me shortly before our trip though he retained the honorary position of 'club captain' until he left just before the double season. He was a dedicated player with a very much 'up-'n'-at-'em' approach that belied his considerable intelligence.

Some players got exasperated with him because he wore his erudition a little heavily and could appear a little fanciful at times – he'd be reading a dense, Russian novel one week, learning Spanish classical guitar the next. I always found him a very engaging guy and the sort of straightforward, reliable player that good, if not great, teams need. Later, I learned that I hadn't been the first choice to succeed him and that Bob McNab had been sounded out. I don't know whether that was because of my contractual stand-off or if the board thought I was too impulsive, but they came to me after Nabbers had declined the position and advocated my candidacy.

The responsibility didn't change me much. I'd always been very vocal and on the field I had a good eye for spotting things about the opposition that we could exploit if we subtly altered the way we were playing. Moreover, I think, the innate aggression that I was blessed with allowed me to push the others very forcefully and, because I was equally hard on myself, there were few recriminations. It's the first principle of leadership – if you're prepared to admit your own mistakes, people take your criticism of them much better.

Indeed, Dave Sexton once told me that he had never seen anyone dish out bollockings as severely as I did yet still be the best of friends with the recipients after the game. I was fortunate, too, that most of the players in the team had developed a very astute tactical knowledge. They knew their jobs and didn't need much telling. My chief concern was the number of speeches I was expected to make at social functions. Terry Neill had been the ideal figurehead for the club. The way he spoke, dressed and conducted himself with impeccable good manners and charm perfectly reflected the board's image of the club and themselves. I had already mastered the natty attire but the rest came only after a great deal of conscious effort.

Inheriting the captaincy, though an enormous honour, was not the critical issue in my decision to stay. I had been troubled by two thoughts, one arising from the fear of instability at the club, the other more superstitious. Primarily I was worried at Arsenal's failure to hang on to Dave Sexton and feared that Don Howe, too, would inevitably wish to 'paddle his own canoe'. I required reassurance that the club were not going to make the same mistake twice and would stick to the long-term plan. Furthermore, while I wouldn't consider myself a credulous person, and certainly not one to feel sorry for myself, the idea that I might be jinxed did make me restless as I speculated whether a fresh start might help to crush it.

However illogical such doubts were, particularly for a good Catholic boy, they had taken hold after a cup final record that left me cursing the fates. I'm phlegmatic enough to recognise that when it's not your day, then it's not your day. But when it's not your bloody decade, you do start to wonder. Ultimately, I did sign a new four-year contract and my decision to do so was based on two important factors. First, I had soon accepted that in the three Wembley finals I'd so far played in we just hadn't been good enough; but I'd also come to realise that if we could win a trophy – any trophy – then the impetus that would give us should ensure it would not be our last. And second, I had Denis Hill-Wood's confirmation that the club would resist offers for Don Howe's services and with Howe staying put as manager I felt ready to sign up for more. It just goes to show how important timing is in football. If I'd been out of contract at the end of the next season I would probably have run so fast that the chairman would have been unable to catch me.

After we had lost to Leeds in the 1968 League Cup, we rallied to win our last five games of the season and began the next campaign in a similar, rich vein of form – winning seven and drawing two of our opening nine fixtures. Don Howe had replaced the rudimentary man-to-man marking system with the more sophisticated, zonal method of defending, and we noticed the difference straightaway. Not only did we let in a mere twenty-seven goals all season but it also freed the full backs, McNab and Storey, from standing toe-to-toe with wingers and pushed them forward.

Midway through the previous season, Bertie had brought in Bobby Gould to strengthen us up front. Gould, a strong, brave and industrious player with infectious enthusiasm, and an emotional, barn-storming, bear of a centre forward. He never had the skill to feature in a team of championship-winning calibre, but he was just what we needed at that stage of our building process when we lacked the sophistication to hood-wink a defence and had to rely on a less subtle route to goal.

Gould's forward partner, on the other hand, was a fabulous talent but such was John Radford's self-effacing nature that he remains probably the most underrated player in Arsenal's recent history. Raddy was a superb athlete: led the line with great guile, took all sorts of knocks, was very unselfish, a powerhouse in the air and he had the courage to compete magnificently with his back to goal. He'd been in London since the age of fifteen but he never lost a trace of his Yorkshire accent or his uncompromising, northern temperament.

Once during a training session Bob McNab, who had come back from an England squad practice, was being effusive in his praise of Sir Alf Ramsey and his enlightened training routines. I couldn't resist asking Raddy what he thought of the England manager and he punctured McNab's eulogy with blunt Yorkshire relish: 'Don't like the booger', he said. It was so funny. McNab stood there totally demolished, utterly crestfallen. John

Ajax and Cruyff in the semi should have been a daunting prospect. But instead we seemed to intimidate them, especially in this first leg at Highbury.

The final. Two down against Anderlecht from the first leg. But we believed in ourselves. 'We will pulverise this team with our mental strength, physical power and heading ability.'

Highbury was electrifying that night. We had all waited a long time to taste success. And it showed on everyone's face.

EMPICS

The fans streamed on to the pitch to celebrate. It was exhilarating, but also fairly scary. A scarf thrown around my neck half strangled me until this policeman came to my rescue.

AMEDEO GUILIANI

'The Battle of Lazio'. All smiles as we begin our defence. But violence between the teams on the pitch and in a car park later wiped the smiles away. Theirs anyway. We won the fight and the tie.

Our mothers must have been exhausted writing all those fan letters.
I wish mine had reminded me not to wear a towelling shirt.
Geordie Armstrong was a terrific attacking winger who formed part
of the nucleus of the double-winning team.

Happy as Larry, with Bertie Mee after we secured our second FA Cup final
appearance in a row. Eight months later, things were very different…

Arsenal Player of the Year, '67–'68. Chairman Denis Hill-Wood is on the left. The guy on the right is probably telling the photographer to hurry up. The bar shuts in 25 mins.

Showing off the Footballer of the Year award in '71.

Don Revie graciously congratulated me at the do, after we pipped Leeds for the title. I knew and admired Don for over 30 years, even after his fireside chat in Leicester and his holiday offer at Highbury.

Delighted to receive my MBE. But top hat and tails I'd rather leave to Fred Astaire.

EMPICS

'71. My first game against the Auld Enemy. My last for Scotland. Giving it my best against Martin Chivers, but I was in no fit state to play. And it showed. He scored twice and we lost 3–1.

C S WILKIN

Enjoying a jar or two with Spurs and Scotland legend Dave Mackay. We had to sing loudly into our 'double-headed mike' to drown out the noise of Dave's shirt.

On a Scotland trip with Wee Jimmy Johnstone. 'Someone's pinched our seats Jinky.'

COLORSPORT

Staring meaningfully into middle distance with Gordon Jago, who brought me to QPR. I had a fantastic four years, but the facilities were very different to Arsenal. We had to dredge our training bikes out of the canal.

And the showers were a bit Spartan as well. 'Henry' Mancini was a brave and uncompromising player on the pitch – but he was no match for a broom.

Giving the many journalists who frequented my Fleet Street wine bar my prediction for the '75 FA Cup third-round replay.

'Total football'
at QPR,
personified by
Gerry Francis.
The Frank
Lampard Jnr
of his day.

MONTE FRESCO

GETTY IMAGES

Last game of the '75–'76 season. Stan Bowles, Gerry Francis, myself and
Dave Sexton celebrate beating Leeds and going top of the table. We'd done all
we could. For ten days we dreamed we could be champions. Then 15 minutes
of football ruined it all.

Happy times at Brentford
Me as the gaffer and John
Docherty as my assistant.

Full of hope as Leicester's manager in September
'77. Nine months of torment was to follow.

Fast forward a couple of
years. Now at Millwall.
John's the boss and I'm
No. 2. About to hit the
big time having won the
'87–'88 Second Division.
Rumours said that
Manchester United
were interested in us.

Fast forward again, 18
months. February '90.
We'd just lost 2–1 to
United. It turned out they
hadn't wanted us and, a few
days after this, neither did
Millwall.

wasn't as effective in his early years as he later became when Charlie George and Ray Kennedy were promoted to partner him but he was such a valuable asset to our team that year, and so shrewd and receptive to coaching that he seemed to improve every month.

We couldn't maintain that opening winning spurt but we put together another run of six consecutive victories at the turn of the year which thrust us up to our highest league position for years. We were still very much a work in progress, with players like David 'Doggy' Court, Jimmy Robertson, Terry Neill and Ian Ure prominent while others – Raddy, Peter Storey, George Graham and I – were still not playing in the positions that we subsequently excelled in. It was also the first season that Bob Wilson became a regular when he finally replaced the smashing 'two-touch' Jim Furnell in goal after five years of arduous dedication to self-improvement.

Poor Bob had waited so long to establish himself and while I felt he had made an unarguable case for inclusion earlier, the boss obviously did not concur. It would have broken the average professional's spirit but Bob is not an average man. Instead of moping about he worked so hard that no one could ignore him any more.

Bob was so untypical of footballers, with the slightly refined language he used, and the way he dressed – in a camel duffel coat and his Loughborough College scarf. It must have been a bit of a disadvantage to him that he didn't conform to the footballer stereotype, wasn't much of a boozer and was from a conspicuously middle-class background. But he never looked down on the rest of us and we just saw him as a one-off. Later, of course – and especially when we discovered that his second name was Primrose – he had to endure the ribbing that everyone gets at football clubs, but it's to his great credit that he fitted in so easily with the rest of us who had gone to school primarily to play football.

I would have expected his academic endeavour to teach him caution. Far from it, as a goalkeeper he was recklessly brave and often put his head where others would fear to put their feet. In later years he used his keen sense of danger to anticipate breakthroughs, operating as a sweeper behind the back four if any holes were bludgeoned through our off-side trap, a ploy which allowed us to keep our line further up the pitch than normal.

With the emergence of players like Bob Wilson and the progress made by Radford, McNab and Storey, we were a much stronger team one year on from our drab game with Leeds. When we qualified for a return trip to Wembley – in the League Cup final again – we felt that we had been handed the perfect opportunity to put things right and could finally get the caretaker to dust off the Arsenal trophy room key. The omens could not have been more favourable – our opponents were Swindon Town. Their form had been good all season and for much of it they had led the promotion race. But it was the Third Division they led, after all. And that's not meant to sound patronising, it's just the way the game was built up in the press. We didn't underestimate them, we didn't really know enough about them to make that error. I wish I could look back and say we were arrogant, ill-prepared and we got our comeuppance. That, at the time, would have been easier to bear than the fact that our composure went out of the window and we were thoroughly out-battled and ultimately out-played.

We did have our excuses but it sounds a bit ropy to trot them out now. Yet it is only fair to point out that six members of the first team, myself included, had succumbed to flu in the weeks leading up to the match, and at the Grosvenor House Hotel the night before we played, it was still touch and go if many of us would make the game. The pitch, too, was a disgrace, the drains having been damaged some weeks previously during the Horse of the Year Show. Wembley was always a punishing surface as I've said, and on top of that, for that afternoon the pitch was flooded and gloopy with mud and my calves were tortured by cramp even before extra time.

It soon became obvious that Swindon were only masquerading as a Third Division team. They were exceptionally well organised and in Frank Burrows, Peter Noble and Don Rogers they had three outstanding players. Their goalkeeper, Peter Downsborough, had the game of his life, which certainly did not help us. They took a first-half lead thanks to a cock-up between Ian Ure and Bob Wilson in a situation manipulated by that pair's lack of faith in the porridge of a pitch. Big Ian tried to shepherd a ball back to Bob but frightened of it bobbling he dribbled it closer instead of passing it. Bob was screaming at him to release it but Ian only did this when the two players had almost converged – Ure hit it unexpectedly late, the ball ricocheted off Willow's shin and was stuck in the net by Swindon's onrushing Roger Smart.

During the interval we were told to be patient, but with half an hour to go we tried to take the pitch out of the equation and hit it long. We made a fair number of chances, most splendidly saved by Downsborough, and were reprieved by Bobby Gould's goal four minutes from time. He was in floods of tears and I was pretty close to blubbing as well. We thought they'd had their chance but we had managed to get out of gaol. I was convinced that the world would revert to its normal axis during extra time.

Perhaps it would have done if I had been able to run but my lights went out almost as soon as the added period began. Don Howe had failed in his audacious attempt to get the match abandoned at full time, arguing that our fatigue would lead to injuries on that boggy pitch, and so we continued, though I could hardly lift my legs. To Swindon's credit they did not brood on the setback of Gould's equaliser and just took up where they'd left off. Don Rogers's skill and persistence won the match for them with two further goals; one a knock-down from a corner that we should have cleared, the second when he skipped through our defence. He was such a classy player, with great balance and a silky touch. I later played alongside him at QPR by which time injuries had left him a shadow of his former self, but that day at Wembley he shredded us.

There's a picture taken after the match which still resonates for me; it captures me in a daze, clutching my tankard, trudging back towards the tunnel through the ranks of the Royal Engineers' band, totally oblivious to the pumping trombones. I was devastated, on the verge of despair. Uppermost in my mind was the indisputable fact that I was now a loser four times over.

Back in the dressing room I was beyond consolation. The good luck telegrams were a ghastly memento of squandered hope. Johnny Giles and Davie Gibson had sent their best wishes but Don Revie, such a well-meaning man, had sent a longer despatch ending with the faux pas: 'Sincerely hope you're first up the steps this time.' He'd forgotten that the winners went second up the stairs.

Later that night at the dinner, and later still at the Playboy

Club, one thought kept recurring, a bitter voice resounding inside my head: 'They've found you out. You think you're good enough but you're not.' It took a few drinks to shift it but there was a heartbreaking moment the following morning when my son Jamie greeted Barbara and me on our return from the hotel with: 'Where's the cup you said you'd bring home, Daddy?' It was purgatory. Losing to Leeds was one thing, taking a thrashing from a Third Division side had knocked me sideways. As I went to bed I distinctly remember thinking: 'Is this how it's always going to be?'

On the Monday morning I still felt hollow but a prolonged bout of self-pity was not an option under Bertie and Don. Our meeting was not an inquest, more an attempt to boost morale with the emphasis on the progress we had already made. European qualification was still possible and that incentive, to prove our resilience and shove our numerous press critics' words straight back down their throats, became a very attractive stimulus.

In Bertie and Don's objective analysis we were very close to success and, as the mood of the meeting gradually lifted with exhortations to remember the pain and ensure that it never happened again, their arguments grew more and more persuasive. I looked into the eyes of my team mates and knew that they hadn't 'gone'. Belligerence and defiance oozed from everyone, and it made us slog our way to the season's end like a team possessed. We lost three of the last twelve games but we scrabbled together enough points to hold off Chelsea to take fourth spot and London's place in the re-named European Fairs Cup.

Five years after a transfer motivated largely by a desire for European football, I had finally got there. Today it would seem like meagre solace but, then, I was so grateful for any success that our achievement cheered me up no end. And, at the age of twenty-nine, I was acutely conscious that opportunities were rapidly running out for me. It was time to shed this jinx crap once and for all.

Towards the end of that season and after the Wembley debacle, I was asked by Don Howe, on the initiative of our chief scout Gordon Clark, to help out the team by filling in for an injured Peter Simpson at centre half. Reluctant even to contemplate their suggestion, I was eventually swayed by the argument that I was a strong tackler, delivered a decent header for my size and that it was a short-term solution and entirely for the good of the team. I had taken the proposal as a slap in the face – at best it was demotion from the cavalry to the infantry, at worst, I thought, perhaps it was a way of easing me out. Clark and Howe quickly convinced me that it was only an experiment and pointed out that if I was comfortable not playing with my foot on the accelerator all the time, then it would probably extend my career.

After my first match at the back, I remember Ian Ure saying that he was knackered. 'You're knackered?' I snorted. 'I've hardly got a sweat on. I could go out and play another game.' Ah, the arrogance of the midfield player. When Peter Simpson came back I returned to my normal position but six months later the switch was made permanent. It took about a year for my body to adapt to playing at centre half and I finished matches just as tired as I'd ever been; and due to the vigilance and unin- terrupted concentration the position demanded I was even more mentally drained than I was physically fatigued.

In another piece of positional alchemy, my move to the back worked to the advantage of my room mate, George Graham. In the late sixties, we two inseparable, Scottish buddies were known to the others in the dressing room as 'Ronnie and Reggie'. Despite our firm friendship, George and I often had explosive arguments – usually initiated by my frustration at his determination to retain his super-cool demeanour on the pitch – during one of which he said, infuriatingly: 'Mind the face, Frank; I'm going out dancing tonight.'

As a forward, George had superb technique, great vision for a pass and was one of the best headers of the ball you would ever see. But his lack of pace, and his blatant dislike of defenders 'clearing him out' from behind, ultimately made him unsuitable for the hard-running role up front that got the best out of us as a team. My friend slotted, majestically, into the gap in midfield that I had vacated; he took the centre-left berth, and Jon Sammels moved across slightly.

George became a highly effective midfield player: proficient in the wall pass, timing his runs to receive possession around the box, and mastering the trick of running with the ball towards the centre of the field to hit a beautifully disguised reverse pass to put McNab into space out wide. George's sumptuous technique enabled him to hit the ball with the perfect weight and in four years McNab rarely had to break his stride to collect a pass.

George Graham always had a quiet knowledge of the game but at that time preferred to emphasise the happy-go-lucky, mischievous side of his nature – if you catch his television appearances, you can still see it in his twinkling eyes. If I was banging on about the game in the bar afterwards he would always say: 'Put the ball away, Frank. Get me a vodka and Coke.' He was never as voluble as Nabbers and me, but he had great ideas about the game if he ever condescended to talk about it.

If you'd taken George at face value you would have been

baffled to see the change in him when he became a manager, but he'd always had that intelligence and toughness. Strangely, he is a model professional now. Never a natural athlete – in fact he used to look near to death after some of the fitness sessions – he goes to the gym three times a week, plays tennis regularly even though he's got arthritis, and fanatically watches what he eats and drinks.

The old George was very much a poser. He always dressed immaculately and groomed himself meticulously. The word suave would describe him perfectly, and I like to think that he saw himself as James Bond. On a post-season tour to Malta, he had me enthralled with tales of his prowess as a diver. He admitted that he was not a good swimmer but, if I threw him a lifebelt after each dive, he would be happy to put on a display from some rocks jutting out above the Mediterranean. Six times he did it, adding flips and somersaults as he grew more confident – I gave him high marks for each dive and provided a running commentary.

There's some dispute about what happened on his seventh dive. George says I didn't throw the buoy out to him, I maintain that I did but that I wasn't as accurate as the previous attempts and it landed several yards away from him. As he flapped out to reach it, he kept pushing it further away and he started to panic. George, from speculating just moments before that he would be Scotland's first Olympic gold medal diver, turned into George the flailing frog. I was so helpless with laughter that I couldn't rescue him but a couple of the lads hauled him out. Spluttering, and with his drenched hair giving him the air of Max Wall, his 007 pretensions never recovered.

If moving to the midfield was the making of George, my move to centre half thoroughly rejuvenated my career. Moving back gave me the space to look at a match properly, just as I had always done at Leicester. The change from the WM formation since I left Leicester had left the midfield areas congested but moving back seemed to give me the space to thrive in. While our defensive tactics were complex – and some of the ploys we used were very cunning indeed – paradoxically, the game recaptured its simplicity for me when my long-lost composure returned as my confidence grew.

It took a lot of hard work to make the transition and I had to confound the scepticism of Bob McNab, who I had asked to help to tutor me. I don't think he was too keen at first but as I responded to his advice, very forthright advice as he was more tartar than teacher, he became more enthusiastic. Don Howe was also a great help, telling me to model myself on Joe Shaw of Sheffield United and helping me to start thinking like a centre half.

If you play at the back with a midfielder's mindset, it is difficult to conquer the inclination to follow the player you're marking, even if he makes a dart out towards the flanks. From day one, Don and Bob hammered home the importance of positional discipline and of holding a compact line.

In the early days I made mistakes, I was suckered out of position once or twice by my desire to make a critical interception or snuff out danger, even if it was not my job to do so. I quickly learned that if I edged a yard or two closer towards our right back than I should have been, then it would set off a chain reaction forcing 'Stan' Simpson and Nabbers to compensate and come closer to me, exposing a huge gap down the left. 'Oi, you knob,' Bob would scream. 'Get fucking back and stop dragging me across.' I only needed to be yelled at a couple of times before it sank in.

Furthermore, we developed the zonal system so that the two central defenders would not be caught out of position. The last thing you want as a defender is a broad channel between you and your partner, or you and the full back, and this is where the tag system came into play. If the forward ran between me and the full back, I would run with him for five or ten yards, then pass the responsibility on to Pat Rice who would tuck in and pick up the run, allowing me to resume a more central position. By maintaining the right shape as a back four, we soon became very difficult to catch out. We never achieved total impregnability, that would have been impossible, but at our best we came as close as anyone has got before or since.

After a few games at centre half I felt totally revitalised and took to defending with a convert's fervour. Once I had grasped the basics I became rapt in the artful plotting of our training ground conspiracy to outwit and deceive strikers. The fabled, if much maligned, off-side trap falls into this category and it was something we perfected only after months of drilling with Don Howe. It was designed to mask our weaknesses as a back four, chief among them our collective lack of speed.

The key to the system was not holding a horizontal line but making sure the space between the four of us was constant, even though the full backs were stationed about six feet ahead of my and Stan Simpson's position. The aim is not to get in a race, particularly not one in a straight line. When a forward made a run, Simpson and I bent the angle of our run to mirror his movement. If it was my attacker, Stan and the full backs would be my eyes and, as soon as one of the opposition pulled his foot back to deliver the through ball, they would give me the shout to step up.

Similarly, if it was Simpson's runner I would shout, or if both made runs the full backs would make the call. Bob Wilson, alert and patrolling the edge of his area, provided the safety net. We snared so many people that way, particularly Geoff Hurst who we fooled on numerous occasions. The other variation, if the opposition played the ball to the forward's feet rather than over the top, was not to mark in the traditional fashion – between the player and the goal – but side-by-side with him. This allowed us to nip in and intercept the pass. Most teams use the trap now but not so rigorously. Back then it drove the opposition crazy with frustration. Simpson was the perfect partner for me and his unruffled approach helped to temper my impetuosity. He was an underrated player; indeed he is the last person, himself, to recognise how good he was. If it had not been for exceptional talents like Bobby Moore, Norman Hunter and Colin Todd blocking his path to the England team, he would have made a very fine international player.

George Graham also settled smoothly into his new midfield role but his occasional bouts of slackness still drove me wild. Pressing requires tenacity and strict discipline, but George sometimes didn't have the stomach for it and sold himself by diving in to a tackle and losing his man. Hustling in a half squat is very tiring, it's far easier to give in and go for the glory tackle but it rarely comes off. When George succumbed to idleness I would go ballistic with him. Moreover, I hated him coming back for a breather to a position just in front of the back four, especially if I didn't have my hands full with a forward and was free. It gives you a false sense of security and if the ball goes back into their midfield George wouldn't be there to pick his man up.

Although we were room mates for seven years, there were

never any holds barred. I would slaughter him if I felt he wasn't doing his job properly and I must have chased him around the dressing room at half time fairly often. My view was that we could have a drink afterwards and pal up again but when we'd got ten minutes to sort it out, then I didn't care if he was my bosom buddy, I was going to let him have it. Of course, with those players without such robust temperaments I would be over-complimentary, gee them up by exaggerating how good they were. But with the ones who could take it, or needed it, I was very harsh and ruthless. I always made sure that it never festered. I said my piece, very forcefully, got back out on the pitch and they responded magnificently. There was no bitterness afterwards.

Our league form in the 1969-70 season was a huge disappointment. We suffered quite a lot of injuries and we had a couple of youngsters, Eddie Kelly and Charlie George, bedding down in regular starting positions. Our Fairs Cup campaign was a different matter. A series of niggling strains meant I missed five legs in the first three rounds but the team comfortably beat Glentoran and Sporting Lisbon without me, and the unsung Jon Sammels won the tie against Rouen with the only goal. I was back for our trip to Romania, our first taste of Eastern Europe.

There was none of the seedy glamour and romance of *The Ipcress File* in Bacau, a Godforsaken part of the communist bloc set in the foothills of the Carpathian Mountains. It was the grimmest place I've ever visited. If in the late forties Glasgow had twenties-style deprivation, Bacau had Dickensian levels of poverty. It was a garrison town, with soldiers everywhere, and when we sat down in the hotel restaurant to eat the food we had shipped with us, hundreds of locals lined up in front of the plate-glass windows and stared at us. I remember the fruit being a particular attraction. You'd be tucking into a banana or a bowl of strawberries and there would be an audible hum from outside as the onlookers, presumably, discussed these novelties.

We won the match 2-0 in front of a large, uniformed crowd – probably a division of the Romanian Army – and our opponents, who were very friendly, just gawped at our clothes as they said their farewells after the match. They seemed petrified when they came to Highbury and we strolled to a 7-1 victory. I felt so sad for them. I think they were overawed and, understandably, wide-eyed from the culture shock they must have felt in London. I hope they at least managed to gorge on fruit during their short stay.

Our semi-final opponents, Ajax, had lost the previous year's European Cup final and would go on the following year to take the first of three consecutive European Cups. With a team that included not only Cruyff but also striking talents like Keizer, Hulshoff, Krol and Vasovic, they should have been daunting opponents but they actually seemed a wee bit intimidated by us, certainly in the home leg at Highbury. That was the night, they say, that Charlie George came of age. And he did score two great goals but I think that accolade was a little premature since the opposition, for all their stars, were very tentative, almost afraid of us. We won 3-1 on aggregate, setting up a final against Anderlecht. This, my fifth final, would be played over two legs. That was great for me as I'd always felt after the previous four that I wanted to play those games all over again. Little did I know how decisive that guaranteed second chance would eventually turn out to be.

Because of the preparation time necessary for that summer's

World Cup in Mexico, there was only a week between the semi-final and final. I sometimes wonder if that had any effect, whether the lack of a traditional, lengthy build-up helped or hindered us. You would think by the result of the first leg, a 3-1 defeat in Brussels, that we must have been undercooked; not so much that we had failed to grasp the magnitude of the game, but that we had not yet worked out how to beat them. I think there was some truth in that. We just went out to play as we'd played all season and didn't modify our approach to compensate for their specific strengths and weaknesses. Consequently, Anderlecht duped us. There's no better word for it. They had the insouciance of a street-corner card sharp.

Even at 3-0 down it didn't feel like a hammering. For two thirds of the game they kept playing the ball into wide areas but never threw a cross into the box. With their constant probing, they explored every facet of our defence except our aerial power. Christ, they were patient. They would pass the ball out to each wing, knock it back to the centre, then back into midfield, and then out to the wing again. They were fantastic at retaining possession but just as you were lulled into thinking they were playing prettily but not very effectively, they'd ping a shot into the bottom corner of the goal.

We had not been getting forward very much but we seemed to have no trouble containing their attacks, yet suddenly they score and you think: 'You lucky bastards!' All they'd done was pass it around, non-threateningly, probe, probe, probe and we were 1-0 down. We were a high tempo team and they were knocking the ball around as though the game was going to last three days. After seventy minutes they'd picked us off for three goals and I found myself thinking: 'Hang on, I haven't got a broken nose, there's no blood, and I don't feel as though I've slogged it out and been battered by three goals.' They scythed through us, beautifully mugged us.

With fifteen minutes to go Ray Kennedy came on for Charlie George. It was only his fourth appearance and aged just nineteen you would think that he might be happy just to get the experience. But he threw himself about and started to win balls in the air, which unsettled their defence so much that Raddy started getting headers in, too. Ray got the 'consolation' goal to make it 3-1 but it didn't do much to improve our dressing-room mood.

Everyone was so downhearted, sunk to the lowest level I'd ever seen. I was just as bad, even worse, thinking it might be five losing finals on the trot for me. But while I was in the shower I started to think about the last quarter of an hour of the match and saw a way out for us. Kialunda, the Anderlecht centre half, was a good six feet two inches tall, but he couldn't head the ball for a free haggis supper. I thought, 'Bloody hell, we can win this,' so I started to gee everyone up in what Bob Wilson calls my *Braveheart* mode: 'Get your heads up. I'll bet anyone we can win this because they can't defend crosses. We need to get our heads straight, really set our stall out to concentrate for ninety minutes and not concede. If we can get the ball out wide all the time and get crosses in, we will pulverise this team with our mental strength, physical power and heading ability.' All of a sudden the mood started to lift and everyone felt so much better. I even inspired myself, I felt so confident that we could take them apart at Highbury.

And that, more or less, is what happened. Highbury was electrifying that night. There were almost 52,000 supporters in the ground and because the stadium wasn't all-seater back then, a good 40,000 of them had turned up hours early to get their favourite spots on the terraces. The fans made a terrific racket even at six o'clock and we could hardly get up Avenell Road on the coach. I think the atmosphere and our performance made it the best night game the stadium had ever staged, a stark contrast with that Leeds United game four years earlier when fewer than 5000 turned up.

We tore into Anderlecht, chased and harried them and got crosses in and shots on goal. The place was heaving and the noise kept growing. We were 1–0 up at half time and remained so halfway through the second half when I threw my arms up to the North Bank to try and get the fans going for the final push. They went so potty it was almost deafening.

We needed to win by three clear goals and we prevailed thanks to three 'screamers'; two cracking shots from Eddie Kelly and Jon Sammels and a scorching header from Raddy. Although they hit the post through Jan Mulder — a great player who could hit the ball like di Stefano, he'd smack a shot in that stayed level at a foot off the ground — Jon's seventy-sixth-minute winner was just reward for a top-class performance from him.

Mulder and Paul van Himst were outstanding that day. We met them afterwards in the players' bar and they couldn't believe how much energy we'd had, how we'd run them ragged because Geordie Armstrong, Jon and Nabbers could push themselves through tiredness. Mulder became a journalist and, many years later, he told me they had thought that we must have been on drugs that night. Needless to say, we weren't, but if you can picture a team playing at their very best, where the physical superiority was married to technical and tactical excellence, that was us that night. It felt like our best ever game, close to a perfect performance.

I would love to have won any one of those Wembley finals but to win that European Fairs Cup at Highbury was special in its own way. When we were awarded that strange, tall, thin trophy thousands of fans came on the pitch, some hoisted me shoulder high and I vividly remember someone throwing a scarf round my neck, but as people grabbed me from either side the scarf became the rope in a tug-of-war and I was half-strangled. I was excited but I was fairly scared too.

I was rescued by a policeman who got me back to the dressing room where my team mates were hugging and kissing and shouting and bawling; they were also slugging champagne and the fags were out. Then the directors came in, toking on cigars, wreathed in smiles, and all the backroom staff who had played their part. As for me, I was relieved more than anything, pleased that Arsenal's seventeen-year wait was finally over and jubilant that, for me, it had been fifth time lucky. That's an understatement, really. I was ecstatic. It was true what great players had told me. It's such a great game but it's immeasurably better when you win.

10

SQUARING UP TO MAKE HISTORY

Some forty-four years on from Spurs' double-winning exploits, whenever Tottenham Hotspur play, someone, somewhere, thinks of that 1961 team. I won't go through the roll call of legends that spring so easily to mind for fans of a certain age, but it is fair to say that Blanchflower's immortal deeds occupy a place in the heart of football purists that ours at Arsenal ten years on could never have hoped to share, never mind dislodge.

This stems partly from the fact that, in terms of winning the double – the FA Cup and the league – Spurs were pioneers, at least in terms of the twentieth century. Acclaim is justifiably more effusive for the first side to reach such a pinnacle. But it was to do with style, too, the impression that double victory made on the country and, not insignificantly, on a generation of football writers. Perhaps the sense that the club has lived in the shadow of that team ever since adds to the romance.

Whatever the reason, there is no doubt that, at Highbury, we suffered in comparison. While emulating Spurs' accomplishments we were nevertheless deemed unworthy, and the words used to describe some of our games throughout the 1970–71 season – dull, sterile, unimaginative – reflect the generally dismissive tone levelled at us. Even the compliments we got – well organised, highly efficient, powerful – had the whiff of back-handed tributes.

It's difficult to be bitter about it when you concede that there's some merit in the argument that, with Arsenal, the whole was greater than the sum of its parts – although the 'machine' analogies did underestimate our players' individual talents. No, it's the 'lucky Arsenal' tag that gets up my nose. Of course you can get the breaks in certain games. But to win the league and the FA Cup in the same season requires a damn sight more than good fortune.

In stating our case to be recognised as deserved inheritors of Tottenham's mantle I do not mean to be disrespectful to our North London rivals. The vibrant hatred the two sets of fans have for each other has never tainted my admiration for the club's achievements. Watching Spurs was always exciting. There was definitely a keen sense of anticipation running through the crowd whenever I went to White Hart Lane and the way Dave Mackay sprinted out of the tunnel, chest puffed out, and booted the ball twenty yards up in the air all made for a great spectacle. Moreover, we regularly used to see the Tottenham players out and about as they tended to live in the same areas of London as us – Palmers Green, Southgate, Cockfosters and Winchmore Hill. While Chelsea players hung out in hotel bars with actors and actresses in their more raffish part of town, we tended to be more pub orientated.

I would have a drink fairly often with Spurs' Mackay or Alan Gilzean as that North London, tribal thing meant nothing to us Scots. I couldn't see great Tottenham players like Bobby Smith and Cliffie Jones as my enemies in the way rival supporters do; we'd tear into each other a couple of times a season but off the pitch we were pals. So I have always understood the affection that team is held in. I just wish that those who sought to beat us with the stick of their graceful elegance had more consideration for the somewhat brutal way the game had evolved in the intervening ten years.

I guess it's ironic that the first full season of the so-called flair decade was dominated by Arsenal, a team then characterised more by its industry than the maverick embellishments that linger so prominently in popular memory of that era. We didn't quite fit the stereotype of the classic seventies team – though when you look at pictures of us off-duty we were all wearing the flowery shirts with massive collars, kipper ties, flares and had bouffant hair that made us dead ringers for Coco the Clown.

We had none of the languid, eye-catching charm of teams that executed short-passing football for the sake of it, or the type of self-indulgent 'fanny merchants' who gloried in pointless tricks. We thrived only at the highest tempo where collective pressing flourished. It was a very technical approach, calculating and mean.

But we also had our fair share of dangerous attacking players. At the back, Stan Simpson and I were both former midfielders who had no fear of passing. Further forward, George Graham had great, subtle skill, Eddie Kelly was fabulously creative and Geordie Armstrong was a terrific attacking winger. Up front,

Charlie George had a Johnny Haynes-like ability to spot an opening, and Raddy and Ray Kennedy had amazing control to go with their prodigious work-rate. We were not a team of big lumps who blustered our way to the title. I know we weren't as easy on the eye as some of our predecessors, and would look like a moose in a beauty contest compared to some of Arsène Wenger's teams, but I remain convinced that we, a team for all seasons, were so fit, shrewd and adaptable at our peak that we could give any side in history a pretty close game.

I wonder whether it was all the criticism about us as a functional team of 'no stars' that persuaded Bertie Mee to invest in Peter Marinello. It was certainly wholly out of character for our manager to spend so much money on an untested teenager, however much he might promise to capture the new, showbiz spirit of the game. There had been rumours before the season that Bertie intended to build a new team around Peter, Eddie Kelly and Charlie George but, despite his goal-scoring debut at Old Trafford in January 1970 that had our mouths watering, the £100,000 signing never made the impact of the home-grown youngsters.

The hype surrounding Marinello's transfer hid his true nature. Sticking him on *Top of the Pops* and all over girls' comics led many to assume that he was a junior playboy ready to knock George Best off his perch. But at nineteen years old Peter was no match for Bestie; he was just a thoroughly likeable lad, a bit naïve, a bit soft, and without a bad bone in his body.

As a winger he was very twinkle-footed, had a jinky way of dribbling and a good, long stride with pace to spare. The way his hair used to sashay from side to side and touch one shoulder and then the other when he ran sent the girls crazy. When he was beating full backs, we would all have been recruits to his fan club. But his tendency to forget to look up to assess his options when running with the ball, as well as his slight physique and lack of strength, marginalised him.

Ultimately the experiment was short-lived because Geordie Armstrong – the player Bertie had initially dropped to make way for Marinello – was at least as skilful, but without the silkiness, and had twice Marinello's consistency and work rate. Flamboyance without stamina and the tenacity to dig in when things weren't running for you was a luxury our team could ill afford.

On one of those essential, team bonding trips immediately prior to the double season, an incident involving young Peter and Eddie Kelly splattered egg all over my face. We were in Cyprus, and there had been some resentment that our daily allowance didn't stretch very far so I began bargaining with Bertie and Bob Wall. I thought I was making a good fist of persuading them that a couple more quid would enable us to get more out of the trip – see more sights, eat better food – when right past our table on the hotel terrace came Eddie Kelly pushing Peter in a pram, both of them absolutely shit-faced, resulting in the instantaneous and embarrassing collapse of negotiations. As Bertie pointed out, if they could afford to be in such a state in the afternoon, then our 'per diems' were probably too generous not too stingy.

We drank a fair bit on those trips, particularly the post-season ones, but they were crucial in fostering team spirit. Though Bertie would have hated some of the excesses, he was always aware of how important they were. Most footballers have big egos but by throwing us all together, and almost getting us to police ourselves on trips like that, he ensured that players did not become too egotistical. As captain I always made sure that cliques weren't formed and refused to allow anyone to go off on his own. Mutual respect and peer pressure are wonderful tools for a manager to unleash and those trips were the laboratory where those elusive qualities were refined.

Our pre-season training before the double took place at London Colney as it always did, before five warm-up games, three of them in Sweden and Denmark. Geordie Armstrong was in his element at Colney; it offered the perfect showcase for his workaholic dedication to fitness. It was baking hot that summer and we would train for two hours solid in the morning, have a ninety-minute break and do another two hours in the afternoon. It was so difficult to start up again for the second session, we put so much effort in on those bone-hard pitches that our limbs would ache and our bones would be literally creaking. By the time I got home at half past four I felt like a cardboard dummy and could hardly get out of the car.

Geordie used to live on the road behind me and I'd sometimes telephone his house in the evenings to find out if he wanted a lift the next day only to be told by his wife, Marje, that he'd gone out for a run. I would need a late afternoon siesta after the day's punishment but he would have gone out and done another five miles. He was like Colin Bell or Forrest Gump, he could just run and run and run. When he played he covered so much ground he was like a left winger, left half and left back all rolled into one. And he'd go on like that, game after game, season after season. We'd take the piss out of him because he had such a zest for hard work, and plead with him on cross-countries not always to bomb to the front, setting a ripe old pace, but he just couldn't help himself.

We were fortunate to have such an athletic team. McNab, Sammels, Radford and Bob Wilson were natural runners and many more, myself included, had reached a pretty high standard. But not Charlie George, Peter Simpson and George Graham. The latter, in particular, thought that the hard slog was for mugs like the rest of us but in reality, fine player though he was, he just didn't have the physical ability to keep up with Geordie. Few did, but our winger had so much more than his prodigious appetite for running. He could ping in a cross with an unerring eye for an unmarked player and could even tailor make it with the optimum heading height for individual attackers.

Off the pitch he was very hard on himself, often commenting in the dressing room that he'd been 'fucking rubbish' when he'd had a perfectly decent game. He was a bit of a conundrum in that he never stopped moaning yet we all still loved him because he complained in such an amusing way. I suppose everything sounds fairly funny when it comes in that rich Geordie accent and he had such a laconic delivery. Generous to a fault, behaving like a millionaire at the bar, he was always great company and would do anything for you. Even if you'd broken down at midnight you could ring him and know that he'd come and pick you up wherever you happened to be. His death five years ago from a brain haemorrhage at the age of fifty-six was such a shock and whenever any of the team meet up today that great, affectionate, wee guy is justifiably celebrated in anecdotes and tributes. God, I miss him.

While I had felt confident all summer that we might be genuine title contenders, it was not until our third match of the season, at home to Manchester United, that we really hit our straps. With Simpson injured in Scandinavia and Charlie crocked in the opener at Goodison Park, we had 'big Garth', John Roberts, standing in alongside me at the back and Ray

Kennedy thrust up front ahead of Don and Bertie's schedule. The style that we became famous for was evident for the first time that afternoon and it had a lot to do with the way the Kennedy-Radford partnership sparked into life.

When Ray went to Liverpool and was turned into a great midfielder by Bob Paisley, some pundits claimed that he'd found his true position – as if he'd been a makeshift striker for us. It was utter crap. He was an exceptionally good centre forward; he was pitiless in the air, had a powerful shot with a short back-lift, would run his legs to stumps before he gave up and had such strength that defenders used to bash him all match long while he barely batted an eyelid. 'Bloody concrete legs', I used to say to him. He was always chunky but, later, if Bertie had stopped him snaffling crisps, takeaways, Coca-Cola and lager, he wouldn't have ballooned, got stuck on the transfer list and a wonderful centre forward Ray Kennedy would have remained.

That season, however, before lethargy and junk food took its toll on the former I wouldn't have swapped Ray and Raddy for any other partnership in the division. If I was ever in trouble I knew I could put my right foot through the ball and the two of them, thanks to hours of extra afternoon sessions with Don Howe, would deal with it in textbook fashion – one would fight for the ball, the other would be 'on his bike' to create space or position himself to pounce on the knock-through. Both of them could face up, back to goal, and collect the ball, something which takes great courage to maintain throughout a season when fourteen-stone centre halves would launch all their bulk into a tackle targeted at your Achilles tendon.

They made such intelligent runs, too, zigzagging all over the place. Defenders hate that, as you have to keep stamping all your weight from one foot to another, and it scrambles your brain since you focus solely on the player you're marking and lose perspective. Furthermore, the two of them had worked so hard at coming short and losing the marker – who would stick to his zone – that I could play it short or, if their man had shadowed them, I could hit it long and they would spin him and sprint into the vacant gap.

They got so good at it that they could bluff and double bluff, changing direction in a split second, moving as if they were going to spin and drive forward and then come short. We worked on this so often in training that I could read their body language and interpret what they wanted me to do, so, even if I had my head down, I could guess their next move by how their feet were placed.

That afternoon when we gubbed Manchester United 4-0 – Law, Best, Charlton, Crerand and the rest – was the first tangible sign that we had real class in attack to complement the relentless defensive teamwork. The two forwards split and terrorised the full backs, letting Geordie and George burst into the box. For all his self-sacrifice Raddy still managed to get a hat-trick that day, and I remember coming off the Highbury pitch and having a very conscious sense that we were going to have a good season. It had taken six years but it was finally coming together.

Shortly after that game we went to Rome to face Lazio in defence of our European Fairs Cup. Rather like Liverpool and the Champions League, there was some controversy regarding our qualification since we'd finished twelfth in the league the previous season, below two other London clubs, and our status as holders did not necessarily entitle us entry into the competition.

Eventually, common-sense prevailed and we were admitted to the draw. It was the only time sanity reared its head in that tie. In a nasty, violent game at the Stadio Olimpico we managed a 2-2 draw but an indulgent referee had allowed all sorts of vicious assaults to go unpunished. There was a lot of hair-pulling but the worst offence was by their sweeper Giuseppe 'Pino' Wilson, a half-English assassin who kicked Geordie flush in the midriff then threw himself onto the turf claiming he'd been fouled. Lazio's equaliser came when the referee awarded a dubious penalty when I'd made a diving, goal-line clearance, which he said I'd handled, so we were brimming with a sense of righteous indignation at the formal banquet after the match.

For us, attending that was a ridiculous obligation, and the fact that there'd been so much argy-bargy in the game meant that the atmosphere in the restaurant was positively hateful. Peter Storey was still seething from Lazio's rough-house approach and he was chuntering away: 'We'll fucking get them back. We'll fucking do them.' Elsewhere, players were eyeballing each other and growling. It was overpoweringly hot, too, so everyone was even more on edge.

Eventually, Ray Kennedy and Sammy Nelson went outside to grab some fresh air and they encountered Lazio's centre half. I've said before that Ray was very stoical when it came to punishment on the pitch. He took the kicks and never rose to provocation. Off-field he would have fought his granny, so when words were exchanged between him and the big Roman and his opponent attempted to knee him in the balls, Ray twatted him. Consequently, a huge brawl erupted, involving not only Ray and the Lazio player but also some Lazio supporters outside the restaurant who quickly piled in to help their centre half.

We were wholly oblivious of this until a flustered Bob Wilson ran in and said in a very anxious yet dramatic way: 'There's a fight going on outside.' It was after this that the name Primrose really stuck to Bob. I rushed outside with Eddie Kelly and a Scots reserve, Jackie Carmichael, and started throwing punches – and I distinctly remember seeing Peter Marinello flying through the air over a parked car. One guy was on my back and punching downwards onto my head as their players and fans quickly outnumbered us. At one point their manager, an Argentinian nutter schooled in the Estudiantes academy of thuggery, picked up Bertie Mee by the lapels and forced him against our bus.

The police came and drew their guns and the fight soon broke up. They started to clear a space to let us back on the bus but, just as I was about to leave, I spotted the little bugger in the maroon blazer with brass buttons who had been pounding on my head. He had become detached from his mates so I sized myself up to whack him. Just as I was about to unwind, two strong arms grabbed me around the neck and dragged me back to the bus with my heels scraping along the flag stones. It was Garth, the strongest man in the club. He'd been fantastic in that fight and laid out about three of them but he knew my temper was still raging and that I wanted revenge so he'd intervened to save me from my wilder instincts.

Bertie stood at the front of the bus and gave his usual 'we are the Arsenal, we don't want any scandal' speech: 'Right boys, we keep this under wraps. We don't speak to the press. We don't mingle with the press in the bar at the hotel. We go straight to our beds.' The last thing I wanted with all that adrenalin flowing was to be sent to bed so George Graham and I nipped out of the emergency exit when we got to our hotel and sneaked off to a party given by Stan Flashman, the ticket tout, in his hotel room.

We both looked like we had been in a riot, which in a way we had, so we quickly became the major talking point. When Fat Stan asked us what had happened, I had to get him to feel the twenty or so bumps on my head before he believed us. Needless to say, the story was all over the press the following morning, leaked either by Stan or one of the other partygoers. At Heathrow we were faced with roughly 200 newspapermen, photographers and television reporters but for once they were thoroughly sympathetic. It certainly helped sell a few tickets for the return leg, which we won 2-0.

Some of my colleagues have looked back on that fight and the way we all stood up for each other almost as if it was the last vital ingredient in binding us together as a team. I am less sure. I think the bond was there that night we beat Anderlecht, but maybe it needed a punch-up and a few battle scars to make it obvious to everyone.

If those two games with Lazio proved our resilience, the way we responded to September's 5-0 defeat at Stoke City was the defining point of our season. They were a funny team, Stoke, and had the knack of getting good results against top teams – indeed they were Leeds United's bogey side for many years – without ever developing the consistency to win things. I suppose it was typical of my relationship with the Potteries club that it should be them that threatened to derail us. I had always had trouble in games against them, primarily because of a feud that had festered between me and Roy Vernon. I know that he had left the club at that point but I'd never enjoyed my trips there since a couple of seasons earlier when he'd 'done' me two years in succession.

Vernon was an excellent player, a free-scoring, chain-smoking Welsh international inside forward, skinny and wiry – a bit like Ken Leek – but with a darker, dirtier side. Looking back, I think I was green when I was younger, quite innocent when it came to bad tackles, and would often give perpetrators the benefit of the doubt. The first time Vernon took me out, back in 1966, was bad enough, but the second time, a year later, just by the touchline, was too much. I'd gone to tackle him, sliding in to take the ball, when he just lifted his leg and hoofed me, deliberately, right under the knee cap. I was bloody furious because I knew I was badly hurt, but more so because it was immediately apparent that I would miss Scotland's end of season trip to Australia and New Zealand.

After the game my right leg was bandaged from ankle to thigh but I hauled myself up the fifty concrete steps to the players' lounge, determined to have a pop back at him. I stood outside the entrance to the bar for about half an hour waiting for him to appear, ready to clock him, not really caring whether I knocked him all the way down the staircase. But after shivering in my thin suit for too long I gave up, surmising that he'd given me the swerve.

Two minutes after I finally went to the bar, Vernon strides in, walks up to me and says: 'That was a bloody good act you put on out there today, Frank.' What a nerve. Talk about throwing petrol on an almost extinguished fire. I threw myself at him and clobbered him full in the face as tables, chairs, cups of tea and the finger buffet went flying everywhere. Women were screaming while Jimmy Magill, Terry Neill and Don Howe hauled me off him, but I was so incensed that I found the strength to pull the three of them back on top of Roy Vernon. I've never seen anyone look so terrified in my life, but my colleagues dragged me off him and put me on the bus. It makes me sound like a lunatic but he had cold-bloodedly injured me twice and was taunting me about it. I prided myself on never going over the top of the ball; I'd rather grab you by the throat than dish out snide tackles designed to wound, but Vernon was quite sanguine about them. He saw it as a 'kill or be killed' game and he was prepared to strike first. Ironically, the public would interpret an unsophisticated slap as far worse than a bad tackle but players are far more outraged by the fiendish use of studs. I had always vowed that I'd get my own back on him but I never got the chance as he died of cancer ten years ago. I would never wish that terrible disease on anyone and I wish that he had lived another thirty years but I would be dishonest if I did not admit that I harboured a grudge against him until the day I heard of his death.

In Jimmy Greenhoff, Terry Conroy, John Mahoney, Peter Dobing, John Ritchie and Gordon Banks, Stoke had enough quality players to beat anyone so losing to them was no disgrace, even if their margin of victory left us with red faces. Teams with flair players click every now and then and Stoke clicked that day in a devastating display where they capitalised on every mistake we made. That Saturday, back in the dressing room, we were more shocked than angry – slightly bemused by what had happened – but Bertie did not lash out at us: 'Before today you went seven games unbeaten. You're going to have to do it again.' That wasn't the end of it but to Bertie's credit he always recognised the futility of an immediate, finger-pointing inquest. We would save that for Monday morning.

What happened on that Monday morning at Highbury after the 5-0 mauling would ensure that Stoke got their come-uppance, thrillingly so, later in the season. We reconvened in a meeting room which used to be located in the tunnel area, halfway between the home dressing room and the pitch. After Bertie and Don's introduction I took the floor and we had a no-holds-barred session during which there was a great deal of criticism, most of it constructive, dished out.

We were an outspoken team, very blunt with each other at times, and I sought to leave no one in any doubt about what we had to do to get back to our gun-toting best. If that meant not skirting around the bushes but ploughing straight through them then I was prepared to do that. It wasn't all yelling, we spoke nice and straight trying to draw lessons from Saturday's loss. I emphasised the basics, and together we reaffirmed our intention to be constant with our discipline and not to allow complacency, and the belief that we were better than we actually were, to take hold. It was a very united squad with a significant number of opinionated people in it and, though the paint might have peeled off the walls with the heat of our arguments, no one sulked and we emerged a stronger team having come through the process.

The consensus was that we should go back to ground rules for the next game and set out our stall for the remainder of the season. That meant imposing ourselves for the first twenty minutes: not letting the opposition win any headers, constantly pressurising the ball and not letting defenders lift their heads up, rattling into tackles with everything we had and flattening opponents with every ounce of our weight. It was all about attitude and tempo and generally not giving any quarter.

Twenty minutes of that intensity and all but the very best teams are knocked out of their rhythm and find it impossible to regain any composure. Then you refuse to yield from that foothold for the next seventy minutes and steam-roller them.

It won us few plaudits from neutrals who would have preferred the game to be as open as it had been ten years previously but we would have been picked off if we hadn't set out to stop the opposition playing. For good or bad, that was the beginning of the dominance of pressing football in England – championed mostly by Leeds and us – but the scorn of critics is easy to bear if you go on a fourteen-game, unbeaten run like we did when we went back to the fundamentals of Don's game-plan.

The other major point of that Monday morning meeting was to reiterate our faith in the defensive principles that had gone missing at Stoke's Victoria Ground. Our one major shortcoming as a team was our collective lack of height at the back, which was a severe handicap at set-pieces. I had a good leap, and can see a bit of myself in the Argentinian, Roberto Ayala, in the way I beat taller players to headers, but on the whole we were not blessed with the physical attributes to withstand an aerial assault from a team of giants. We plugged this hole by getting our two centre forwards back at free kicks and corners and they became very brave auxiliary defenders. Most strikers are lackadaisical when they have to do the humdrum tasks, like marking up, but our lads were always alert.

We adopted the touch/look method, where you would keep the attacker under scrutiny by digging him with your arm to make sure he was still there while looking at the rest of the penalty area and getting ready for the ball. If you execute this manoeuvre properly it should mean that your man never gets the space to have a proper running jump against you for the cross. If it looked like he might try and get away, I found a quick whack in the solar plexus with the forearm worked wonders for your defensive security.

All this was played out to a chorus of instructions from me, Nabbers and Raddy to make sure everyone was on their toes: 'mark in front', 'step into his run' and 'watch him!' Those constant words of encouragement may seem banal or superfluous to some readers but they are like a comfort blanket to a defender. They are spoken almost as much for your own benefit as everyone else's. It is a good tool for clearing your head and reinforcing your immediate priorities. I doubt whether any British team had ever put as much effort into defending as we were doing then. But it took masses of concentration and commitment, as well as tactical awareness, to get it right. That double season, and that season only, we got it spot on.

The team that came closest to stopping us in the league in that season were Leeds United, the team we are also most frequently compared with. There were certainly some shared characteristics but the view that Arsenal were a lighter, more palatable version of Leeds United does us both a disservice. I think we were mentally tougher than Leeds, less emotional and we didn't worry so much about the opposition. We would stick to our game-plan, particularly with regard to compression and our use of the off-side trap.

Moreover, we were the fairer team. Leeds had improved since their ultra-violent, mid-sixties heyday but they were still prone to dirty tackles and devious tactics – like buying time through feigning injury or collectively hounding the referee. But they also had qualities in abundance. In Johnny Giles and Billy Bremner they had arguably the best midfield pairing in the world at the time, and every other member of the team was of the highest calibre. In the seventies, Leeds were the team of the decade but, of course, they will never win the plaudits their skill and consistency deserve because of their cynical approach.

Most football teams eventually come to resemble their manager in terms of their strengths and usually, also, to reflect his quirks and foibles. Don Revie was among the most complex men I have ever met and his many contradictions – warm, mistrustful, confident, cautious, charming, defensive – must have perplexed his players at times. I knew him for nearly thirty years and I have only one bad memory of him. From the moment he door-stepped me in Leicester until his death in 1989 we only fell out once. That happened at Highbury in the late 1960s – in the marble halls of all places – before a late-season Arsenal v Leeds league game. As ever, Don was very solicitous about Barbara and the kids, whose names he remembered, and was very considerate in his tone. I was just about to leave to go and get changed when he became rather furtive and whispered: 'You know, you and Barbara should have a nice holiday this summer. In fact you could go anywhere in the world you wanted as a guest of Leeds United. Just take it easy out there tonight.'

I've thought long and hard about revealing this so long after the event. I've never had any wish to join the massed ranks of his detractors because I retain a great deal of admiration and affection for the man. Nonetheless I lost my rag and shouted: 'You come up to me and ask me to take it easy. Are you fucking crazy?' Everyone stared at us and he went bright scarlet as I stormed off to the dressing rooms.

Halfway through the first half I got the chance to steam into a tackle on Billy Bremner and I was still so angry I went sliding in with the intention of hurting him. Billy was too canny for me and jumped out of the way and, as fate would have it, my slide took me right to the edge of the pitch in front of the Leeds dug-out. As I got up I bellowed at Don and Les Cocker:

'You'll be fucking next.' I hit a great angled shot that night that lodged in the stanchion, possibly my finest goal in an Arsenal shirt. We won 4–3 and nothing else was ever said about the matter.

There was no ambiguity about what Don had said, though I can accept that it was more of a 'floater' than an overt bribe. I continued to respect him even if I could acknowledge that he was a flawed man in flawed times. He was so anxious to do well that it pushed him over the edge sometimes. I didn't hold a grudge against him, but I remained pissed off more by the fact that he might have thought I was the type to take a bribe rather than by the actual offering of one.

A lot of journalists hated him but I maintain that he was a fantastic manager. I still think that on balance his good points outweighed the bad and I feel the same about his team. They were driven but it would be daft to portray them all as going over the top all the time. Cooper, Gray, Lorimer, Madeley, Charlton and Jones were not dirty players. The others could put it about when they needed to but by 1970 they had curbed their worst excesses.

We, by contrast, were never as bad as them but I also have sympathy for the argument that we never reached their consistency or their occasionally sublime heights in the way they tore teams to pieces. They were formidable opponents and it says a lot for our team that we were neck and neck with them all season before our resolve and tenacity finally put us in the ascendancy.

11

THE DOUBLE

When writing about the double season I'm always drawn back to the word 'resilience'. I am keenly aware that it's not a particularly sexy concept. Teams that glitter in the memory – The Busby Babes, Real Madrid, Brazil, Holland, Ajax and even the unbeaten Arsenal side of 2003-04 – had superior qualities. But they also had enormous amounts of durability allied to their creative gifts.

Our attacking credentials have been downplayed by laymen but without our ability not only to endure pressure but also to dish it out, we would never have achieved what we did. It is most evident in the way we came back from defeats – the fourteen-game unbeaten run that took us from the beginning of October through to mid January, followed by nine consecutive wins in March and April after the first run was broken at

Huddersfield. We also had ten 1-0 victories that season, a sequence of results that forms the basis for that defiant North Bank anthem.

You would think that such a narrow margin means that you live on your nerves in those games but that was not the case. I felt quite comfortable defending a slender lead and I don't think that we ever felt much psychological pressure. We were good at soaking up attacks and I was confident that Raddy, George, Ray or Charlie could always nick us a goal if we stood firm. It might have looked like we were in danger of wilting on occasion, especially when we invited attacks by keeping our line so high up the pitch, but it was all part of our defence master plan.

Our opponents could huff and puff all they wanted, but after the 5-0 Stoke debacle no one ever blew the house down. There were plenty of hairy moments, sure, but we had a magnificent goalkeeper and a system working at its optimum. If we played in top gear from the whistle, and by that I mean we were a team who could not dominate by gradually ratcheting up the tempo throughout the ninety minutes, we were unstoppable.

Crucial to that nine-match winning trot – which enabled us to build momentum and eat away at the seven-point lead Leeds had over us in February – was the return from injury of Charlie George. He was one of the best players of his generation, Arsenal's own bespoke George Best, but partly due to injuries and partly because of his volatility he did not sustain that early impact throughout his career. He did, however, have more natural ability than anyone else in our team and a safecracker's eye for spotting chinks in the opposition's defence.

When Charlie came back into the team his contribution was immense – slotting in behind the front two to create chances with his short, quick passes and the ease with which he could hit a powerful twenty-yard shot with either foot. It's almost heretical for a Scot to say that Charlie had the potential to be as good as Denis Law, but he was that special as a teenager. Like Denis too, he was a bit of a firebrand, plenty of mouth, quite impetuous at times, with the priceless knack of getting the crowd going.

Because of his background as a fanatical Arsenal fan, he was taken to the supporters' hearts and lauded as if he was their on-field representative. When he had the ball in home games, that old quip about the 'Highbury library' was never more ridiculous. I don't think our crowd was ever as consistently intimidating as some of the Northern teams' but there was a boisterous and throaty element that Charlie's performances often whipped up to a frenzy. In the closing games of the season, when we regularly had 40,000 plus in, you could close your eyes and get a sense of what it must have been like at Anfield or Elland Road most Saturdays. That longed-for, raucous and vocal support played a significant role in driving us over the finishing line.

The first evidence of the dynamism, guile and sheer insolence we had missed in his absence came at Maine Road in the FA Cup. Charlie was very headstrong and tended to be very black and white in his assessment of people. As far as he was concerned there were only two categories: you were either a 'diamond geezer' or a 'c★★t'. I decided to play on this before our game with Manchester City when I told him that their manager, Malcolm Allison, didn't rate him much as a player: 'He thinks you're a fancy dan, a flash in the pan, someone who can't last the full ninety minutes,' I claimed.

In fact, Malcolm is exactly the sort of person that Charlie

would normally like. He admires talent and brashness but on this occasion I thought it might help us if Charlie thought City's manager fell into the other category. My little wheeze fired Charlie up no end and he was outstanding that day, scoring both goals in our 2-1 victory on a very heavy pitch. When he came off at the end he started screaming and gesturing at Malcolm, who must have thought him a head-case.

I quickly tried to bundle Charlie down the tunnel in case my trick had greater repercussions than I'd planned. I told Malcolm what I'd done and he was great about it. He liked to use psychological stunts to get the best out of players and was gracious enough to have a laugh when the tables had been turned on him. Captaincy isn't all about cajoling and bollocking, sometimes it requires subtlety and the occasional mind game, too. Charlie, because of his temerity, was always the ideal candidate for the less straightforward approach.

Charlie also scored the winner in the quarter-final replay with Leicester which set us up to face my old pals Stoke in the semi-final at Hillsborough. Once again, it looked as though they had the beating of us when they took a 2-0 half-time lead thanks to a pair of farcical goals – one a ricochet from a Peter Storey clearance, the other coming from a panicky and ill-judged back-pass from Charlie.

We were quite calm in the dressing room considering the way the first half had gone and Don was adamant that we could get back in the match if we kept our composure and upped the tempo. Storey nabbed one back almost immediately and though they had chances on the break we bombarded their goal for most of the next forty minutes. Our equaliser came in injury time when I caught the ball sweetly above my right eyebrow, and sent Geordie's corner way beyond Gordon Banks into the bottom left-hand corner of his goal before it was slapped out again by John Mahoney. Storey wrong-footed Banks to equalise with the penalty and send us all giddy with relief.

I don't know what it was about Stoke and me but as we were going back to the centre circle for the restart, their centre forward, John Ritchie, head-butted me on the bridge of my nose. He was not usually so vicious but he must have been trying to get a reaction out of me in the hope that I might retaliate, get sent off and miss the replay. A couple of years earlier I would have chinned him but I was now more aware of my responsibilities to the team. I merely growled at him and walked back, confident that they'd blown their chance, spunked it as we used to say, and that we'd finish them off at Villa Park.

Four days later, a trademark, towering header from George Graham and a tap-in from Ray Kennedy gave us a 2–0 win in the semi-final, a game we commanded from start to finish. We followed this with six wins on the bounce in April which finally took us to the top of the league after Leeds' infamous defeat to West Bromwich Albion at Elland Road and that notorious off-side goal. I have certainly never seen much wrong with Ray Tinkler's decision that Colin Suggett was not interfering with play, even if I would have gone ballistic if it had happened to us.

Managers often try to downplay their team's prospects so as not to increase the pressure on their players, but the unavoidable fact that we were on to repeat Tottenham's achievement prompted Bertie to address the issue in a team meeting halfway through our unbeaten run. 'Gentlemen,' he said, as was his typically formal habit, 'you have the chance to put your names in the record books. But to do that you have to make football the priority of your life at the expense of everything else. Are you ready to make that sacrifice?' It's easy to say 'yes' in such circumstances. Our performances in the last few weeks of the season show that we meant it as we emphatically gave everything we had to make history.

As fate would have it, our last three league games of the season were against Leeds, the team we had to fend off, Stoke, the team that seemed to have a vendetta against me, and Tottenham, not only our fans' most bitter rivals but also a team that would sweat blood to defend their club's proud record. Because of our appearance in the FA Cup semi-final in late March, we had a game in hand over our Yorkshire rivals and led them by a point. The maximum return they could achieve by beating us and their final-day opponents, Nottingham Forest, was four points. If we matched them and won two of our remaining games, the league was ours by the slenderest of one-point margins – a comforting thought but one we sought to banish. Whenever we were on the bus to Elland Road, it could be quite revealing to look around at the faces of your team mates; playing away to Leeds was, after all, the most intimidating fixture in football at the time and I will admit that there were occasions when I could tell that certain players were quivering.

That night, as we left the Queens' Hotel by coach to go to the ground I turned in my seat and quietly cast my eye over each of our players, mentally ticking off the ones who were up for it. There were no crosses; I knew they were all mentally tough enough to withstand everything Leeds could throw at us. We might not win the match but we would be cowed neither by the ferocity of their assault nor the blood lust of their crowd.

The match was a ferocious affair but not as violent as we had come to expect when we resolved to go toe-to-toe with them. I was extremely proud of the way we withstood our opponents' pressure and kept our discipline, sticking to our off-side trap in the face of wave after wave of attacks in the second half. The game turned in the closing minutes when Jackie Charlton scored the only goal – but from a position which looked to me to be at least six yards off-side.

Norman Burtenshaw, the referee, was one of the best around, the sort of guy you could have a go at and – like his colleague Gordon Hill – he'd just say: 'Piss off, Frank, you're not playing very well yourself.' All niceties and banter were put to one side that evening when we surrounded him to let him know, very firmly, how wrong his decision had been, but there was no chance of him reversing it and the match finished with Leeds back on top of the league with one to play and us only one point behind with a game in hand.

We turned the air blue on our way back down the M1, cursing the linesman, the referee and, above all, the giraffe – Jack Charlton. Given our game in hand we were still in pole position and, in some ways, a sense of righteous anger at the perceived injustice could spur us on in the final two games. I was very keen to exploit that so I wasn't very sympathetic at all when Bob McNab sheepishly admitted that, in his view, it had been a fair decision. In fact, he had been at the angle of the six-yard box and inadvertently played Charlton on-side. When we had pushed out to trigger the trap, we had not noticed that Bob had been injured and he could not quite get up to our line.

I immediately lost my temper with him, not for his positioning as he subsequently thought – I would never have a go at anyone for a genuine mistake – but for puncturing my attempt to rally the team around our grievances with Leeds and the referee. Television replays later showed that Bob's analysis was accurate but at that point I couldn't help but feel that the legitimacy of the goal was beside the point. He may have been right but it was an untimely and unhelpful intervention.

Had we got a point at Elland Road, a win in our Saturday home game with Stoke would have given us the title. Instead, we had to make sure we won at Highbury to allow us to be still in the race when we went to White Hart Lane for the final game of the season on the Monday night. The game against Stoke was, understandably, fraught – and marred, too, by a bad injury to Peter Storey early in the second half when we were still 0-0. As a defensive shield sitting just in front of the back four, Peter was a key player, particularly in that string of 1-0 victories.

As a bloke, Peter – 'Snouty' – is quite enigmatic and of all my team mates he is probably the one I know least well. Despite his reputation as a hatchet man, he was an excellent footballer and would have been equally at home in any position in midfield or defence. The fact that he won more caps than any other member of our team speaks volumes for his ability but – in the same way as Nobby Stiles – he's been underrated because of his fearsome qualities in the tackle; indeed, again like Stiles, on the pitch he was not very nice at all and could be quite frightening.

Cold and focused, Peter was great at sensing danger and was unflappable when we were under pressure. His gift for the simplest, but most vital tasks – winning the ball then giving it – gave a framework for the way we operated. With a drink inside him, he was funny and approachable. At parties, if you glanced in his direction all you could see was his tonsils as he threw back his head and roared with laughter. But the rest of the time he would be monosyllabic and even grunted those solitary words, working on his image as Arsenal's own Clint Eastwood.

It was a huge blow when Peter limped off but luck was with us that afternoon and the substitute, Eddie Kelly, made an immediate impact. Stoke had seemed to approach the game as if it was their express intention to pay us back in kind for their defeat in the FA Cup semi-final replay and give us a taste of falling flat on our faces at the final hurdle. Stringing five men across midfield and leaving Jimmy Greenhoff to forage alone up front, they seemed happy to play for the draw which would leave us to grapple with the vagaries of goal average if we were to take the title. At 0-0 the crowd's anxiety was palpable and the knowledge that a breakaway Stoke goal could hand the title to Leeds added to the tension as the news that Leeds were beating Forest 2-0 quickly spread.

Stoke's policy of packing their midfield meant that George Graham and Charlie George did not have their usual freedom to break forward to support Raddy and Ray and they were left isolated as our midfield diligently tried to strangle Stoke of possession. In the sixty-eighth minute, our left-sided triumvirate, stifled for so long, blew Stoke's defence apart with a safe-cracker's resourcefulness. McNab delayed his pass long enough to set Geordie Armstrong free from his marker and his bludgeoned cross was glanced on by Graham, controlled by Raddy and sweetly laid into the path of the on-rushing Kelly who spanked the ball past Gordon Banks to put us 1-0 up. The usual certainty I had of victory when 1-0 up during that season was tempered slightly for the last twenty-odd minutes of the match. For once

I would have been reassured by another goal and, indeed, extreme caution crept into our play which nearly let Stoke in to equalise but Radford was expertly placed on the line to repel John Mahoney's late shot. At the final whistle we heard that Leeds had duly won their game through goals from Bremner and Lorimer, putting them, with their season completed, top of the league by one point from us with only Monday night's game at Spurs left to play.

Our only trophy to date, the Fairs Cup, had been won in North London. I desperately hoped that the fact that the opportunity to surpass that feat lay at White Hart Lane – just a few miles up the Seven Sisters Road – would prove to be a happy omen.

Late that Monday afternoon, before the Tottenham match, our team congregated at South Herts Golf Club in Totteridge, our usual home match rendezvous. Arsenal had very strong links with the club, largely through Dai Rees – runner-up in the Open, a former Ryder Cup captain, Harry Vardon's successor as club professional and a fanatical Arsenal supporter – and thanks to him we always had lunch there before a Saturday match. I think Dai must have had a reciprocal arrangement with the Arsenal board because we got free membership at the golf club and he got complimentary tickets to Highbury, where he never seemed to miss a match. (As soon as I left for QPR, though, fee-free golf became a thing of the past and I had to stump up the full whack.) We went through our normal routine, with no member of the team noticeably suffering from nerves on the journey down through Palmers Green and Edmonton. The coach ride should have taken half an hour but it seemed to go on for ever and, no, that wasn't down to my mind playing tricks on me.

The scene as we crawled through the congestion up Tottenham High Road was like those newsreel films of VE Day. White Hart Lane held just over 50,000 people but there must have been a tide at least 90,000 strong inching their way towards the ground. Within 100 yards of the main entrance, in the midst of the crush, I spotted Barbara and Marje Armstrong and leapt towards the coach door to drag them to safety. Needless to say, Bertie wasn't too pleased with this serious breach of match-day etiquette: 'Women aren't allowed on the team bus', he said but I told him, in no uncertain terms, to stop his chirping.

It took us a good twenty minutes to make the last eighty yards. At one point, the driver switched off the engine in case it overheated but the bus still moved forward due to the pressure of the crowd. In the end we had to get out and run the last few yards. All in all, the journey proved far more traumatic than the game, though it probably did us a favour as we had no time to brood on the magnitude of the task ahead. We barely had time to get stripped and strapped before the referee summoned us into the tunnel.

One of the problems you face when you look back at a career spanning 700 games – the vast majority of which were played more than three decades ago – is that some start to meld into others. That night at White Hart Lane, though, is an undimmed pleasure that I can recall in minute detail.

Moreover, I remember that, long before Alex Ferguson became famous for his mind games, Don Revie tried a similar tactic prior to that title decider. Laughably, as if he thought there was a (highly improbable) cockney conspiracy afoot, Revie had let it be known that Spurs would far rather we won the league than Leeds. Nothing could have been wider of the mark and the Spurs players, Alan Mullery in particular, were bristling with defiance. We were the last team on earth they wanted to appear in *Rothmans Football Yearbook* alongside the sainted Blanchflower and company.

It was a real ding-dong game with Mullery, and even Gilzean – very much a result of the situation as it was so out of character for him – kicking lumps out of us. The ball seemed to go from end to end as Spurs threw everything at us and we countered through Charlie and Geordie.

A curious anomaly of the goal average system still in place then was that a 0-0 draw would have given us the title but a 1-1 draw would hand it to Leeds. We approached the match, as Bob McNab reminded me, as if we were already 1-0 down and went for the imaginary draw, i.e. a 1-0 win, but we were never able to feel comfortable as one lapse could cost us everything.

We had by far the most possession and got a firmer grip on the game halfway through the second period. Then with fifteen minutes to go Geordie played me in at the edge of the penalty area. I saw a gap in the bottom right-hand corner of the goal and I thought, 'Jesus, it's going to be me. I'm going to win the league.' If there had ever been a moment when I felt almost fated to make history, it was then, just for a split second. I pulled back my right foot, opting for the no-nonsense approach of 'putting my laces through it' and pile-driving the ball, when Bang!, the referee, Kevin Howley, ran straight into me. I absolutely clattered into him and sent him sprawling on his back as Cyril Knowles prodded the ball away. 'Christ, Frank,' he shouted, 'you've loosened my front teeth.'

'I ought to knock your teeth out, you daft bastard! I was

just about to score the goal that would have won the league,' was my rather unsympathetic response.

I was still cursing my luck five minutes later when we made the breakthrough. Charlie George robbed Cyril Knowles and dinked a cross into the box which Joe Kinnear spooned back towards the goal. Jennings's save pushed the ball into space on the left flank where Geordie raced to receive it and whipped in his cross towards Ray Kennedy lurking outside the six-yard box. Ray's powerful header grazed the underside of the cross-bar to make it 1-0.

We were delirious but, with four minutes to go and a further four minutes of injury time, we had little chance for a premature party as Spurs unleashed a furious assault to try and deprive us of the title. People talk of those closing minutes as if they lasted half an hour and I, too, remember the surreal experience of thinking the game was never going to end.

When Howley blew the final whistle, there was pandemonium. Thousands of Arsenal fans streamed onto the pitch and swamped us. Those players nearer the tunnel barged their way into the dressing rooms relatively unscathed. I was mobbed and, like a year earlier with the Fairs Cup, it was a claustrophobic and unsettling experience despite my obvious euphoria. I'm not one of those precious footballers who think that the game is primarily about the players – I recognise the importance of fans. But, however much I valued them, I must admit that in my exhaustion I would have preferred the chance of celebrating with my team mates first, rather than getting repeatedly pounded on the back by a swarm of semi-hysterical supporters.

At times like that you just hope that a mounted copper will plonk you on the back of his horse and get you to safety but such a rescue was out of the question that night; there were too many people on the pitch. It took me a quarter of an hour to get back to the dressing room. There, the party was already beginning to swing; there was a lot of jumping up and down, hugging, and shouting that roar of triumph that comes from somewhere pretty deep inside you.

In terms of my career, it was the greatest night of my life. Cups are wonderful but to win the hardest competition of all, and getting the weight of my so far thwarted expectation and the monkey of the club's proud history off my back was an amazing feeling. It was everything I had ever dreamed it would be, an overwhelming sense of elation that almost makes you pulsate with joy. It gives you a raging thirst, too.

We got to our regular haunt, the White Hart in Southgate, just before midnight and celebrated for about five hours. Several drinks were taken, and the alcohol combined with my weariness had its customary retribution the following day as I lay in bed late into the afternoon. That day off was a godsend and I spent most of it with a broad grin plastered across my face. There are some people in football who think that smiling takes up precious time but I had the rare luxury that afternoon of thoroughly indulging myself. We still had the cup final to play, of course, so it was back to Colney on Wednesday to devour George Male's dossier on Liverpool, along with some loosening up and a bit of shadow play on a lush practice pitch – Bertie had ordered that it be cultivated to replicate Wembley.

On Thursday and Friday we went through our familiar training routine, trying to keep it all low key and not overstate the importance of the game but the press had latched on to the fact that it was my fifth Wembley final and, keen to speculate on my chances of breaking the duck, were peppering the press conferences with questions about my dismal Wembley record. On the Thursday night, however, there was a happier meeting with the press when I went to the Royal Lancaster Hotel to pick up the Footballer of the Year award from the Football Writers' Association.

It was an enormous honour, to be the first Arsenal beneficiary of the award since Joe Mercer almost twenty years earlier. I was too preoccupied with the cup final to enjoy it as much as I should but I scored a few points after an extremely tedious address by Harold Wilson, then leader of the opposition. He went on and on for so long that those among the well-oiled audience who hadn't actually nodded off were wearing tortured expressions of utter exasperation. It was a funny sight to behold from my top-table position but I was so desperate to get up and get it over with that I could not revel in their discomfort – though it helped to settle my nerves. Wilson had been so useless that I knew I could do better, and so it proved. My speech, in which I paid tribute to my team mates and Leeds United, went down very well and I was congratulated on it by a procession of the great and the good including Brian Clough, Bill Shankly and Don Revie.

Later that night at home in Winchmore Hill I remember lying in bed, unable to sleep – and the two glasses I'd rationed myself to at the award dinner were hardly going to knock me out. My mind was buzzing with all that had happened that week and with what was about to happen in less than forty-eight hours.

We spent the night before the game at the Grosvenor House Hotel and it was hard not to let the sense of anticipation overwhelm me. Our need to focus on the league had spared us much of the hype of the build-up to the cup final but in the ensuing five days that led up to it we had gradually become more excited as each day passed, particularly as wherever we went we seemed to be pursued by the constant refrains of *Good Old Arsenal*, our Top Twenty hit.

I still like to tease my team mates that it would have gone even higher in the charts if Jimmy Hill, the lyricist, had let me sing it but I was confined to the choruses with the rest of the squad. The fans had picked up on it quickly and when they sang it as we drove down Wembley Way just after noon on that baking hot day, it certainly added to the drama of a nerve-jangling moment.

Contrary to what you might think, I didn't dwell much on the previous four lost finals. My poor streak had weighed far more heavily on me in the past and I think that my ridiculous notions about a jinx must have been obliterated by those two victories – the Fairs Cup and League Championship – in the past twelve months. Dumb as it may sound I had a very real sense that the law of averages had to be on my side this time, even if most pundits had made Liverpool favourites for the game. Nevertheless, I could have done without having to leave the dressing room fifteen minutes early for the long walk up the tunnel and the formal presentations to the Duke of Kent. Looking back I wish that I had made the most of every moment but at the time I just wanted to get it over with and start the game.

For years my recollection of the game was that it was fairly free-flowing, but when I watched it again recently I realised that both sides played cautiously and, while there was a high degree of technical competence, it didn't liven up until extra time. The heat was horrendous and the stadium's new roof meant that there was very little air circulating which made it difficult to catch your breath.

Moreover, if you include the pre-season friendlies I'd played, it was my sixty-seventh match of the season and I was running on empty. And, in addition, the fact that I had to mark the six-feet two-inch Toshack was a heavy burden on my legs. Constantly jumping against him and trying to project my voice across thirty or forty yards – and loud enough to be heard above the noise of 100,000 supporters – consumed all my energy.

On the whole, we kept Liverpool's forwards very square by retaining our discipline and holding a high line, but George Graham was our only player who seemed to have the composure to shine. Indeed, George had a tremendous game and his probing passing and darts around the edge of Liverpool's box made the few chances we had, but we weren't able to capitalise on his inventiveness. When it came to time up I was gone and as we lay sprawled on the pitch waiting for extra time, even though Bertie and Don were adamant that we would win, it was always in doubt.

When, thanks to Bob Wilson's misjudgement, Steve Heighway scored for Liverpool in the opening minutes of extra time my mind went back to those earlier lost finals as I thought: 'Not again, no!' For those few minutes it was like I wasn't really there. The physical torment was one thing but I was also dumbfounded by the prospect of failure. Bob had been trying to cover the cross and been caught out low at the near post. But I couldn't blame him for long as moments later he pulled off a startling save to keep us in the match. Bob's save snapped me back to normality.

We quickly regained our grip on the game and our midfield pressure continued to force Liverpool backwards, allowing George Graham and the substitute, Eddie Kelly, to get into dangerous positions. Eddie's equaliser was the most bizarre goal I've ever been involved in. Raddy had hooked the ball over his head and it bobbled just in front of Eddie who shinned it towards goal. Liverpool's goalkeeper, Ray Clemence, thought that the onrushing George Graham was going to redirect it and dived, anticipating a touch. But George, or so we thought at the time, cleverly made a far fainter contact than Clemence had prepared for and the ball trickled into the net.

George, of course, ran off to claim the goal and we all thought that it was, indeed, his until later that night when Jimmy Hill put it under the microscope with countless slow-motion replays. Though George had swung his leg at the ball, he'd missed completely. I'm happy to credit George with one of the greatest dummies of all time – even though he didn't intend it – but his repeated assertion that the goal was his is said with such a mischievous smile that I'm convinced he knows he didn't score it. He's such a funny bugger, though, that even when you pin him into a corner he'll say: 'Well, who would you rather have hugged, me or Eddie?'

I doubt whether anyone with Arsenal in their heart ever tires of Charlie George's winning goal. It was him at his best; his class and arrogance combined to rifle an unstoppable, twenty-yard shot high past Ray Clemence. Ray told me recently that the reason he didn't save it was because it took a slight deflection but I'm not having that. I can still picture it perfectly. As the ball fell to him I remember thinking: 'Thank God it's gone to Charlie. He's the only one of us left with the energy to hit it.' He had the talent, too, of course, and the cockiness to try it. It took me ages to get up to him to join the celebrations – I was as weary as an eighty-year-old.

I have no memories at all of the last eight minutes. I think

I must have run around purely from instinct and when the final whistle went my legs buckled with relief. The television cameras caught me quite clearly mouthing: 'We've fucking done it' as everyone converged on me but I felt so listless I could not summon up enough energy to go wild.

Everything else is a blur: the walk up the steps, the hoisting of the cup, the parade around the ground and the numerous television interviews. And on the television footage my blank eyes reveal my feeling of detachment from everything that was going on around me; I had given everything I had and there was nothing left to give. I was an empty shell, even though everyone was chuffed for me because I had finally won at Wembley. Bertie, in contrast, was deliriously happy and he even forsook his usual, muted handshake for hugs. But no matter what was said I still felt like a zombie.

Back at the Grosvenor House Hotel I had changed for dinner and just flopped on the bed while Barbara was getting ready. When the time came to go downstairs I couldn't actually get up for a few minutes. I so wanted to enjoy it but I felt flat, like a candle that had been snuffed out. I thought a few drinks might give me a boost but the alcohol didn't have its usual effect. When we went on to Danny La Rue's club with George Graham and his wife Marie I started to liven up more with every glass but there was no exhilaration, none of the elation I had felt when we'd won the league five days earlier. It was a strange experience. The more I chased happiness that evening, the more elusive it became.

The following day we had a bus procession through the streets of Islington – Arsenal's home borough – that ended at the town hall. There's a photograph of me, sitting on the town hall steps, which featured in the following day's newspapers with the caption: 'Frank McLintock: Overcome with emotion.' In fact I had a terrible hangover and felt like death. It's a bloody exhausting, long drawn out day when you've got a sore head and you're absolutely knackered.

There must have been 250,000 people in Islington that lunchtime and every one of them seemed to want to grab me and congratulate me, but all I wanted was to go home. Back in Laburnum Gardens, when we were finally released from our official duties, the families in our cul de sac had erected banners and threw a street party to welcome us home. It was in that low-key environment that it finally began to sink in and I started to cheer up. Nine months of intense focus had taken such a toll that only after a few weeks of total idleness did I recapture my normal verve. Ten years on from my bit-part in the 1961 FA Cup final which clinched the double for Tottenham, I had taken centre stage. By the middle of the month following our final I could, albeit belatedly, bask in the profound sense of satisfaction that it and our double victory had brought me.

12

NOT QUITE CAPPING IT

Football should have been the last thing on my mind that summer of 1971. If I had been sensible I would have immediately taken Barbara and the boys off to Europe as soon as the season ended. Doing nothing at all for a few weeks, recuperating in the sun on the beach or the golf course was the logical prescription for my shattered mind and body. I had never felt so fatigued; the emotional high coupled with the temporary erosion of all my physical and mental resources had left me feeling like an old man, thoroughly burned out.

But I wanted more. That 1970-71 season had culminated in a kind of redemption song for my career, banishing for ever the notion of McLintock, the nearly man. An unforeseen side effect of my form that year was the surprising opportunity to conquer my other major disappointment, my long-abandoned international hopes.

When the call came from Bobby Brown to join the squad for the Home International Championship, the prospect of playing three games in seven days – my sixty-eighth, -ninth and seventieth matches of the season – exhausted me just to contemplate it. But the thought of adding to my paltry six caps in eight years was far too enticing. Last season had proved that miracles were possible. Why not put myself through the mangle one last time, and see if my remaining unfulfilled ambition could be salvaged in a similarly thrilling fashion?

I have written in chapter three of Tony Knapp's prediction on my Leicester City debut in September 1959 that I would 'play for Scotland, son, before the season's out' . He was a year too early. My first representative game was with the Under 23s in a match against a Scottish Second Division Select XI and it set the tone for the rest of my time with the national team.

Before the game I made the mistake of reading the newspapers and one Scots daily brought the full weight of the anti-Anglo-Scot debate down on me: 'Who is this McLintock?' the journalist wrote. 'Why do we need him when we have players here in Scotland who are much better?' That was a typically warm welcome from that parochial bunch.

The game itself was a walkover – I think we won 9-2 but that did not spare me from a second mauling from the same reporter, who gave me a roasting for lacking composure on the ball. Was there any wonder that I couldn't settle properly? I was always relatively free from nerves but his diatribe the day before had left me tense and desperate to prove myself in front of my friends and family who had travelled to Fir Park to mark what should have been a special moment for me.

The selectors kept faith with me, however, and picked me for another Under 23 international against England at Aberdeen. Bobby Moore and Jimmy Greaves played that day for England and Greavsie, in particular, ran us ragged. I remember him running through on goal as I speculated: 'How's he going to do this?' He got to within fifteen yards of the goal – perhaps a bit too near I hoped – and leaned to his left, the goalkeeper followed suit and Jim just opened his body slightly and slotted the ball a foot to the keeper's right; he didn't have enough time to shift his weight back to make a save. 'You jammy sod,' I thought, but after seeing him execute the same trick at least another fifty times in his career I had to recognise the intelligence, economy and cruelty of Greavsie's finishing.

He got a kick out of tantalising goalkeepers, putting them in a position from which they could not make a quick enough adjustment, then poking the ball just out of reach. One against one you would put your bank book on him and he scored with the calmness of someone who had just heard the final whistle but thought he'd put it away in any case. He scored twice in a 4-2 win for the English team. And for all his outgoing, jocular personality and genuine levity at times on the field, I will never forget the hardness that lay beneath it and the ruthlessness he exhibited that day. Don't let his joshing around on television fool you; Jimmy Greaves was the slyest and most merciless forward England have ever had.

A defeat, even in a junior friendly, brought an all too predictable demand from the press for the selectors to stop wasting their time with us exiles. Every time a result did not go Scotland's way it seemed they wanted us blacklisted from the squad, as though our desertion of the homeland was a wicked act of betrayal for which we could never make amends. It was different for the likes of Dave Mackay and Alan Gilzean, who had played for Scottish clubs and had built up some good-will with the press and the public. Real vitriol was saved for serious transgressors like Denis Law, Billy Bremner and me, who had flaunted our flagrant lack of patriotism by joining English clubs without paying our dues to the country of our birth.

Denis and Billy eventually made it into the Hampden Hall of Fame, deservedly so, but no one should forget that after some defeats the press would launch venomous attacks on them and their lack of commitment. When Scotland drew with West Germany in 1969, one report slaughtered Law's contribution under the headline 'Goodbye, Denis'.

More than thirty-five years on, it makes the mind boggle to contrast the view the press held then about the strength of the domestic game and now, where a player with a quarter of Law's talent would be lauded as the saviour of Scottish football. Scotland did have a relative embarrassment of riches in the sixties but that was no reason for provincially minded bigots to slate us merely to shore up their own perverse sense of national pride.

The pattern was set when I won my first full cap in 1963 as a substitute for the injured Dave Mackay against Norway in Bergen. I went on with twelve minutes to go and Scotland leading 3-2. I touched the ball four times in total as we contrived to lose the game 4-3 but I made no mistakes and stuck with the man I had been told to mark. Norway were still considered a soft touch and so the result was seen as an ignominious one but I was still shocked to read the following morning that the consensus among the travelling reporters was that I hadn't 'looked the part'. Twelve minutes and I'd been written off. The vast majority of them had never before seen me play but my record in English football had been good up to that point. I also thought that two FA Cup finals in three years might persuade them to give me the benefit of the doubt but there was no chance of that happening. Anglos made very convenient scapegoats in those days.

Another member of our party was treated with more discretion. Jim Baxter was the darling of the Scottish press. He was an outrageously talented footballer, dripping with the arrogance and cheek that Scots love. The 'gallus' that made him so mercurial as a footballer also made him intolerable, occasionally, off the park, particularly when his savage sense of humour had been aroused by a drink or two. To give you a flavour of the esteem in which he was held on the day the team left for Scandinavia, the main headline on the front, not the back, page of the *Evening Times* read in two-inch bold type: 'Baxter forgets boots'. One single column down the side of the page had the much smaller heading: 'Harold Macmillan seriously ill'. In a toss up between the health of the prime minister and the possibility of Jim having to play in borrowed boots, the editor knew which story would shift most copies.

The drunk and disorderly side of Baxter has been well-documented since his appallingly early death in 2001. I only witnessed it once at first-hand and that was at the banquet in Bergen after my Scotland debut. We had a competition where you had to eat three water biscuits without the help of fluid, and if you failed you had to neck a pint of strong, continental lager. Three of us – Jim Baxter, Davie Gibson and I – had several goes and failed every time, so we'd drunk three or four pints in a oner in the space of about fifteen minutes. It was a good laugh but thoroughly daft as we still had the formal part of the evening to get through.

Baxter was wonderful company most of the time but, as I've said, could be a right nutter once he'd had a few and it didn't take him very long into the meal before he started with his antics. I was his first target. Every time I tried to take a bite of food, he'd thump me on the back and burst out laughing. I stuck it for a while but after about the fifth time as my forkful of food went flying I lost my temper and threatened to put him 'through that fucking wall' if he didn't stop.

Turning his attention to his Rangers' colleague, Jimmy Miller, he jostled him for a while then upped the ante by picking up a large stainless steel tea pot full of hot water, opening the lid and drenching him. We were sitting at this big T-shaped table, like the ones you used to see in a school refectory, with the players either side of the long stem and the selectors and management team facing us from the top table.

That, incidentally was very representative of the system in place at the time; the selectors, some good men but with a few passengers – duffers from county associations – enjoyed the old hierarchical structure. They travelled first class while we went in second and they had wine while we had water. Some took advantage of it and it was quite common to see them enjoying their jolly to the full as they stumbled around slightly glassy-eyed.

They were busily gorging at the top table when Willie Henderson, Baxter's great friend, stood up to defend Miller and started on Jim, telling him he was out of order and threatening to take him outside.

Baxter responded by launching a water-jug missile and it was only when the dignitaries were splashed that they decided to take some action. One old guy stood up and said in a precise

THE DOUBLE

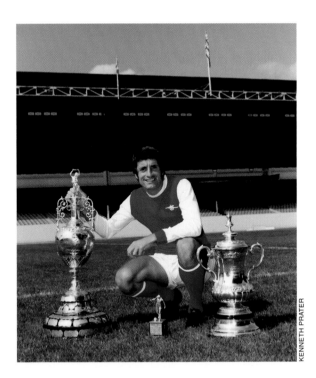

KENNETH PRATER

The 1998 reunion.

EMPICS

First game of the '70–'71 season. I was just
about to catch George, honest. Our 4–0
victory was the first tangible sign that
something special was happening.

Celebrating a vital goal
against Southampton
which gave us a 2–1 win
with seven games to go.

DAILY EXPRESS

Tension is building as we take
on and beat Chelsea in April.
Peter Osgood had a few words
to say about my challenge here.

Three to go and facing our rivals for the title. Charlie sees the funny side of Bob's injury, but Bremner is in no doubt what I think.

Disaster strikes. Or Jackie Charlton does at least, scoring in the dying seconds in controversial circumstances. Leeds top.

Last game. Against Spurs. I've got a clear sight of goal then, Crunch! 'I ought to knock your teeth out you daft bastard. I was just about to score the goal that would have won us the league.'

But it didn't matter. Ray Kennedy's goal soon after brought the Championship to Highbury. And thousands of Arsenal fans savoured celebrating on Spurs territory.

DAILY EXPRESS

The dream looked over. 2–1 down in the semi with seconds to go. But I met the corner just right. My header was goal-bound until slapped off the line. But not by the hand of 'keeper Banks.

Penalty! And Peter Storey slots it home.

FA NEWS

The double is on. Only Liverpool stand in the way. Charlie seems relaxed enough.

Into extra time and knackered. Then Charlie unleashes his wonder strike and sinks to the ground. No shortage of arms to help him up again.

The final whistle. Exhaustion and elation. The double was ours. Charlie raises his arms. John Radford and I can only scream at each other.

The celebrations continue. Ray Kennedy, John Radford and me in the Wembley changing rooms.

Opposite: The day after. The newspapers said I was overcome with emotion at Islington town hall. The truth … a stinking hangover.

That's my boy.

That's my boys. Left to right: Neil, Jamie Scott and Iain.

Grandma and Grandpa with the grandkids. At the back, Ruby and Robyn; front, Frankie, Thomas, Finlay, Ellis.

and pompous teuchter accent: 'Mr Baxter, would you kindly sit down and behave yourself. We will see you first thing in the morning.'

Jim was riled by this and stormed off to bed but not before shouting: 'Ah fuck off you old bastards.' Anyone else would have been shipped back to Glasgow the following morning and we all thought that Jim had played his last game for Scotland. But nothing was said at breakfast and everyone carried on as though the incident had never happened. That was the first manifestation I saw of the way different rules applied to him.

He was such an exceptional player that he was treated leniently and for that, thinking like a player, I was grateful. But I cannot help thinking that it might have been better for his long-term health if those in authority had applied the same disciplinary code the rest of us had to adhere to.

Our summer tour continued with a game against the Republic of Ireland in Dublin where I made my first start in place of the still-ailing Mackay. Another defeat did not fill us with the confidence necessary for the next match with Spain in Madrid, and by the time we had spent an hour sitting in the Chamatin stadium (later re-named the Bernabeu) watching the Spanish squad train, I thought we were about to face the biggest tonking in Scottish history.

You have to remember that we were very unfamiliar with co-ordinated and scientific training sessions. We were still rather rag-bag in the way we ran about while there was so much precision in the Spanish approach that it made us feel like a bunch of amateurs playing in the park. For twenty minutes Spain were like an elite army display unit as they responded to the coach's whistle to do all manner of sprints, leaps and jerks. If that wasn't intimidating enough, they then got the ball out.

Splitting into groups of threes and fours, their training session began by knocking the ball on the volley to each other, controlling it with their chests and knees. The group I watched dropped the ball once in a quarter of an hour. As we sat in the shade of the massive stand we all looked at each other in disbelief and most of us were muttering a rueful expletive. Then, our prospective opponents went down the bottom end of the pitch and proceeded to put on the most amazing exhibition I have ever seen.

We had to climb further up the vast stand to get a good view and what we saw terrified us. Del Sol put the ball down by the right-hand touchline and hammered in a cross with the outside of his right boot. Gento, the best winger I have ever seen, ran into the box quicker than the bloody Road Runner, dived forward, executed a perfect hand spring and belted the ball past the goalkeeper with both his heels. He did it five times in all, missing the goal twice but making a beautifully sweet connection every time. We sat there slack-jawed and could only say: 'Fucking hell.' I would have been happy just to head one of those bullet crosses! Even Baxter, who had more skill in his left foot than a barrelful of Brazilians, was quietly impressed.

Di Stefano took over next, getting Del Sol to hit a more conventional out-swinger at hip height. He did a 360-degree pirouette and smashed it in with his right foot. He, too, did the same trick five times on the trot – deliberately taking his eye off the ball every time in the most complex manner imaginable yet still hitting it crisply every time. Discipline, phenomenal skill and arrogance. It had been an incredible matinee performance. They obviously knew we were there and it was designed largely to make us crap our pants. If it hadn't been for our injured skipper, Mackay, that's exactly what we would have done.

An hour before the match the following evening we were out on the pitch taking in the atmosphere of that enormous stadium. The Spanish players were there too, just milling around, when Jim Baxter decided to show them that we were not all clod-kicking mugs in Britain. We all knew Dave Mackay's party-piece and Baxter decided now was the right time to unveil it.

Jim called over to Dave, using his nick-name, 'Hey Marquis, see if you can catch this.' With that, he tossed a coin thirty feet up in the air. Mackay didn't let his stomach-muscle tear prevent him from giving the Spaniards a dose of their own psychological warfare. 'Give me some room,' he shouted. 'Don't crowd me.' He thrust out his right leg, bent at the knee, and caught the coin on his toe. He stood there for a second, for show, then flipped it back up in the air, caught it on his forehead, knocked it back up and caught it in his left eye, then rolled it down his shoulder into his open blazer pocket and waltzed off back to the dressing room to thunderous applause. We'd seen him do it many times before, indeed Davie Gibson and I had practised for three weeks solid just to get the toe-catch spot on, but his timing was perfect because it showed our opponents that we weren't frightened of skill and that we might have a few tricks up our sleeves, too.

In some ways both shows had been part of the phoney war as neither Mackay nor those three Real Madrid geniuses – Del Sol, Di Stefano and Gento – actually played in the match. I took Dave's place at right half with Baxter alongside me. Up front we had Willie Henderson, Davie Gibson, Ian St John, Denis Law and David Wilson – probably as good a front five as Scotland have ever had – and, astonishingly, all five of them, plus me, scored.

Our 6-2 victory was truly remarkable, especially since we didn't have any tactical plan at all. Ian McColl's position as a manager without any input into selection was confined to a little fitness work and telling us to go out and beat the opposition. There was none of the chalkboard analysis or protracted strategical discussion that was later so prevalent. After eight minutes we were 1-0 down but then put on such a scintillating display of old school, brash, attacking Scottish football that we were up 4-1 by the half hour.

My only international goal came straight from Filbert Street: a shot from a Davie Gibson cut-back corner that I met just by the edge of the box, a regular point of rendezvous in First Division games. We were fantastic that night and I don't think that it was any coincidence that the five Anglos were magnificent in an away match. Far from Hampden and the attendant pressure of your family, friends and the full press corps, we played without inhibition. I was, as they say, chuffed to bollocks and it remains the one outstandingly happy memory of my turbulent, nine-cap career.

That result was probably Scotland's greatest away result to date yet only four of that team, me excluded, were retained for the next match four months later, and it took a further eight years and a switch of position before I got to play back-to-back internationals again. I have no argument with that when I reflect on who I was up against for the number 4 shirt all those years: Dave Mackay, Paddy Crerand, John Greig, Bobby Murdoch, Pat Stanton and Billy Bremner. I was usually in the squad – 'You've been in more pools, Frank, than Johnny Weissmuller,' as Baxter put it – but found it very hard to break into the team and played only three more times until the end of Arsenal's double season: once in 1964, again in 1967 and, finally, in 1970.

For a long time I thought that the 1967 Hampden friendly against Russia would be my last international match. I hadn't played for Scotland for three years and reports of our 2-0 defeat were accompanied in one newspaper by mug shots of the guilty men: Eddie McCreadie, Jim McCalliog and me. All three of us were based in England and that sort of treatment by the press can make you feel like a terrorist.

I know that I didn't play particularly well but I didn't do any worse than a couple of the Celtic lads who'd escaped that sort of denunciation. I wish, so badly, that I had handled it better, that my temperament was closer to Denis Law's. As a player Law was electrifying, skinny and sinewy in physique and with the right haughty look to match his shock of aristocrat-ically blond hair. He used to live on tea and cigarettes but his apparent frailty was an illusion; he was as tough as the granite from his native Aberdeen with the cocksure confidence to dismiss all that anti-Anglo nonsense that I let get to me.

I was too uptight ever to enjoy playing for Scotland. I was so tense when I played that there was no fluency to my game. I was desperate to prove a point to my critics and I got too fired up, wasting my energy haring about in straight lines and trying to tackle everything that moved.

To any sane person, it was far more trouble than it was worth. OK, the players were fun to be around, the managers gave their all – even though they did not get a free hand in selection until the early seventies – and the fans were generally fine. But the majority of the press had disappeared so far up the Old Firm's arses that they could never be objective about English-based players and the Scottish Football Association (SFA) often treated us like the shit on their shoes.

On one occasion, when Ian Ure and I had joined the squad for a European Championship qualifier in Belfast, we took a taxi to Heathrow for the flight at half past eight in the morning; we also had the gall to take a taxi back to North London on the return leg. When we sent our joint expenses chit, with receipts, to Glasgow asking for the eight pounds to be reimbursed, we were summoned to Bob Wall's office at Highbury to take a telephone call from Willie Allan, secretary of the SFA. Allan was out of control, shouting and accusing us of having airs and graces for taking a taxi and attempting to defraud the association. Ian took the call and screamed back down the phone, trying to enlighten him on the difficulties two professional footballers faced in trying to get from North London to Heathrow, and back again, on public transport in the early morning rush hour with suitcases and boot bags. But Allan was unmoved. He'd happily sign the bar bill for some blazered geriatric from Renfrewshire but we got the sum of two pounds and ten shillings to split between us.

It would have been easy to walk away at that point. I hadn't played in the Belfast game and I didn't play for another two years but, though I admitted in interviews that my international career was probably over, I was still hopeful of making a breakthrough – despite the grief. In the absence of Leeds and Celtic players given time to recover from their European Cup semi-final, I was rewarded for my patience with the captaincy for a British Championship game back in Belfast in 1970 but I had to wait another year for my next cap even though we won.

It was the proudest day of my parents' lives and, for that, I am glad that I persevered. Actually, that sounds too non-chalant. I used to get carried away with the frustrations of it all because I yearned to be a super-hero in the national team and never got there and that has coloured my memories. No, it was not just my mum and dad who were proud that Saturday afternoon: I felt the biggest sense of personal honour that a game ever gave me. Anyway, few others can boast a 100 per cent international captaincy record!

My final fling in the Scotland jersey, all three games of the British Championship in the summer of 1971, probably came too late. It wasn't down to my age since I played on in the First Division until I was thirty-seven, but I was too tired to do myself justice.

I played fairly solidly in the first game, a 0-0 draw with Wales at Ninian Park, but having to mark Toshack for the second time in a week following the FA Cup final left my legs feeling like two flaccid rubber bands. We lost the second match to Northern Ireland at Hampden and, though Bobby Moncur and I had forged a decent understanding, we lost to an own goal, then halfway through the second half I had to come off with a pulled hamstring.

Looking back, I wish that I'd had the courage to cheat and pull out of the Wembley game with England. On the Thursday morning, two days before the match, I'd thought there was no way that I would be fit but I'd never played England before and I could not bring myself to pass up the chance. I was massaged all day Thursday and most of Friday before pushing myself through an arduous fitness test. I knew that I wasn't right but Bobby Brown, the manager, convinced me that I could get through the game and I was blinded by the excitement of taking on the Auld Enemy.

It was a daft decision on both our parts; I was in no fit state, either mentally or physically, to mark Martin Chivers for ninety minutes. Martin was one of the most difficult forwards to jump against. He wasn't gigantic but he was a freak of nature in that he seemed to have a ludicrously long back and very broad shoulders, which made it difficult to get your head up to the height of his. By half time my hamstring was aching and I was dead beat.

We were 3-1 down and Chivers had scored two goals, a topic that Bobby Brown naturally sought to address: 'Chivers is winning everything in the air, Frank,' he said. I told him that I was aware of that but Bobby Moore was hitting flat balls at head height for Martin; he wasn't floating them in and giving me the opportunity to challenge for them. Martin was so tall and stocky that I had no way of getting up to fight with him as I could have done if Moore had tossed the ball up. Bobby was such an intelligent footballer he could spot that I was struggling and had the wit and dexterity to exploit it.

In addition, we had not worked on grooving our defensive system properly. Full backs schooled in the Scottish First Division habitually liked to tuck in, which left huge gaps. Similarly, I was used to passing the centre forward over to a full back when they ran into wide areas but our full backs rigorously stuck with their wide player even if he was miles from the ball. It meant that the way I had successfully played at Arsenal went out of the window and, instead, I ended up running hundreds of yards further than normal on repeated darts to the corners with Chivers and Hurst.

Attackers can play spontaneously but a defence has to work as a unit. But for our squad, thrown together just eight days earlier, everyone simply had to rely on instinct rather than planning. We shored it up in the second half and kept it to 3-1, but I was half lame by the end. If I had been clever and pulled out I am sure I would have played again the following season. As it was, I limped off the pitch at Wembley knowing that my rashness and enthusiasm had probably put the kibosh on my international career.

I would never have had such a good career without my passion and commitment yet, ironically, these two attributes were one of the main reasons for my failure to have the international career of which I dreamed. At the time of writing, Scotland is in an awful predicament and they would probably give fifty caps to a solid professional from Outer Mongolia who had a Scots granny.

Back then, the competition for places in the national team was too strong for me to cement a place and that, coupled with the Glasgow press's dim view of native Scots playing for English clubs, meant that whenever I got the chance – apart from the Spain game – I got too wound up to perform without inhibition. It's such a wonderful feeling to be picked for your country, and it was particularly important for my family who had been denied the opportunity to watch me regularly.

I was desperate to make my family proud of me and – like at Arsenal under Billy Wright – because of the criticism I tried too hard and found myself stuck in a no-frills rut of competent, but ultimately frightened football. I was too sensitive and it became soul-destroying as I got myself into a downward spiral where the harder I tried, the more unnaturally rudimentary my game became. And that state of affairs continued to blight my international career long after I had recovered my confidence and form in domestic football.

Still, it was nine caps more than a lot of players have managed and while some people might say I had a very modest international record, no one could say it was disastrous. There was a little relief when I accepted that it was over but my major feeling remains one of regret.

On my long-delayed holiday that summer to Val de Lobo in Portugal, I tried to clear my head of football. But to my surprise, and delight, that proved impossible because no sooner had we arrived at the resort than we discovered it to be a sort of English First Division enclave and we soon hooked up with Bobby and Norma Charlton, Martin and Cathy Peters and, of all people, Don and Elsie Revie. It was the ultimate busman's holiday, I suppose, but one which helped me put the Scotland disappointment into perspective. At least I had Arsenal to return to, a club that most predicted was bound to build on the double and go on to better things. Little did I know that within eighteen months the club would be in turmoil once again and a team feted to be on the verge of greatness would be making a straight line for the knacker's yard.

13

DROPPED

Few football teams achieve sustained success and it is no real shame on us that we did not manage it at Arsenal. But the sense of waste is difficult to shake. When a football team starts to decline, the early symptoms are often the hardest to spot. It is not complacency but blind optimism that persuades you to ignore the evidence provided by seemingly insignificant but telling signs – like noticing that one or two players had started to look a bit podgier.

Indeed, the lack of discipline and focus that kicks the foundations out from beneath a football team is a gradual process characterised by lots of daft little things – occasional breaches of punctuality, constant speculation about wage differentials, and even too many biscuits, crisps and fizzy drinks. In contrast, a dread sort of pettiness takes hold and ridiculously trifling 'crimes' are jumped on – it's as if the manager is trying too hard to show he's still firmly in charge. In our case this took the form of Bertie's declaration that, unless he shaved off his summer holiday beard, Charlie George would never play for Arsenal again.

Given the age of our squad when we won the double and the momentum we had built up over the preceding four years, we had a better chance than most of establishing ourselves as consistent competitors both at home and in Europe. We had the players, we had the system, we had the confidence and now, in 1971, we had the trophies to prove it.

But above all, we had a work ethic and, in Don Howe, a martinet to enforce it. Our faith in him and his methods was the bedrock of 'the Arsenal way'. I sat through the summer of 1971 slowly regaining my strength and appetite for the game, convinced that the double was only the beginning. But the muesli-spitting shock I had one morning when I read that Bertie had, once again, rolled out his canoe analogy and let Don Howe go to West Bromwich Albion as manager meant that it was, in fact, the end.

Nothing was the same after that moment as the creeping indiscipline that Don would never have stood for started to erode our edge. In a little under two years I would go from Footballer of the Year to playing in the stiffs. I, at least, eventually recovered. The team honed by Don Howe never did.

Footballers can be precious about the relative importance of coaching. The old line, that a good team depends solely on the quality of the players at a manager's disposal, is still trotted out regularly. But our team's decline disproved that; without Don Howe at Arsenal we were no longer able to replicate the intensity that had led to our dominance. It's probably unreasonable of me to expect the ultimate act of self-sacrifice from Bertie, but if he had been prepared to signal that Don would eventually inherit his job, I am sure that would have been enough to stop him leaving.

Don's lack of success as a number one would not normally make him a candidate for manager. However, I think he had already done the hardest job and we, already faithful disciples of his fiery, zealous approach – because he had demonstrated its value with tangible results – would have continued to follow him, always.

In Don's place we got Steve Burtenshaw, a fine technical coach and as good a judge of a player as there has been in the game. But he was very softly spoken and relied too much on trying to be reasonable with us. To imply we needed a dictator to get the best out of us makes us sound like children, and is not quite what I mean. But winning the double had bred a sense of self-satisfaction among the squad and I think it required a much tougher stance than Burtenshaw's to combat it.

We had won the 1971 league by only one point and to achieve even that narrow victory had demanded our rigid adherence to an exhausting defensive system of pressing. Unless every single member of the team was willing to put his body on the line – training session after training session, game after game – for another year, we could not hope to gain the optimum benefit from the pressing strategy that suited us best. We all knew where we were supposed to be in terms of fitness and commitment but we just weren't mature enough to achieve it without the man we trusted, Don Howe, to flog us there.

Bertie, of course, did not see it that way. He had come through the loss of one coach unscathed and must have felt that our protestations about Don's departure were a re-run of those we voiced four years earlier when Dave Sexton went back to Chelsea. I don't wish to downplay Bertie's contribution to the team in organisation and structure but when it came to coaching he had relied so strongly on Don, his right-hand man, that without his influence things inevitably started to deteriorate.

For example, the change made by the FA in the way referees were to interpret tackling – especially the tackle from behind – was not addressed quickly enough; an apparently minor matter in the scheme of things, yet it made an enormous difference to us. We were not a dirty team but we were hard and played at the limit of the old interpretation by being very aggressive in the tackle. With the new clampdown we were picking up more cards and yet, despite the fact that we became hesitant and less robust in physical challenges, we failed to work on a way to compensate for the loss of what had been one of our most potent weapons.

Add to that our status as champions, which gave our opponents an extra but unfamiliar incentive to beat us which, in turn, meant we needed to be at our best to respond. In the 1971-72 season our old watchwords – discipline, team-work, commitment, desire – were there when we outplayed Leeds and eventual title-winners, Derby County, at Highbury, as they were when we trounced the likes of Chelsea, Manchester United and Newcastle. But we could never achieve the long, winning runs that we'd enjoyed the previous year.

Of our four watchwords, desire was the hardest to renew. How do you keep a team at the top when deep down the players are grateful to have got there once and can't face pushing themselves through the pain barrier again? As the season went on some players started to resort to their old ways and a hint of selfishness and self-protection trickled in. On three separate occasions we lost three league games on the trot, a sure-fire indicator that something had gone badly wrong. What's more, in 1970-71 eight of us had played forty or more league games; in 1971-72, as we struggled with injury and suspension, only two of us played this many. It was clear that we lacked a stimulus. In previous years we had cranked it up in training which ensured our unmatchable physicality – the vital resource, or magic ingredient, which we could fall back on. This time, as we struggled against defeat, Bertie overlooked the traditional remedy and decided on a radical solution. He got his chequebook out for the first time in years.

Signing Alan Ball, a magnificent footballer and pugnacious competitor, looked like a no-brainer on paper. While I was thrilled at the news of his transfer – and relished the prospect of having a World Cup winner in our team – it raised two significant issues: first, would his playing style and attitude suit our well-established game-plan? And second, his record transfer fee along with our speculation about the size of his salary threatened to open up that old dressing-room fault line – Arsenal's contentious wage and loyalty bonus policy.

Off the field Alan was marvellous company; on the training ground he was like a strutting peacock and he oozed class. Settling him into the team, however, proved problematic. Although playing at the back, both Peter Simpson and I were converted midfielders, adept at dropping balls in, directly from back to front, to Raddy and Ray Kennedy. It was one of our most frequently used tactics – Raddy and Ray held the ball up so well and liked to get it early to bring the midfield into play in the attacking third. Alan, on the other hand, was used to being the fulcrum of every team he had played in.

He liked to take the ball from the centre half, run with it, then play it to a midfield colleague, get it back, play it to a forward and maybe get it back for a third time. He was not a play-maker in the Glenn Hoddle mould. Teams did not use him as the hub of sophisticated passing but he was used to setting the tempo of play and the ball repeatedly going through him. Our inclination, at times, was to bypass the midfield and Alan hated it.

Always an extremely emotional person, after only a couple of games he got down in the dumps, saying we were making him look poor. At that point I had to intervene: 'Look, we've been playing this way for seven years,' I told him, 'and you can't expect ten players to switch overnight to accommodate the eleventh man. You will have to be patient and adapt to us and we will try to adapt to you.'

His four years at Arsenal must have been a huge disappointment to him. He must have taken a great deal of satisfaction from being the main cog at Blackpool and Everton but we just could not marry our contrasting styles. I felt for him, and though he was still dangerous we never saw the best of him until the style that had brought us our previous success was disastrously ditched.

Abandoning our pressing game enabled Alan to shine but the team as a whole went rapidly downhill. He was an excellent player but perhaps – like Charlie Nicholas, later at Arsenal, or Rodney Marsh, famously, at Manchester City – it did not matter how superb any individual player was if the rest of the team were more effective playing in a way that did not necessarily spotlight its superstar's superior talent. Man City, for example, were a dynamic, fast-moving team and Marsh slowed them down. It was the same with us and Alan Ball, but not with such drastic results.

It was not Alan's fault – a wee bit of our team's desire had already gone – but that Bertie had brought in a superstar to solve our problems was representative of his flawed thinking. It was clear that some players were resting on their laurels but instead of kicking them up the arse, as he and Don had always done, he panicked. The fact that he opted for the doomsday scenario, and at the first sign of trouble, dismantled the team, showed his essential lack of expertise in purely football matters. In the face of some players' lethargy, and the team's demonstrably falling standards, he could have tried more of the sergeant-major-type bollockings that had driven us on in the first place rather than this uncharacteristically meek resignation to ship in fresh talent.

If Bertie was not prepared to do it and Steve Burtenshaw was temperamentally unsuited to the severe approach, that left only one person with the authority to try to get things back on track. So I took up the baton but, in the long term, my attempt to confront the issue backfired on me. I still had the hunger, and the prospect of winding down my career after the double appalled me. There were undeniable signs of laxity in our team: some players got chubbier, some gave up the chase too quickly and others cheated by throwing themselves into tackles instead of staying on their feet.

I called a team meeting and specifically asked Bertie and Steve not to attend: 'I don't think we're playing well and I think some players will hold back if you two are there,' I explained. Bertie was puzzled by my request but let me call the meeting all the same. With hindsight, I think he interpreted it as interfering and possibly resented what he took to be empire building on my part. Nothing could have been further from the truth.

I steamed straight into four or five of the lads, Ray Kennedy and Raddy in particular – they were the best front two in the country and had been formidable only months before. Now, however, they were letting defenders get on top, bully them out of headers and consequently we had lost our cutting edge. Ray had piled on the pounds, too. In the past, Bertie would have given him the Alan Skirton treatment and thrashed the lard off him, but now it was down to Ray – he'd have to respond as a professional and get back to his fighting weight. Both Ray and Raddy took my tough talk in good part, and it was only Peter Storey who responded with the legitimate quip: 'How the hell do you think you're playing, Frank?'

I admitted straight off that I had not been exactly uprooting trees and said that the purpose of the meeting allowed any of them to slag me off all they wanted. I had called them in because we were a tremendous side that was not performing and I wanted to find out what had gone wrong. The common consensus was that we were missing Don – that fiery presence that was in your face in training and could be unleashed when needed at half time. Everyone agreed that Steve was a good coach, arguably the equal of Don tactically, but he was too respectful of our feelings and prone to backing off when he should have been doling out hard words.

I reported back to Bertie and told him how we felt about Steve's attitude; Don would have shaken us out of our complacency and unless Steve was more forceful we would not recover. Perhaps Bertie thought I was a trouble maker for questioning his recruitment choices – our relationship was certainly diminished thereafter.

I didn't want Steve to be sacked; I just wanted him to tweak his approach. And the last thing I wanted was Bertie's job. I just wanted to do something about our team before it was too late. My ambition was to play on in the First Division for as long as I was physically capable – which I did. At the age of thirty-two when we had the clear-the-air meeting in January 1972 with our title defence all but gone, the thought of managing Arsenal had never entered my head and any fears Bertie may have had about my motives were ludicrous.

I wish I could use the European Cup as an excuse for our form that season but it was not much of a distraction since the competition was still reserved only for true champions and there were not many ties. We played only four games in the run-up to Christmas and had won comfortable aggregate victories over Stromsgodset and Grasshoppers before, in early spring, Ajax took their chance to avenge the defeat we had dealt them in 1970.

In the intervening two years the Dutch team had improved beyond recognition, and now played a keep-ball game of crisp cruelty to match their marvellous individual skills. We took the lead, however, through Ray Kennedy and only lost the match 2-1 to a Gerrie Muhren penalty. The referee should never have given that penalty; Piet Keizer clipped my feet – not the other way round – and fell on top of me.

It was an unpleasant echo of our loss to Cologne the previous year in the Fairs Cup which put paid to our defence of the cup at the quarter-final stage. That day we were the victims of some extraordinarily strange decisions, including several free kicks awarded against us for ungentlemanly conduct when, in fact, we were just shouting to each other for the ball. With regard to both the Ajax and Cologne matches, we were, to say the least, very unhappy with the standard of refereeing.

Marinello missed a sitter in the Highbury leg before George

Graham sealed the tie for them with a powerful headed own goal. He managed to laugh it off later by saying that we should have been marking him because we all knew what a beast he was in the air.

The defence of our league title had floundered on a lack of drive and consistency and Bertie's European pipe dream had been dashed after only six games. However, in the run-up to the FA Cup, we had mustered up enough of our former class to knock out Derby and, for the second year running, Stoke City in a semi-final replay. This meant we were in with the chance of, once again, emulating Tottenham if we could follow up the double by retaining the cup.

I honestly feel that had we stuck to the high tempo, attritional game that most of us were comfortable with we could have beaten Leeds in that centenary FA Cup final. But in order to allow Alan Ball the space to make his mark we had become more ponderous and this gave Leeds the time they needed to exploit their superior technique. In the build-up to the game we had paid a great deal of attention to the threat posed by Allan Clarke and Mick Jones. Mick was a hard-running player's player whose prodigious appetite for hard work never gave you a moment's peace. Clarke was more eye-catching, with that snotty look he perfected, brilliant close control and only slightly behind Jimmy Greaves as the best finisher in the game. Simpson and I had been resolute for much of the first half, and it was only when Giles and Bremner started to dominate Ball and Graham that I began to realise we were getting a hiding.

We'd had chances – when Bally's shot was cleared off the line by Paul Reaney and I had a rasping free kick saved at the second attempt by David Harvey – but we were never really in the game. So, we had managed to hold on until half time;

our long familiarity with our opponents' players enabled us at the back to anticipate their likely moves.

A lucky ricochet gave Leeds' Mick Jones space to cross for Allan Clarke from the touchline. One against one, few players ever got past Bob McNab but on this occasion he dived in to the tackle but the ball bounced fortuitously for Jones, who wrapped his right foot around it for Clarke to spear past me and Geoff Barnett with a ferocious, diving header. We did all we could to get back in the game but they were far too canny. Charlie, later, hit the bar but they ran us ragged at the back on the counter-attack.

I had met the Queen Mother earlier that year – and felt patently ridiculous dressed in morning suit and top hat – when I collected my MBE at Buckingham Palace. Now, I would meet her daughter, when I collected my third FA Cup runners-up medal. I can value those medals today but at the time they were worthless trinkets to me. They served only as a stark reminder of our inability to match Leeds' game in that final; we missed a unique opportunity, given the similarities of the way both teams played in the early seventies, to be the one club to take them on at their own game.

I suppose, in some ways, that it was a fitting end to an anti-climactic season. After winning the double in 1970-71, we had promised so much but we'd failed to capitalise on our strengths and adopted a sort of half-cocked, wishy-washy style of play that had more pizzazz but lacked our old punch. It seemed to me, as I had yet another consolation drink at the Grosvenor House Hotel, that the next season, 1972-73, had to be about getting our fire back – and the critics could go to hell. But when the boss keeps throwing water on it, you have not got a hope of rekindling the flame.

My view was pragmatic rather than romantic. Returning to the nuts and bolts of an effective, defensive power game would not have won us many new fans but it was the most practical approach to take on the basis of our players' strengths. But after the summer, Bertie came back to pre-season training a convert to the sort of enlightened, expansive football that Ajax had mesmerised us with. It had been clear from the start that to remodel the team so it revolved around Alan Ball would take years. It was, however, an audacious gamble, foolhardy perhaps, that Bertie seemed intent on making – and contrary to all our misgivings. I could see how it might have worked if he'd signed three or four players, but he made no purchases during the summer and, instead, to spice up our wing play, relied on recalling Peter Marinello for an extended run in the first team.

When, in October 1972, Bertie eventually entered the transfer market to sign Coventry City's Jeff Blockley for £200,000, it made little sense in his 'total football' scheme. People still ask if the signing of such an expensive centre half unnerved me and it didn't; I did not feel personally threatened and, without being disrespectful to Jeff, it was obvious after a couple of training sessions that I had very little to fear. Yes, I was coming up to thirty-three years old by then, I'd lost some pace in my late twenties but my form and fitness had not deteriorated in the previous three years.

Jeff was a big, strong defender, the type of player we had not had since Ian Ure left. But to buy him to play like a Dutch centre half who would initiate attacking bursts with short probing passing from the back? Bertie must have flipped his lid. No wonder Joe Mercer, Coventry's manager at the time, told me that getting that fee for Jeff was the greatest transfer move he ever made.

Yet the size of the fee should have been a warning to me and, as I've said, my relationship with Bertie had grown more testy since that team meeting I'd called in the wake of Don Howe's departure.

The only aspect of training that remained as intense as it had been under Don and Dave Sexton were the mock England v Scotland games that we played every Friday on Highbury's indoor, red ash pitch. Primrose, Eddie Kelly, Peter Marinello, George Graham, Jackie Carmichael, me and Geordie Armstrong as our ringer piled into that game against the Englishmen with all our usual fervour. And they gave it back, none more so than Bally. It was often mayhem in there, just like the old days, but the unrestrained ardour on show was one of the very few remnants of the indomitable qualities that had defined us as a successful team. Pointing this out to Bertie only lowered my stock still further in his eyes. An incident on the pre-season trip to Switzerland also did me little good.

We had been to a wine tasting and several bottles which we'd secreted under the tables before lunch were swigged when Bertie's head was turned. The manager had always liked a sing-song on the bus and I found myself up at the front, belting out *Strangers in the Night*. Perhaps it was my decision to borrow the female courier's orange jacket to wear while I conducted the singing but, whatever the reason, Bertie was particularly sour-faced that afternoon.

When we got back to the hotel I said: 'Did you see wee Bertie, the little Hitler. What's his problem?' I was pretty sloshed and had no idea that the boss – sitting two seats away from me – had overheard everything. I'd thought I was being funny and entertaining the lads, but comparing the manager to Hitler was not the wisest thing I'd ever done. The following morning on the bus to training Bertie stood up and said: 'I'd just like to mention that I've never been so embarrassed by a team's behaviour and our captain was a bloody disgrace to the Arsenal.' It was a fair cop and I apologised but I wonder if he really took it in the spirit it was made. I know that football culture has changed so that our occasional episodes of boozing on pre-season tours looks unprofessional now. Back then it happened every year and while it was not officially sanctioned, management turned a blind eye as it was seen to be good for team spirit. But I regret opening my big mouth and sincerely hope that the incident did not play too significant a part in the continuing demise of my relationship with Bertie.

When we lost 5-0 to Derby at the Baseball Ground in late November, it was time for the experiment with a new model Arsenal to end. In a Sunday newspaper interview, Brian Clough had said that if every Arsenal player had shown the same commitment as me then we would not have taken such a hammering. That didn't change the result, though. I was injured for the next game, which we won against Leeds, but had returned in time for back-to-back victories against Spurs and West Brom. These games, also, saw Geordie and Ray Kennedy restored to the team – they had been dropped to facilitate the fluent style Bertie had decreed he wanted at the start of the season.

As we travelled to the Midlands on the following Friday in advance of our game against Birmingham it seemed everything was returning to normal; we had gone back to basics and won three games on the bounce. Now, surely, was the time for more of the same.

On the Saturday morning, in a private lounge at our Birmingham hotel, we were killing that dead time between breakfast and the team meeting. Some of us played cards, some flicked disinterestedly through newspapers while others waited to watch *Grandstand*. When Bertie came in and asked to see me in private I thought he wanted one of those quick captain/manager chats about off-field arrangements, something about bonuses or future trips. I followed him into the oak-panelled corridor where, without a hint of emotion, he said: 'I'm leaving you out of the team.'

To say I was caught completely unaware would be a gross understatement. If he had told me that he was going to join the French Foreign Legion it would have come as less of a shock. I wasn't exactly crestfallen by the news – that would come later – I was livid: 'What? You're leaving me out of the team? Why?' And he just repeated himself: 'I'm leaving you out of the team. I've made my decision. That's it.' I went mad and smashed my fist with such force into the wood panel next to him that I splintered the oak and pulverised my knuckles. He may have thought that I'd thrown a punch at him and missed, but I hadn't. I was distraught but I wasn't insane. Anyway, he was flabbergasted by my reaction, his face momentarily turning a pale, chalky grey, and he scuttled off back to his room damn quickly.

I spent the rest of the time before the game brooding on what had happened. I had never been dropped in thirteen years as a professional. This was my ninth season at Arsenal, I had been captain for almost five. I didn't always agree with Bertie but he knew I was honest and straightforward. I had been a conduit between him and the team and we had never got to loggerheads. Moreover, I had been a good ally to him and worked tirelessly to galvanise team spirit. Now it was two days before Christmas and he hadn't had the courtesy to tell me in

London, before we left for Birmingham; he had treated me, instead, like a seventeen-year-old apprentice.

Of course he had every right to drop me, I can't contest that, but having known me so well for nearly a decade he could have had more compassion in the way he did it. If he hadn't caught me off guard I would have been able to keep that foul temper of mine in check.

When Denis Hill-Wood came into the dressing room at St Andrews before kick-off and saw me slumped on a bench, still in my clothes he came straight over and asked: 'Frank, come on. Why aren't you getting stripped?' I just muttered in reply: 'You'd better ask that little bastard over there.' I was completely out of order, totally disrespectful and I regret my choice of words – but I couldn't help it. For years they'd exploited my passion for the club's benefit and now they'd dropped me; surely they couldn't expect me to take it lightly.

I was put in the reserves the next week and had an absolutely dreadful first game. I had been moping around at home, full of self-pity and I just couldn't motivate myself. Then, as ever, my gloom lifted and, not wanting to be thought a bad professional, from then on I gave my all – even though it was killing me playing in front of 300 when I was used to crowds of 50,000. I played pretty well in the next couple of games and my calming influence on the young professionals was commended by David Smith the coach.

Reports of my form got back to Bertie, and Bob McNab asked him to put me back in the first team only to be told that I had 'burned my bridges'. But Nabbers persisted on my behalf – I could not have wished for a more forthright advocate. He told me later of his conversation with the manager: 'I can't believe you, Bertie,' he'd said. 'Look at us without him.

There's a lack of understanding at the back, the off-side trap's all over the place – one's pushing up, the other's holding – there's no communication. I know I've been made captain, but Frank's still the captain of this club and everyone knows that and wants him back in.

'He's been your lion, done the job for you properly and then you expect him to take it on the chin when you drag him up to Birmingham and tell him three hours before kick-off that he's out after all those years' loyal service. He only reacted with the same qualities you've used to get the best out of everyone else.'

But Nabbers' words made no difference to Bertie, I was still in the reserves. When Blockley was injured in February, I did get back in the team and we won five of the seven games I played. But Bertie had let me know that I was only a stop-gap and, anyway, I had already made up my mind: I couldn't hang about in the reserves at my age hoping for the occasional first-team game.

So, one day in March, I knocked on Bertie's office door and went in at his call. Stiff and officious as ever, he glanced up from his paperwork: 'Yes?' he barked. I asked him if I could sit down and told him: 'I'd like to go.' I had come to that decision reluctantly and I thought that I had got over the hurt, but when the words actually came out of my mouth it felt like a sort of death.

Tears were rolling from my eyes, streaming down my cheeks and bouncing onto my navy blue blazer. I'd heard of people wearing their hearts on their sleeves but this was ridiculous. I was furious with myself for letting Bertie see how upset I was but he did soften slightly. He agreed to my request – said it was probably for the best – and asked if there was anything else he could do for me. I had been at Arsenal for nine seasons; if I had kicked my heels in the reserves, and I'd stayed on for another six months I would have qualified for a testimonial by reaching my tenth. When I put this to the manager and asked if he could bring my benefit match forward, he said he'd put it to a mini board meeting and get back to me. We parted that afternoon more amicably than I thought we could, both of us seemingly relieved to have brought my position to a head.

A fortnight later Bertie had still not come back to me so I went to see him for, as it turned out, the last time. Back to his curt and clipped best, he gave me a withering stare when I asked about the decision on my testimonial. 'What on earth are you talking about?' he said. 'We have accepted your transfer request but you can't have a testimonial. You've only been here nine seasons. You have to be here ten to qualify.'

I did not go into Birmingham corridor mode this time but I was just as pissed off and tore right into him verbally, saying that if I ever became a manger I would treat people a damn sight better than he had. Questioning his honour, though, just made him more resolute. That was me and him finished, and I told him that the sooner I was transferred the better.

The least I felt the club could do was give me a free transfer, meaning Arsenal would ask no fee for me from whichever club took me on. This way, I could pick up a bigger signing on fee which would compensate in a small way for the more than £80,000, tax free, that I was giving up by not holding them to contract and hanging around like a spectre at the feast for my testimonial.

Bertie, however, was adamant that I was worth money to the club and a free transfer was out of the question. The price put on my head after all my service was £25,000. As I left Bertie's office I vowed to myself that, whatever it took, over the next few years I would sweat blood to prove the wee bugger wrong.

14

INDIAN SUMMER
IN WEST LONDON

In the process of looking back at my career for this book, I have become acutely aware of how emotionally robust a professional footballer has to be. One of football's great sayings is that there is no sentiment in the game; this is not only a cliché but it is also wrong. I was broken hearted when I had to leave Arsenal and, though that rawness has been soothed by the passage of time, there is still a great deal of sorrow – not only about the manner of my departure but also about the premature break-up of our magnificent team.

My friend George Graham had left some months before me and within a couple of years Raddy, Nabbers, Ray Kennedy and, most astonishingly of all, Charlie George had also been shipped out. It did not take me long to become reconciled with Bertie Mee. After a few weeks of the most wonderfully surprising recuperation at Queens Park Rangers my bitterness towards him had gone and we got along fine on the rare occasions I bumped into him.

Bombing me out at the age of thirty-three made sense if he sincerely believed that my best years were behind me – though I still contend that he made a huge booboo. But the way he dealt with Ray and Charlie was beyond my comprehension. Both of them hung around for a couple more years during which Bertie shunted them between the reserves and the first team. He had lost faith in both players when they were still in their early twenties – a cardinal waste of his resources, in my opinion. In the Don Howe era, he would have worked so hard on motivation and fitness, constantly trying to educate them. Now, it seemed, he had just given up on them. At the time, I likened it to investing in a great yacht, pootling about in it for a bit, getting sea sick, letting it rust in the harbour then sending it off for someone else to salvage. Neither Ray nor Charlie were the easiest of people to handle, but management would be a doddle for everyone if it did not throw up a few difficult temperaments.

I think we all left the club aching to show Bertie the error of his judgement and I hope I don't sound too petty when I say that his decision not to bend the club's ten-year testimonial rule gave added impetus to my mission. It is important to note how much players relied on the testimonial benefit before the era of mega-buck wages. No Premiership player should need one now but back then when my annual salary was £8000, it crucified me financially to miss out on the possibility of banking ten times that amount, tax free.

I know it's difficult for some people to sympathise with professional footballers when they gripe about money, but

£80,000 would have come in very useful to me, particularly when I had business troubles at the depths of the recession in the eighties and, just to keep my mortgage payments secure, found myself making ten-hour, 400-mile round trips to places like Oswaldtwistle to make an after dinner speech. Fortunately, my finances have recovered significantly since then.

It occasionally rankles when I see some of my colleagues from the double side struggling financially and I know how much a collective testimonial would mean to them, but as a spectator at David O'Leary's second testimonial match, I was struck by how much it would have meant to me on an emotional level, too. To see David parading around the pitch, a big smile plastered across his face, acknowledging the warm tributes of a massive crowd while *Simply the Best* played over the tannoy, I could not help but envy him. That would have been such a great way to finish, but it was not to be.

I still have great affection for Arsenal and like all its former players feel enormously privileged to have played for such a great club. The fans have always been magnificent to me since I left; indeed one group arranged a testimonial dinner for me in 1975 for which I remain deeply touched. The board and management, though, can be rather distant in the way they deal with ex-players, possibly a result of Arsenal's background as the establishment club, but I don't think that it is deliberate, it is just their way. Nevertheless, I will be delighted if, when they move to Ashburton Grove and have much more room, they make as much fuss of some of the older boys on match days as most other teams do. It would be nice, sometimes, to be reassured that you haven't been forgotten.

Nowadays, most transfers are openly preceded by a courting process in the press. Back then, however, I had to go through the old rigmarole of waiting for Arsenal to 'circulate' my availability then sitting back and waiting to see who might want me. There was a gap of a few days before I heard anything during which time I was asked so often on the street about my reasons for leaving Arsenal that I tried to put out my version in London's *Evening Standard* or *Evening News*, but neither was willing to jeopardise their cosy relationship with the club and print the interview.

Of the five offers that Arsenal told me about, only West Bromwich Albion and QPR appealed. The financial package on the table from Don Howe at West Brom was staggering, and I would have been very happy to hook up with my old mentor had it not been for the chance, with QPR, of staying in London. Barbara was settled in the capital, two of my four sons were already at a good school nearby and I had just bought the tenancy of a pub between Camden Town and Finsbury Park, so it made sense to stay.

But those were not the only reasons. In terms of my career prospects, West Brom were on the brink of relegation from the First Division while QPR had already clinched promotion from the Second. I didn't fancy lower league football one bit. With the end of my professional career in sight I was far too impatient to play with players who didn't have the vision to read your game properly and make the right runs – I'd had my fill of that in exhibition games and testimonials. The older you get the more you need right, classy players around you or you end up with too many wasteful, speculative moves.

The fact I also enjoyed living in London was an added attraction to staying put, but that was never the be all and end all. Indeed, months later, I met Brian Clough in the Sportsman's Club on Tottenham Court Road and he badgered me about the mistake I had made in spurning his offer to join Derby. Apparently, Bertie Mee had told him I wasn't prepared to leave London and that he'd already agreed a fee with QPR so there was no point taking it any further. Never leave London? I would have bloody well walked to Derby to play for the new League Champions.

Incidentally, I asked Brian why he had wanted me when he already had a peerless central defensive partnership in Colin Todd and Roy McFarland. He replied that I would have played at the back with Roy for a couple of seasons while Colin was 'such a good player he could play anywhere. I'd use him all over the place.' I certainly landed on my feet with QPR at Loftus Road but I can't help wondering what an Indian summer it might have been at the Baseball Ground.

If I had been looking for a greater contrast to the atmosphere at Arsenal I could not have chosen better than QPR. Where Arsenal were austere and regimented, QPR were boisterous and carefree. The club reflected the attitude of its chairman, Jim Gregory, a successful car dealer. Jim was a complex, west London character; shrewd and sharp, fun-loving and sentimental, and, despite his natural charisma could be blunt, abrasive and occasionally explosive.

It didn't matter that the manager Gordon Jago wanted me; I had to pass an audition with the chairman – at a hotel in Hendon – before the deal went through. We didn't get off on the best foot when he responded to my opening gambit about money with: 'Nah. I'm not paying that,' and stormed out of the room, and I had to backtrack quickly to get him back. It was more a test than anything else as we soon came to a compromise not far short of my opening position.

Less than forty-eight hours after agreeing a deal, the chairman and I were celebrating QPR's promotion to the First Division after their last match of the season against Sunderland at Roker Park. At one o'clock in the morning, Jim and I were racing each other down one of Sunderland's terraced streets, he having bet he could beat me if I gave him a yard for every year in age difference. QPR's Terry Mancini said we caused such a commotion that he woke up and was amused to see from his hotel bedroom window the obviously pie-eyed chairman and his new signing sprinting, in our smart suits, down the street.

If Jim liked you, he was a marvellous chairman from a player's point of view, far more likely to insist that you accompany him to a night club than crack the whip. He loved the whole concept of 'flash' football and both worshipped and indulged no end Rodney Marsh and Stan Bowles. It wouldn't surprise me to find that they were paid twice as much as the rest of the team. Yet if you crossed him or even if he felt that he wasn't getting his say in selection (and he was very opinionated about players), he could be fearsomely intimidating and combative, as many managers found to their cost.

Now, it's amazing to think that apart from the occasional cameo – perhaps on Sunday television's *Big Match* – that game at Roker Park was the first time I'd seen QPR play since I had faced them with Arsenal four years previously. I think my lack of knowledge about the team increased my enjoyment of the next four years, because it was so unexpected. I had heard that Rangers had some decent players but right from that afternoon on Wearside I was genuinely thrilled and surprised at just how good they actually were.

Dave Thomas caught my eye immediately. That daredevil way he dribbled the ball, with his socks rolled down and no shin pads – as though he were actually inviting someone to try to break his leg — was admirable enough, but the accuracy of his crossing and the George Armstrong-like unselfishness of his tireless defensive work was very impressive indeed. It was obvious, too, that Gerry Francis and Stan Bowles were special talents. Instead of spending the summer licking my wounds over Arsenal, the evidence I gleaned from that one match at Roker Park replaced most of the heartbreak with a lovely, sparkling sense of anticipation. I couldn't wait for pre-season training.

After nine years of driving up to Arsenal's training ground at Colney, it was a strange experience to head west on the North Circular out to QPR's near Ruislip. Moreover, where standards at Arsenal's facilities leaned towards the Old Etonian, Rangers' were as rough and ready as our chairman. We used some pitches near the Polish war memorial, out near Ruislip, and often had to pick our way through the dog shit when out running.

Our kit would be dried every day after training sessions but washed only once a week so if the weather had been wet you'd have all this brittle mud caked on your gear and putting on your stiff socks would be like shoe-horning on a pair of Nancy Sinatra's kinky boots. It definitely took some time to get used to after the meticulous approach at Arsenal. Nonetheless I was desperate to show my new team mates that I wasn't a snob and that I was happy to pitch in.

I was just as keen to impress in the training itself and in the first week, despite my age, was right up at the front in the cross-country, trying to show that I wasn't a big shot who had come to slum it for one last pay day. I felt my Achilles tendon almost straightaway, that nagging soreness that you half know spells danger but, deluding yourself, you try to run it off. The next morning I tried again to ignore the pain and ground out a circuit, but I was making it worse by the step. By the end of the session I'd done enough damage to be out for six weeks. When you're trying to prove yourself and fit into a new group, you do some pretty foolish things.

The day the physiotherapist gave me the all clear to resume training, I had the boundless energy and deranged enthusiasm of a springer spaniel. I did all the physical work with a big grin on my face and no sooner had our five-a-side kicked off than I flew into a tackle with Terry Venables and thoroughly crumpled him. He must have thought at best that I was a lunatic, at worst that I was after his position as captain. After assuring him when he asked me what the hell was wrong with me that: 'I'm just so pleased to be back. I love it!' Terry shook his head and knew it was the former.

Not having the captaincy didn't bother me at all and I had great respect for Terry and his influence on the team. Sadly, as a player Venners is remembered more for the disappointing time he had at Spurs rather than for the glittering promise of his early days at Chelsea or the clever efficiency of his later years at Rangers. His reputation as a coach has also helped to over-shadow his football career but I have a strong memory from the year we played together at QPR of his bustle and guile and that funny way he ran with sticky-out feet like Robert Pires's. Off the field he was great company – just as proficient with the wind-up as he was with the many tactical suggestions he made in such a lively and thought-provoking way.

That first year with QPR – 1973-74 – I played alongside Terry Mancini at the back. 'Henry' makes fun of himself for his lack of ability as a player but he was actually more than useful. He was brave, uncompromising, good in the air and always cleared the ball in the direction he was facing. He was heavily criticised when he moved to Arsenal at the end of that season for his 'rudimentary skill' but, at QPR, his assets complemented mine – he was always an easy player to read and made few mistakes, which made him a decent partner. His transfer to Arsenal was still quite a strange move, given his age, and the fact that he struggled there illustrates the gulf in expectation between the two clubs. Don't get me wrong, QPR were a better team than Arsenal at that time and under Dave Sexton – who had joined QPR in 1974 - we would widen the gap further. It was the vice-like pressure at Highbury that unsettled Henry and led to scorn for his wholehearted attributes.

Almost at once I found myself thriving in a more relaxed atmosphere and I realised that you can play football without all that intensity. We were focused yet there was such buoyancy at training. Both our manager, Gordon Jago, and coach, Bobby Campbell, encouraged us to spend twenty minutes each day in groups of four, playing with the ball, keeping it off the floor and honing skills, so that even at the age of thirty-four my touch improved. At Arsenal we had won by training like lunatics and in my early years there I felt an all-consuming rage to win. You grow accustomed to the presumption that you must be challenging for trophies and all that goes with it – hatred from opposition crowds, an expectant and occasionally volatile 50,000-plus crowd at home games, a large travelling support to away matches, media attention and, not least, your personal ambition. That level of stress grows to feel so normal that, after a few months at Rangers, I noticed it only by its absence.

But there are many ways to skin a cat and at Rangers we did it the Liverpool way – with five-a-sides and technical work. It was so refreshing for me and I basked in my team mates' excitement; they treated the First Division like an adventure, and without fear. The players and fans were wholly unjaded and went with a mixture of eagerness, innocence and enjoyment to grounds such as Anfield and Highbury. It sounds funny but I would liken my experience at QPR to what I imagine it would be like going to college: I was a mature student but every day, learning and joking at training, I was just as invigorated as the youngsters.

The manager who signed me, Gordon Jago, resigned after a year when his relationship with Jim Gregory became intolerable. Considering he'd hardly had any money to spend on the team – apart from the £200,000 transfer fee for Rodney Marsh two years earlier – he had done a remarkable job. He was an excellent coach and a well-spoken, polite and kind man who went on to enjoy a fantastic career in the United States but if your face didn't fit with the chairman he would get rid of you. So, regardless of his marvellous league record – QPR's best ever – and the fine team he had assembled, Jago went. Only weeks before Jago left, Venables and Mancini had been sold and there was an argument about incoming transfers. Under the benevolent dictatorship at Loftus Road there could only be one winner, Jim Gregory, but Gordon Jago deserves all the credit for laying the sound foundations that Dave Sexton so stylishly built on.

The lads at QPR adored Dave. They were good professionals – young, eager, hungry for knowledge – and Dave, more mature and a more rounded person than he had been at Arsenal, was dedicated to the point of vocation to imparting his knowledge. The squad soon became the perfect audience for Dave's extraordinary coaching ability. After his experiences at Chelsea, I think Dave had become sick of compromising. If he was going to manage Rangers, then he was going to do it his way. He spent a few weeks taking stock of what he had, then we worked on a plan in training. Gradually, we developed a new method of playing which combined the Dutch principles of slick, attacking football with the pressing and off-side game we had refined during my Arsenal days.

That Dave first took careful stock was vital, for he needed to ensure that he had enough players of sufficient quality in his squad to execute such a bold and intricate style of play. Thanks to Jago, QPR was awash with technically accomplished players and that encouraged Dave to aspire to his dream.

I had played in front of Banksie for five years at Leicester, Bob Wilson for my last four years at Arsenal and I had the good fortune to make it a trio of outstanding goalkeepers in front of Phil Parkes at Rangers. Tall as a steeple, great at snatching crosses and extremely agile – despite being built like Man Mountain McGurk – he had an intimidating presence in the box, like Peter Schmeichel's.

In front of Parkes, the full back pairing – Dave Clement and Ian Gillard – was as good as anything in the league. Because my friend, Dave Clement, committed suicide at the age of thirty-four, it seems flippant and irrelevant in the face of such a tragedy to mention his gifts as a footballer, but I don't think that his life should be defined by its terrible end. He was a dedicated player, something of a perfectionist and was brilliant at making those endless, powerful, shuttle runs demanded of the attacking full back. Like his colleague on the other flank, Ian Gillard, Clement was smart and canny, and a great disciple of Sexton's who contributed so much to our slick, passing game.

In the wake of Terry Mancini's move to Arsenal, David Webb

slotted in alongside me and it was then that I was given my head to boss the back four a bit more and get it properly organised. Webb is a very affable, articulate and astute man. Off the pitch he, like the chairman, was a classic Del Boy figure, happiest when he was wheeling and dealing.

Although he was very solid and there was a punishing sting to his tackle, when Webby first arrived at the club, he was something of a death or glory merchant; over fond of the slide and scissors tackle. I certainly helped to cure him of that – it's a dangerous ploy because there's no consistency to it and it's only effective if you get it spot on, otherwise you take yourself out of the game. Within a few weeks Webby had taken my advice and become better and better at staying on his feet, so that we started to work the back four as a unit – advancing and retreating together as we had in our heyday at Arsenal.

Once the defence was fixed, Sexton's coaching took the team up to the next level. I suppose it was Stan Bowles, Don Masson and Gerry Francis that really made the team tick but everyone contributed a great deal, as they had to, if our version of total football was to live up to its billing. As for the skill of Bowles, Masson and Francis: there's a training routine where six players stand in a circle and pass the ball while two players in the middle try to intercept it; you're only allowed one touch and if your pass is picked off you have to go in the middle. In the four years I was at Rangers I don't think Bowles, Masson or Francis ever went into the middle because of a misplaced pass. They were that good.

I'd never even heard of Don Masson before he signed for us. Already in his late twenties, he'd played the majority of his career with Notts County in the Third Division but he was a great little player. Like Johnny Giles, Masson was tough and arrogant and he was two-footed, loved responsibility, was a good passer and had a nice, clean shot. Masson's midfield partner, Gerry Francis, always had a quiet confidence about him and in the dressing room, he held his own as captain, despite his youth – although if you saw him on television, his reluctance to look into the camera might make you think he was quite shy.

His father, Roy – QPR's kit man – had been a professional, too, and Gerry had been groomed to be a footballer. He had a broad knowledge of the game, and before his career became ravaged by injury, he was one of the most complete midfielders I have ever seen – as dynamic a runner as Frank Lampard, a good tackler, a fine shot and with great imagination around the box. As he strutted around the penalty area, striking little passes with the outside of his foot or setting up Bowlesey for one of their trademark one-twos, I'd watch him from forty yards away and I'd be like a fan, wondering what he was going to do next and savouring every moment of it.

Stan Bowles, of course, is the one player everyone remembers from that team, the one the crowd took to their hearts. I sometimes think all those after-dinner anecdotes that portray him as a rascal or Casanova have done him a disservice as a player but those are the stories people love to hear. Stan was a good team man and wasn't in the game for personal glory; he was never self-indulgent on the pitch, though his laidback, super-confident demeanour might fool people into thinking that.

He was mercurial and full of bare-faced cheek, but he always laid the ball off at the right time, took up clever positions and, in front of goal, he was as cool as you like. The stories about Stan being in the betting shop until twenty minutes before the match on a Saturday afternoon are true but they sell him short – he didn't shirk in training and he never let a team mate down. I roomed with him for years and he always took the bed furthest from the door so that if anyone he owed money to came looking for him they'd have to go through me first; still, the company he kept didn't affect him as a player. Bowlesey and his big pal, Don Shanks, were the life and soul of the club and both have hardly changed in thirty years. Both of them were gambling fanatics and would have us in hysterics at stories of their losses and various antics: they'd think nothing of hitching a ride in the back of a van to some obscure dog track and travelling home with an incontinent greyhound for company – it wasn't clubbing at Tramp every night of the week for those two.

That kind of vagabond charm was integral to the way we played at Rangers and, in some ways, it defined us as a club. Emboldened not to be straitjacketed by the numbers on our backs or by the orthodoxy we had learned before, we were encouraged to take more daring positions when we were in possession.

Stan would be constantly dropping off deep to take the ball, making it very hard for a centre half to mark him – a move we took advantage of at every opportunity. Another move we worked out to perfection started with the ball in Phil Parkes's hands. As soon as Parkes picked up the ball our two full backs would race up to the halfway line and turn inside, and the two wide midfielders would take up a position beyond the full backs and also turn to face our goal. Stan would come short, Gerry and Don Masson would place themselves wide of him, then Phil would throw the ball to me. I filled the Beckenbauer role as it was down to me to set up the play – I could flip the ball to one of the four wide-placed players if any of the opposition's markers advanced on me, or I might chip it at an angle to Gerry or Don, drop it into Stan or drive a pass further up to Don Givens.

We had so many players with good control and superb passing ability that I could always offload the ball to any one of them, confident they'd be able to cope with the pressure of a potential challenge. It was an absolute delight to play that way. At Arsenal our game had, at times, been predictable, but though opposition teams could read us, they couldn't stop us. At our best, we were indomitable; powerfully athletic, a team for all conditions. In contrast, at QPR we annihilated teams with sheer skill – at times, and especially on decent pitches, we were by miles the best football team in the country. During the three years Dave Sexton was in charge at QPR we played some wonderful stuff and his second season, 1975-76, was QPR's best ever – before or since – as our methods and performances deserved.

John Hollins was drafted into the side and he slotted really well into midfield. Olly was the consummate professional. Infectiously enthusiastic, he approached every training session as if it was his first, and chief among his many qualities were his ability to cover incredible amounts of space during a game and his accurate, long passing. He was as chirpy as 'get out', as we'd say in Glasgow, and everyone loved it when he used to take me off – he'd put on a thick, impenetrable, Gorbals accent and could mimic, brilliantly, all my expressions, like the flared nostrils when I got angry. Hollins, and poor old Mick Leach who died so young, were the unsung heroes of that side; Leachy, in particular, did such crucial work as a box-to-box 'boiler room' midfielder and had a happy knack of scoring important goals.

The 1975-76 season, our annus mirabilis, began in the best possible way with a 2-0 win over Liverpool at Loftus Road. Our first goal, scored by Gerry Francis, was like a statement of intent, a slick, multi-player passing move that was efficiently capped by a withering Francis finish. It certainly set the tone for our home form as we comfortably remained unbeaten at 'the Loft' all season and we entered the Christmas period neck and neck with a Liverpool team looking to win their first championship since 1972-73.

Our momentum built throughout the early weeks of 1976 but, after losing to Manchester United at Old Trafford and an uncharacteristically sloppy display gave West Ham a 1-0 win at Upton Park in January, we had a team meeting designed to get our quest for a UEFA Cup place back on track. Although we were still in the top three, we were realistic enough to recognise that winning the league was unlikely, so there was no specific talk of such an implausible ambition at that point. We had drawn five and lost two games in that mid-winter lull, giving rise to speculation that our style of play was not equipped for the rigours of a full season and the harsh pitch conditions of the English winter at its worst.

But our determination to prove our detractors wrong, allied to a greater emphasis on our defensive strengths, soon reinvigorated our league position. Indeed, from the end of January to the first week in April we didn't lose another game, winning ten and drawing one of our eleven fixtures. Though Manchester United occasionally threatened to make it a three-way race for the title, by March QPR and Liverpool were clear by a defendable margin. I, for one, thought that Liverpool's greater experience and bigger squad would be the decisive factor but when they managed to take only one point from three games in early

March – a dismal run which enabled us to overtake them at the top of the table – I started to believe that the most improbable of championships since Ipswich's in 1962 was within our grasp.

We kept our nerve with six consecutive wins in March and April to cling on to our one-point lead with three games to go. Our run-in – Norwich, Arsenal and Leeds United – did not look too daunting on paper but we had to concede that Liverpool's – Stoke, Manchester City and Wolves – was probably easier. Three wins and the title would be ours and our first match at Carrow Road should not have caused us too many problems. Our final surge had been building for four months and we approached the game with the utmost confidence in our ability to prevail but quickly came unstuck in the face of a ferocious Norwich onslaught. Those who claimed we were a fair-weather team should have seen us that day as we battled as gamely as any scrappers could in a disjointed and error-strewn game. Having been on the back foot for so long, at 2-2 we were still confident that we could go on to win but as we threw midfielders forward in old-fashioned, gung-ho desperation, an uncharacteristically mistimed header from Dave Clement let Norwich in to nab both points at the death. The transistor radios in the dressing room confirmed our worst fears: Liverpool had beaten Stoke 5-3 and, for the first time in eight weeks, our destiny was not in our hands.

We regrouped quickly to play Arsenal on the Monday night following our Saturday set-back. Dave Sexton was quick to point out that while Liverpool's one-point lead in the race obviously made them favourites, we had to play as though our dream was still alive. And we did, easily beating a moribund Arsenal in one of Bertie Mee's last games in charge of my old club, a game in which I scored the opener with a firm header. But Liverpool also played that night and their 3-0 victory at Maine Road meant that everything came down to the final Saturday.

Or at least it should have done. We played Leeds United at Loftus Road and put on the sort of performance that had characterised our season, toying with a team that had set the benchmark for cruel, penetrative passing. Goals from Dave Thomas and Stan Bowles gave us a 2-0 win, which put us back at the top of the league and sent us into an excruciating and surreal limbo for ten agonising days. Because Liverpool had qualified for the UEFA Cup final against Bruges, the Football League had given them permission to postpone their final league game until after the first leg of the final at Anfield, a match they won 3-2 on Wednesday 28 April, four days after the First Division's scheduled close. The following Tuesday they took on Wolves, needing two points to become champions.

It's a strange feeling knowing that there's nothing you can do to affect the result of such a crucial football match and that ten-day hiatus was awful to endure. It was a bit like being in church waiting for a bride you feel will probably not turn up but you live in hope that she'll prove you and the doubting congregation wrong. Everywhere I went people wanted to talk about it, conversations I tried to avoid at every opportunity.

On the Tuesday night, BBC's *Sportsnight* sent a camera team to my pub, the Sutton Arms, and though the place was packed with Arsenal supporters, there were huge celebrations when we heard on the radio that Wolves had taken a 1-0 lead. Such were the obtuse restrictions placed on live broadcasts by the Football League that only the second-half commentary was relayed live. With fifteen minutes to go and Wolves still leading, the camera crew had started to set up their lights and I had allowed myself a couple of light ales as I prepared to get the party in full swing and capture my thoughts for the television interview. As we listened intently to the blaring radio broadcast, the whole pub fell silent when Kevin Keegan equalised with thirteen minutes remaining and then John Toshack put them 2-1 ahead.

By the time my old Arsenal pal Ray Kennedy had applied the *coup de grâce* in the final seconds of the game, the BBC's lighting rig been dismantled and I was heading for my car. It was the biggest anti-climax of my career and I was keen to get out before the drink-addled commiserations started. As I pointed the car north towards Winchmore Hill I was not quite as inconsolable as I would have been had I not anticipated that Liverpool would probably pip us over that ten-day period of tormented speculation. But it was extremely disappointing nonetheless and the fact that we never had the opportunity or the desire to celebrate QPR's best ever season was a sad reflection that it had finished in such an 'after the Lord Mayor's show' fashion.

Liverpool's result was the ultimate party pooper. After our defeat at Carrow Road we'd tried to accept that we'd already blown the championship and we'd tried, in advance of that last game of the season, to reconcile ourselves to coming second to Liverpool; still, it hit me hard. On a more positive note, when people get all nostalgic about the skilful soccer of the seventies, most recognise that our QPR team were England's best exponents of silky, flowing, continental-style football, and when Sky television screens football retrospectives, you can guarantee that pictures of us, wearing those iconic blue and white hooped shirts, will feature prominently. Once you've had thirty years to get over the initial misery, that level of recognition does provide some consolation.

Though during the course of that 1975-76 season I had started to feel exhausted after matches, I played on through the following one and we reached the quarter-finals of the UEFA Cup, only losing on penalties to AEK Athens. But I knew that the end was coming. I tried to ignore the unmistakable signs of age – the heavy legs, cramp and the struggle to get out of third gear – and I really pushed myself through training, but it took a skin-shrivellingly long soak in the bath before I was ready to go home after matches. I was coming up to thirty-eight years of age and had begun to feel something akin to a generation gap between me and my team mates. These guys were, after all, fifteen and sixteen years my junior and I was noticing I no longer dressed the same or listened to the same music or wanted to play the same daft games as they did. Not that they treated me like a grandfather, and the banter did not cease but it was apparent that something was different.

A wee bit of distance had opened up and I had begun to feel more comfortable hanging about with people closer to my own age. Two years previously I would have pushed all thoughts of retirement out of my head but the nagging truth that my days as a professional were numbered was creeping up on me. Perhaps, if I'd taken it easy, done only two hard training sessions each week and spent the rest of the time stretching and resting, I might have been able to extend my career – but even in the late seventies no one, least of all me, knew much about the physiological benefits of that. Appearing to wind down slowly, as it were, would have gone against the grain of everything I'd been as a player, too, so I had to accept that enough was enough and announced my retirement in May 1977.

I could not have wished for more than I got out of those fantastic years with QPR in west London. And though, as I've said, I did not hold a grudge against Bertie Mee for long, it was nice to put two fingers up at him by playing for four more years at the highest level. It wasn't until much later, when Bobby Robson told me he'd noticed that every club I joined went for a championship and competed for cups while those I left took a downswing, that I realised I might have been quite an influential player.

In 1974, QPR were eighth in the league, Arsenal tenth; in 1975 we were eleventh, Arsenal were sixteenth and in 1976 we finished second and Arsenal were seventeenth. I never thought to reflect on that until it was pointed out to me but it is nice to know that I made an impact as a player even in those so-called twilight years. In 1979 on the eve of the new decade, Bob Paisley gave an interview to the *Sun* in which he picked me as his player of the seventies, even though I'd been retired for two seasons. I shrugged it off at the time but it is gratifying to know that someone I respected so highly would pay me such a compliment.

It's not something I dwell on or have allowed to swell my head, but it is great to be able to tell the grandkids that their grandfather was once, many years ago, quite a tidy player – and for that I have to thank QPR for the camaraderie and technical excellence that rejuvenated my career.

15

OUTFOXED IN MANAGEMENT AND BUSINESS

A common lament among ex-footballers is that their careers don't mirror those of golfers – who manage to play on well into middle age with a lucrative seniors' tour to sustain them through their twilight years. Our sport, unfortunately, is far more brutal. If you have a bad game at the age of twenty-eight, you're 'garbage', play badly at thirty-five and you're 'finished'. Like most of my contemporaries I lived in denial until at least a couple of years before I finally retired. I couldn't bear to talk about it and thrust it to the back of my mind, trying to kid myself that things would take care of themselves once that sorry day arrived.

However, I could not ignore the indisputable evidence provided by the persistent aching of my legs after games, not to mention the necessity for some sort of plan to provide for four young sons who shared their mother's great common-sense but their father's great appetite. I couldn't get away with the ostrich method indefinitely. Yet what was I going to do? I certainly didn't fancy getting my overalls and brushes out from the garage once again. No, the two, well-trodden paths followed by my peers – stay in football or go into the pub trade – were still the most likely roads for me. Which one should I follow? With four kids, one job wouldn't have been enough to maintain our standard of living. So I did both . . . simultaneously.

Professional footballers are always popular recruitment fodder for those seeking capital investment. There's always someone promising to combine your money with their expertise to produce incredible results and it can be difficult not to get sucked in. Promises of riches can be tempting but, as I later found to my cost, you have to be very careful. My first proper business deal was done in partnership with Ian Ure and Maisie Mather, my Arsenal landlady in 1966. Together, we bought three Victorian houses in Muswell Hill and rented them out but we soon disposed of them. Forty years on, each of those properties is worth over £1,500,000 but no one, then, could have predicted the subsequent boom in the London property market.

Then, during the late sixties I invested in three wine bars – in Fulham, Chelsea and Fleet Street – but realised quickly that all three investors, me included, were looking for an income from the businesses but did not want to work in them so I got rid of those, too. The Fleet Street bodega was quite fun; I'd pop down there fairly often and a good crowd of reporters used to come along – Norman Giller, Peter Batt, Jeff Powell, Reg Drury, Hugh McIlvanney, Bernard Joy, Ken Jones et al.

Incidentally I think this helped to restore Arsenal's relationship with the press at this time because the club's policy in the late sixties that we should not mingle with them had caused a great deal of frostiness. This gradually started to melt once press and players began to socialise together.

My next venture was by far my most successful. During my last two years at QPR I took over the tenancy of a couple of north London pubs. One I sold almost immediately but the other, the Sutton Arms in Copenhagen Street in upper Holloway, the heart of Arsenal country, I kept for nearly ten years. The main problem was that to make it a success I had to be there a lot of the time which, as I was still training and playing full time, was not exactly easy. But while the bar was becoming established, I had enough energy – even though it was unbelievably knackering – to work behind the bar most evenings and still help propel the team to that heartbreaking second in the league with Rangers. For the first six months I'd been being ripped off by the barmaids and had to sack them all. But things really took off after I installed my business partner Harry Hicks' sister-in-law, Jean, as manager. We replaced the dolly birds behind the bar with a slightly older staff, taught them how to greet and treat the customers and paid them almost double the wages our competitors were offering – which put a stop to all the pilfering.

For a time, the Sutton Arms was one of the busiest pubs in north London. I had its interior re-designed to the tune of £24,000 – a fortune in those days – and installed the best sound system I could afford. The pub became well known for its music – we had a resident band with two singers, and on a Saturday night lots of the regulars would get up to sing – and that was in the days before karaoke. I'd be up there, too, of an evening with George Graham, and I'd croon through the Frank Sinatra song book.

Some Sunday mornings I'd find myself up on stage with the Nolan Sisters, one of our most popular bookings, harmonising away with the girls. Later on, the bar became a haunt for celebrities looking for the authentic London pub experience. My pal Joe Dunne, who lived around the corner, was a stuntman in the movies and he used to bring all sorts of people in – actors Tom Selleck, Kevin Costner and Bob Hoskins all supped there. I served Islington faces such as singer Johnny Rotten, actors Pauline Quirke and Linda Robson quite frequently, and television comedy star the late Richard Beckinsale came in a few times.

North London was more parochial then, a forgotten world of market traders and dodgy characters. Sometimes my pub was half *My Fair Lady* half *Guys and Dolls*. Ronnie Knight was around a lot and colourful characters – some discreet, some proud hoisters – rejoicing in names such as 'Morrie the Head', 'Ted the Printer' and 'Dancing Charlie'. At its best, the place was very lively and I have some great memories of the sing-songs and the post-closing time fireside chats with the band and staff. But running that pub was very tiring, especially as 'afters' were customary in the area and my customers expected me to keep the bar open for as long as they wanted.

As I contemplated retirement at the end of the 1976-77 season, the pub was to be my immediate priority while I considered my job options in football. There were quite a few whispers surrounding my future; Billy Bingham, who was angling for the Arsenal job, asked if I'd be his assistant should Denis Hill-Wood come calling and Lawrie McMenemy also contacted me about working alongside him at Southampton. Most intriguingly of all – but I only heard about this when it was too late – Dave Sexton, who had just been appointed to succeed Tommy Docherty at Old Trafford, had wanted me as his number two. I often wonder what would have happened if Jim Gregory had told me the way Dave was thinking because I could not have wished for a better mentor in management. But Jim, who had hoped to persuade me to prolong my playing career, only told me when I'd already fixed myself up and the opportunity had passed.

Instead, I got a call from my old chairman at Leicester, Sid Needham, with the tempting, if premature, offer to go straight into management in the First Division. Not for the first time I let my heart rule and took the job in June 1977, setting myself up for nine months of such torment that my stomach still flips over whenever I think of it.

I must admit that I was quite tempted to gloss over this episode. I have no wish to jab a stick into that wound but when I see words like 'unforgivable' and 'inexcusable' bandied around about my time there in the official history of City, it adds insult to injury. I am determined, therefore, to set the record straight. It might not excuse my failure to die-hard Foxes but it could help to explain it.

The thing I find 'unforgivable' was my naïvety. Though I'd walked into the manager's job with my eyes wide open my self-confidence had blinded me to the scale of the task I'd taken on. The pub was bringing in a fair amount so I'd accepted a year's contract at a modest £14,000 and did not even quibble at the transfer kitty of £100,000 – despite having been told that the club required four or five new players and knowing that transfer fees had already begun to spiral. I appointed my former colleague Ian MacFarlane as my assistant and started work with my usual optimistic fervour. It didn't take too long for it to fall apart.

Although I hadn't had any formal experience as a coach, I believed that my best qualities as a successful former captain would equip me for management. I had always been good at organising players on the pitch – knowing when to switch tactics, being quick to sense danger and able to exploit weaknesses in the opposition's game. Neither was the 'vision thing' a problem nor, I felt, my man-management skills.

Furthermore, I wasn't a one-dimensional skipper – I had encouraged and cajoled those who needed a softer approach and steamed in to those who responded best to a kick up the backside. And I knew, both in theory and in practice, how to put on training sessions and believed that the lessons I had learned from Matt Gillies, Bert Johnson, Dave Sexton and Don Howe were the football equivalent of an Oxbridge degree. Finally, I knew I had a good man alongside me in Big Ian, a talented, canny and loyal deputy who would cover any areas where I might struggle. What I didn't have, of course, was the experience and like poor old Billy Wright at Arsenal, the best intentions and qualities soon go out of the window without a bedrock of know-how to fall back on.

City had finished eleventh under Jimmy Bloomfield the previous season, a reasonable achievement even if the eight points that cushioned them from a relegation place were not all that impressive. The trouble was apparent from the first day of training when I got to meet the two most influential players at the club, Keith Weller and Frank Worthington. Weller, who had given the team width and penetration down the right-hand side, had a chronic knee injury; we managed to strap him up and mollycoddle him through a few games but he wasn't able to make the enormous contribution the team had relied on in previous years. Worthington, the club's poster boy, posed less conventional problems.

As soon as I took over at City, he came along and told me his desperate financial plight. So indebted was he that the club had confiscated his chequebook. His only way out, said Worthington, was to get a transfer, pocket his percentage of the fee and bank a signing on fee and higher wages to clear his debts. I was flabbergasted but the board were more sanguine. They loved to watch Worthington play but had grown sick of the embarrassment caused by his inability to control his and his then wife's extravagance. They were happy to let him go and would have taken the £20,000 offered by Leeds United if I hadn't encouraged them to hold out for more.

The decision to accede to his request – my 'act of betrayal' in the eyes of Leicester fans – was not mine. I would have loved him to stay, even though he didn't have the practicality of my ideal type of centre forward. In the end, he played a few games at the beginning of the season, in which he sporadically displayed his crowd-pleasing tricks, but as soon as Bolton Wanderers offered enough money, he went there and I went into the doghouse.

I wish it was as simple to explain what went wrong at City by hanging the blame on that transfer but long before that there were signs that it would end badly. I'd had a good summer, eating and drinking far more than I had done in my previous eighteen annual holidays when I was a player. And I'd certainly foregone all the pre- pre-season work I had normally done in advance of the official fitness programme. But in the first day's cross-country I was in the leading pack all the way round and some players who had a fifteen- to twenty-year advantage trailed in up to ten minutes behind me.

I brought in a specialist fitness coach to work with the team that first week and at the end of it he came over and said to me that I was the best player there, and that I should consider playing. I was flattered but – if that, indeed, was the case – I should have been petrified. I wish I had listened to his advice.

Then we played a friendly in Sweden against Tottenham, a team that had been relegated the previous season. Glenn Hoddle apart, they were a pretty average side but they demolished us 2-1 – not a representative scoreline – and toyed with our players in the manner of Leeds' famous show against Southampton in 1971. At times we couldn't get the ball off them. I turned to Ian MacFarlane in the dugout and said: 'Jesus, what is this?' He just looked shocked and said: 'You've got a huge job on here.' How right he was.

There were some good players at City – especially Mark Wallington, Steve Whitworth and Steve Kember – but I just couldn't get the team to gel as a unit. My great friend Jon Sammels from my Arsenal days was also there, and there is no bigger fan of his in the game than me, but by that point his influence had started to wane and he couldn't recapture his thrust. Who could when chaos reigned all around?

I started off by trying to get the team to play like Arsenal but we didn't have the right players to make it work. I eventually went out and, from Liverpool, bought Alan Waddle, a six-feet-four-inch centre forward, and tried to get him to match the work rate of John Radford and prowl the channels; he could do it in training but he was incapable of doing it in matches. But it wasn't his fault – I should have been pragmatic and seen the bigger picture. I should have discarded my preferences and got him to stand up there like a lamp-post and use his existing attributes rather than try to mould new ones in a couple of weeks.

In training, I split the squad into eight-a-side and I would get them to play for thirty minutes, always keeping the ball below waist height. They would play some lovely stuff and I would emphasise that in my team talk before a game, highlighting how good they were at short passing and how promising their movement was. But five minutes after kick-off those comforting words had turned to ash in my mouth as they'd panic and hoof it Buckaroo-like out to the wing.

We could not stop ladling the ball back to the opposition whenever we had it, almost as if we were saying: 'Here you are. Have another go.' The daft thing is that I was too idealistic, but not in the sense of being a purist, rather I wanted to do it my way, the Arsenal way. I might have stood a chance if only I'd had someone like Matt Gillies alongside me to say: 'Hold on. Calm down. This is what you've got to work with. Cut your cloth accordingly.' Without that insight things got even worse and by the turn of the year we were bottom of the league with only eleven points from twenty-three games.

I tried to shore up the team by using up the entire transfer budget and bought Eddie Kelly, David Webb, Geordie Armstrong, Geoff Salmons and Lammie Robertson as well as Alan Waddle. They all cost peanuts and I remember a board member telling me: 'You can't go wrong at those prices.' Unfortunately, you can. The new transfers all tried hard – and the first four had great pedigrees – but the reason they were so cheap to buy was that they were coming to the end of their careers. Lammie was a speculative punt from Third Division Exeter. I had hoped he might turn out to be another Don Masson, and there's no doubt that he had the skill, but he couldn't adapt to the lack of time and space at that level and made little impact.

When you make enough transfers, even for paltry fees, they add up and it didn't take long for that same director to tell me that I'd wasted 'his' money, despite his earlier statement. And it's mistakes like these that are the nails in your coffin. We found it very difficult to score and in the end the board released further funds to buy a striker to replace Worthington. I could not get the two I fancied; Bobby Robson would not sell Trevor Whymark and Liverpool's David Johnson wouldn't take the wages offered, despite his club's willingness to sell.

Both my chief scout, Ray Shaw, and Ian MacFarlane made glowing reports on the ex-Derby County centre forward, Roger Davies, who was by then playing for Bruges, but my scouting mission proved fruitless as he didn't feature in the game I went to watch. I had played against him many times and thought that he could be devastating but that he was also inconsistent. I wish I'd done the sort of research that Bill Shankly did and watched the player at least six times and assessed how he coped in different situations – what he was like away from home, how he fought when his team were 2-0 down, and so on, but I was at the end of my tether and took the plunge at £250,000. By half time in his first game I had the terribly sobering realisation that I'd made a massive booboo because while Davies could be very good on his day, he was more likely to be awful. It was poor judgement on my part.

Our dreadful form really gnawed away at me but however tirelessly I worked to plot a revival nothing came off. I felt ashamed and could not face going out and about in Leicester. Since Barbara had stayed in London with the children, I used to go back to my room at the Holiday Inn five nights a week and sit there, staring into space, almost on auto-pilot, anticipating the conversations I would have the next day. I had wanted the crowd to think of me as City's manager with just the same fondness they had had for me as a player but, given the team's predicament, that was impossible.

If the earth had opened up and swallowed me I assure you that I would have been relieved. At that stage I just did not know enough about how to put things right from the touchline and I wish I'd carried on playing for that year. I should have left the majority of coaching to Ian and, if that's all I could manage, played only seventy-five minutes because I'd have made a difference had I been in the players' ears all the time, telling them when to push up and when to hold their line. At the time, however, I just didn't think it was feasible.

The end came when relegation was all but confirmed in early April 1978. I was called in to see one of the directors, Dennis Sharp, and he informed me that I had to move up to the city permanently instead of going back home to London on Saturday nights. I'd already had a run in with him when he boasted about the qualities of Leicester's reserve team and I countered that not one of them would make it, highlighting, instead, five in the youth team who would – Trevor Christie, Larry May and Tommy Williams among them – and I was right, but I should have been more diplomatic. Anyway, I said that moving up to Leicester would not be a problem but if they expected me to sell my pub and my house and take my four children out of school then they would need to give me a longer contract than the one that expired in three months' time.

Sharp's refusal to offer any extension to my contract while continuing to insist that I uproot to Leicester felt like he was taking the piss. 'You want me to sacrifice all my interests in London?' I said. 'Sell up and move here but you won't give me any security and then you'll sack me in a few weeks? You must be crazy. You can stuff your job.' I handed him the keys to the club car, and despite his protestations that I was now in breach of my original contract, I told him to look at my back as I left, for confirmation that I was off. It was a hell of a relief, actually. I would never have quit but I could not bear his shamelessness and I would have been in terrible straits if I'd accepted his proposal.

Yet it remains the biggest regret of my career that I did not make a success of my time as manager at Leicester. I became very introverted and tore myself to shreds with worry, and that anxiety swiftly translated itself to the players. I felt sorry for them because they seemed frightened to play, inhibited by a lack of confidence but I just could not raise their game. It still galls me when I hear Frank Worthington on the after-dinner speech circuit talk about the 'great' side he played in at Leicester; it just goes to show how far apart their standards and mine really were.

They were a decent team but never a great one. And without Worthington and Weller to mask their weaknesses, the virtuosity that got them up the league disappeared, leaving no structure to fall back on. It was my job to provide that and it is my greatest sadness that I failed, but it wasn't for lack of effort and mental torture. Perhaps they were a team that needed relegation. Certainly, they needed the sort of systematic restructuring they eventually got under the vastly experienced Jock Wallace. I did my best but my inexperience hobbled me from day one.

I was glad to be out of it, happy to go back to my pub and to spend a few weeks in the revitalising company of friends and family. When Jim Gregory rang that summer to offer me the QPR job, I was still too raw to take it. After ten days of courting I had to turn down his offer, admitting to myself that I was too shell shocked to contemplate it. My appetite slowly returned, thanks to my first forays into broadcasting with the BBC where I worked in the Jimmy Armfield role alongside *Sport on Two* greats, Peter Jones, Bryon Butler and Peter Lorenzo. I loved it, especially the World Cup in Spain, but I was still intent on redeeming myself in management somewhere down the line. Apart from running the pub and the intermittent media work, I got involved in various business schemes, each, on paper, promising riches. The nearest I came to establishing myself as an entrepreneur was in the advertising business. In 1979 I invested in several billboards in major cities in the south of England and rented them out to advertisers. I stuck with it for a few years but the business never took off and I was happy to pack it in when a job offer in football finally materialised.

It was Terry Venables who persuaded me to go back in December 1982 and I had a great fifteen months as youth team coach at QPR. Terry was a magnificent tutor, a very expansive man and not precious about imparting his knowledge. I learned a lot and our youth team won just about everything we entered. Unfortunately, this was the time that QPR had a plastic pitch at Loftus Road, which meant my young charges had perfected devastating close control and ball skills but were less proficient on mud-heaps away from home. Even so, I liked working with the kids but missed the responsibility and, God help me, the pressure of first-team work, so, when Martin Lange, Brentford's chairman, rang to say that Bertie Mee had suggested me for the manager's job at Griffin Park I was ready to go.

When I took over in February 1984, the Bees were second

bottom of the Third Division but we managed to stabilise in the last few weeks of the season and avoid relegation. It's a cracking club but I did not expect the celebrations when we were safe from the drop to be so ebullient. I felt that it was something we should be embarrassed about, not partying like mad about. I had to get used to the different levels of expectation and I sincerely believe that I did a good job at the club. It quickly became apparent that the tools required to thrive in that league were: a strapping centre half; a pacy winger; a tall, quick centre forward and two tenacious central midfielders. It meant compromising my principles somewhat but I think I got it just about right, apart from the centre forward. And I am sure that we would have been promoted if I'd found the right man for that job.

The constant gripe of managers, and I am no exception, is that they are hamstrung by cash restrictions. I did some great deals at Brentford, getting Terry Evans from Hillingdon Borough and both Andy Sinton and Robbie Cooke from Cambridge United. Robbie's signing was almost scuppered by a stand-off over a twenty-pound-a-week discrepancy between how much he wanted to be paid and how much our chairman was willing to pay. The situation was only settled when I took a wage reduction of the exact amount to finance Robbie's salary. That's how football was in the lower divisions and Martin Lange was hypersensitive about the dangers of spending too much money. Who can blame him given the problems faced by spendthrift clubs?

Our young team was relatively successful, finishing in the top half of the league in my two full seasons there and reaching the Wembley final of the Freight Rover Trophy, where we lost to Wigan. Terry Hurlock and Chris Kamara played manfully in midfield and if Francis Joseph hadn't had such a bad injury we might have scored enough goals to push on further up the league.

Terry Evans adapted brilliantly to the professional game and the manager of almost every team we played against used to ask: 'Where the hell did you find him?' but I wish I had used Chris Kamara – later a colleague at Sky television – in a different role. I should have stuck him as a shield in front of the back four every week, because he was a strong tackler and a good header of the ball and he could have stopped most of the teams from using their fifty-yard missiles all the time. All in all, though, I am proud of my time with the Bees and think I made a useful contribution to that great little club's development in the eighties.

As my three-year deal was coming to a close in January 1987, Martin Lange thought that the club had not done well enough to justify my £25,000 annual salary and told me he would be looking to make a change at the end of that season. I had brought in Steve Perryman as player-coach, and to be my voice on the pitch and, in a way, I'd slit my own throat because Martin thought he could economise by giving the top job to Steve. So, I decided to walk, regretting only that I hadn't been decisive enough in that elusive search for a centre forward. I don't have any bitterness and Martin and I have remained good friends.

It must have been around this time that my Islington pub started to go slightly downhill. Fashions change and many London venues have only a limited shelf life. I'd had plenty of great years but the takings had begun to slide and I was looking for other business opportunities to make up the shortfall. I was impressed by a proposition from Frank Warren who was very keen to cash in on the City's boom years by opening a restaurant and night club in the Barbican. While I knew nothing about silver service or maitre d's I decided that Frank knew enough, and reckoned that between us we had enough charisma to make it a success so we went into partnership.

It was an absolute fiasco. We invested a great deal of money in getting the look of the place right, and it was a beautiful venue, but it was too small to coin it in, even if it had been packed out every night of the week. I hadn't realised that the Barbican becomes deserted at weekends so that we would have no business really from Friday to Monday night. The venue was too night-clubby to attract much of a lunchtime trade and too small to pack in enough people at night to compensate.

I still had the Sutton Arms at the time, and a lot of my customers would want to go to the club after an evening's drinking. I thought that it might have been one solution to our dilemma but Frank discouraged that plan, saying oil and water don't mix. He was probably right: City types didn't want hairy-arsed rascals from north London socialising in their midst. So I would go to the pub, which was still fairly busy, and then pop down to the club, which would be empty.

I would sit in there watching the door and if it opened my heart would leap, hoping that a big group would come in, but invariably it would be just a couple and I would sink back into despair. I tried to do the genial 'mein host' *schtick* but inside I was crumbling in the knowledge that the writing was on the wall and I could lose my life savings, my pub and even my house.

Then we had a robbery where £4000 was stolen and we discovered our insurance policy covered us only as a restaurant, not as a night club, and that just put the tin hat on it. In the fourteen months it was open I lost £140,000, had to sell the pub and only kept hold of the house by the skin of my teeth. That loss rattled me like nothing else and, ever since, has left me insecure about money, despite the fact that financially I have bounced back strongly since then. For the next few years, I turned into a workaholic, juggling a combination of after-dinner speaking, punditry and a coaching job at Millwall just to restore what I'd lost. After my, albeit happy, time at Brentford I thought I'd had enough of management but when the Millwall opportunity arose I was intrigued. The small salary would come in useful as well.

Millwall had poached my former Brentford assistant, John Docherty, to succeed George Graham in the summer of 1986 and when I, also, left Griffin Park I'd been offered a coaching job at the Den as well but had turned it down. John is an exceptionally good manager but it's his personality that is his real strength. He is so endearing and he loved to tell minutely detailed stories. You would know that you were in for a long night at Griffin Park or at the Den when he settled back in his chair, lit up a cheroot and said something like: 'On the day we played Cowdenbeath . . .' He loved an audience and he would think nothing of grabbing players after games to join us in the office while he held court. Some of them escaped after a couple of hours in time to make it back to their wives but I often stayed there until midnight, spellbound by his tales and nattering incessantly about the game.

He made telephone calls to me that summer of 1987 until he hooked me, and in a very subtle way. He'd start out by asking my opinions about various players and chatting about tactics. We would be on the phone for hours. Then, later, when he had assembled some of the players we'd been discussing he'd invite me down to take a look at them. By the time he offered me the job a second time I had become so excited by our talks and his plans that I couldn't say no. I stayed at Millwall as John's assistant for two and a half years and we had tremendous success. Of all the clubs I've been involved with, Barbara liked Millwall best, finding a genuineness and warmth in the people that reminded us of Glasgow. We had some great times in Bermondsey and, despite their fearsome reputation, I never had any trouble from the club's fans. There were lunatics aplenty, of course, but in general people were proud of their club and thrilled at the results we were getting.

John and I were very disciplined in our approach, we timed training to perfection and had the players working on their fitness with a Don Howe-like intensity. Being the second in command can be frustrating, even more so if, like me, it is not in your nature to keep quiet. John was very studious and had developed an affection for the back-to-front ball from the works of Wing Commander Reep and his theory of how to score goals. In the dressing room at half time during one game, after I had become frustrated by the amount of aimless long balls played, I instructed our centre halves to try dropping passes into zones where Tony Cascarino and Teddy Sheringham could flick the ball on or control it with their chests instead of having to leap and fight for it all the time.

John went mad, screaming that he didn't want 'fanny football' at his club. I responded in kind, knocking the blackboard over and covering myself in chalk dust, spluttering about his hoofing tactics and explaining that long balls were all well and good as long as they hit the right target. He ended up apologising and we made up but that was part of our relationship too – two fiery Scots guys with the same intense passion.

We stormed to the Second Division title in the first year of our partnership. In our forwards, Teddy and Tony, we had a dynamic and prolific goal-scoring duo served brilliantly from the wings by Kevin O'Callaghan and Jimmy Carter. Unsurprisingly, since they scored forty-two goals between them, the two forwards took all the headlines but the work put in by Terry Hurlock and Les Briley in the centre of midfield was just as important.

Forget the haircut, Hurlock was a very good player, far better than he has been given credit for. Initially, Briley and he used to work like stink at getting the ball back then lash it up to Big Cas. But I encouraged them to think more about their options and drilled them to inject more variation into our play by looking for one of the wingers, or the onrushing Nicky Coleman.

We also had to work on Terry's aggression because he persistently fouled and got far too many bookings. It was more a fault of positioning than any nastiness on his part, and we succeeded in getting him to use his presence as a weapon rather than a slide-tackle. Eventually, when I became an agent, I took him up to Rangers where he was superb and it is a pity that so few English fans saw him at his very best.

At Millwall, the team spirit throughout the club was tremendous and something we always tried to foster. The facilities were rough and ready but we got everyone to muck in. We'd get the players up to sing a song or do a routine and I remember a teenaged Neil Ruddock lapping up his colleagues' applause. When I had been a player I had always treated myself to one cigarette after a game as a little calming ritual. At Millwall, perhaps because of John's cigars, I started smoking more regularly and John and I became like a pair of Italians, puffing away in the dugout and filling it with smoke – much to the bemusement and disgust of our coughing substitutes. Together, these seem to be very vivid memories for all Millwall players at that time; they always mention the sing-songs, the laughs and the fumes.

In our first season in the top flight – 1988-89, which was also the club's debut season at that level – we were third with nine matches to go but finished tenth. Cascarino and Sheringham continued to work very well in tandem; Tony caught the eye more on first impressions, but you could tell that Teddy was going to be an awesome player. Arrogant, sometimes hostile and never a yes man, Teddy Sheringham harnessed all that abrasiveness to his wonderful technique and it was that which made him such a special talent. John and I had done so well in our first season together that there was some newspaper speculation that we were on the shortlist to replace Alex Ferguson – who was having a very rocky time – at Manchester United. Our chairman, Reg Burr, came and told us that we were the best managerial team in the country and he had no intention of letting us go for less than £1,000,000 compensation. Nine months later he sacked us.

Millwall had such a small squad that any injuries were always going to be costly. By September of our second season in charge we had climbed up to third in the league but, over the course of just a few weeks, lost the services of Briley, Sheringham, Carter and Steve Anthrobus through injury. We never recovered, we failed to get a settled team and lost our momentum. In eighteenth spot in early February, having won only one league game since September, John and I were kicked out. I felt that it was unjustified and I vowed not to go back into management. Even as an assistant the job had become engrossing. I was like a zombie, thinking about football all the time, worrying about systems and players. You think that the whole world revolves around your side and how it is faring, and you want to talk about it the whole time. You look at people, imagining they know intricate details about your concerns. Once you've been out of the game for a few months you realise that ninety-nine per cent of people don't give a toss about the world you inhabit. So why send yourself loopy and be at the beck and call of a trigger-happy chairman for £17,000 a year? Finally, I had accepted that it simply wasn't worth it.

16

AGENT PROVOCATEUR

My outlook was fairly bleak at the beginning of the nineties. I had been battered in business and football, battered so thoroughly I could have been a piece of haddock. The loss of the night club business followed so closely by being given the sack at Millwall had left me scarred. To this day, if I walk past an empty restaurant it instantly transports me back to the worry of that time and I feel sick to the stomach for the helpless proprietor. It is not hard for me to imagine them lying, terrified, in bed at four in the morning in silent, sleepless torment because it's something I went through myself as my business went down the pan.

I was, therefore, slightly apprehensive about taking another plunge. But looking for a job in football was out of the question – although George Graham did offer me some work with the reserves at Arsenal – but I just could not face going back to that world. I felt Millwall had stitched up John and me, probably to shore up their flotation and deflect criticism from the board. Both of us had put our hearts and souls into the club. You give so much over two years, get the club to the highest position in its history and your reward is the sack. 'That's football,' people say. 'Get used to it.' I wasn't prepared to put myself through that again so I steeled myself to get started back in business.

We had lost our jobs in February 1990 and I spent the rest of the season doing the after-dinner circuit and working for radio but the income wasn't nearly enough to support my family now my savings had been wiped out because of the situation with the restaurant. I was approached by Graham Smith, who had worked for adidas for a number of years, and invited to join his agency, First Wave. I wasn't too keen at first because as a manager I had felt that some of the people involved in representing players were exploitative and the agency business itself was murky. But I found Graham a very persuasive advocate of a new style of working and said that I would be interested in a partnership if I could be the sort of agent that did not seek to get players agitating for transfers all the time.

I felt that we could build a reputation for First Wave as a company with integrity. I knew I had the experience to judge what sort of players would be right for a particular club and had picked up a lot from sitting on both sides of the bargaining table over many years. It was a naïve position to have taken because I soon became aware that the quickest route to wealth was the merry-go-round approach – shifting players as often as possible and getting your cut of their improved packages. But I wanted to be a genuine agent; I would be honest with players and try to act as a mentor as much as anything else. I did not want to cheat anyone and stir up the shit just to line my pockets. That just wasn't my way.

And despite how it ended I think I achieved that. We had a good roster of clients, a lot of them from my contacts at Millwall – Teddy Sheringham, Jimmy Carter, Neil Ruddock and Terry Hurlock. But we had some players, too – Mark Robins, Gary Penrice, Danny Wilson and Dion Dublin – who joined us after they had heard we were a decent firm. Others we recruited from scouting missions. I went out to Australia and took on Mark Bosnich and John Filan, quickly getting both of them signed to clubs in England.

Some players had contracts with us, others we worked for on a handshake basis – which I found a very precarious arrangement. At one point I had gentleman's agreements – football's ultimate meaningless phrase – with Stan Collymore and Andy Cole, only to hear that they had joined Nottingham Forest and Newcastle respectively without telling me. That was the main problem in the agency business then; it was unlicensed, so it was like the Wild West at times with everyone scrambling for position and to hell with morals. The legal status was blurred and there were a fair few characters with the whiff of the used car dealer about them.

A good agent should be fair to his client *and* fair to the club he is dealing with. Through my work with Teddy Sheringham and Neil Ruddock I was, occasionally, at Spurs' training ground. There, both Pat van den Hauwe and Vinny Samways told me they had heard good things about me and invited me to work with them. I was delighted but when I asked how I could help, both players said that they wanted me to find them new clubs. Neither were in the first team at the time and I told them, straightaway, that it was unlikely I could get them a better club than Tottenham, or better salaries. At that stage in their careers they should stay and fight rather than hastily take a step down.

In my opinion, if they knuckled down they could get back in the team – and I even said to Vinny that he should not try to pick the ball up off the back four all the time because he was getting bogged down. I told him to have the patience to receive the ball further forward, where he could get the best out of his passing strength. That's not how agents are supposed to operate but I was giving them the best possible advice I could. Within a couple of weeks Pat and Vinny were back in the first team and stayed there for months. I could have encouraged them into asking Terry Venables for a transfer but it would not have been the right thing to do for either player. I believe that, from the players' point of view, such integrity is clear evidence that I was a good agent. But by the prevailing standards, in business terms, it also made me a bad agent because I had talked myself out of two potential commissions. Those were the topsy-turvy ethics of the football agent's world.

Some clubs were fine to deal with, treating me and the player I was representing with respect. When I took Terry Hurlock to Rangers Graeme Souness was top class. He was 'big time', and was very open yet firm in his stance and I admired him for that. Other clubs were very patronising and bumptious, haggling over every single clause and trying to play hardball as if they thought I was wet behind the ears. Clubs like to blame agents but they were equally culpable. There were an awful lot of dodgy practices that the clubs condoned as the trade in players quickly became a free-for-all.

Some clubs paid no heed to the contract between player and agent and would try to involve other agents in the deal if it suited them. One particular agent was notorious for being parachuted in by certain 'friendly' clubs halfway through a transfer and he would hijack the negotiations. Rumours that he was in cahoots with some managers and chairmen abounded and I am sure that he engineered cuts for them to secure his position. Some others had tremendous power at individual clubs, and it was not uncommon to see a transfer where one agent represented the manager of the buying club, the club itself, the selling club and the player – all on an ad hoc basis, of course.

When I was an agent the average fee for negotiating a new contract and signing on fee was about £8000, which I split fifty-fifty with my partner. Look at some deals now and you see £500,000 commissions as the norm in the Premiership, not to mention the £2,000,000 fee mentioned in a recent deadlocked court case. I am sure that some of you will think that £8000 is far too generous but the amount of work entailed was enormous. Take the case of Neil Ruddock, for example, whom I took from Southampton to Tottenham. It was common knowledge that Terry Venables was looking for a centre half and I knew that Southampton were willing to sell Neil so once I heard that Spurs' chief scout, Ted Buxton, had recommended Neil to Terry I set to work.

I had worked with Neil at Millwall and knew his strengths and weaknesses in intricate detail. At his best, Neil could be a commanding figure at the back, the sort of powerful, dominating defender that Spurs had not had since they sold Richard Gough. Neil was also a tremendous asset at attacking set-pieces and was no mug with the ball at his feet. At Millwall he had scored the best goal I have ever seen – a forty-five-yard shot that was like a ballistic missile. He's a lovely guy, a very lively professional to have around the place with a nice sort of cockiness, but he was also lazy, in my opinion. He used to step up and stick his arm in the air, trying to play off-side regardless of where his team mates were placed because he could not be bothered to chase back. I knew Terry could handle him and coach his wilder instincts out of him. For three months I was like a stuck record, continually impressing upon Venables the positives about Neil's potential and outlining how his faults could be corrected until, eventually, he was convinced enough to make a bid.

The contractual negotiations were not difficult because Neil desperately wanted to play for Spurs – in fact, even before we had stated our position he had called Terry 'Boss', which had weakened our bargaining hand considerably. I arranged a deal at £2500 a week, a healthy signing on fee, and even got him some extra for a car on top of that. That night, I took a telephone call from Neil's father-in-law informing me that they were unable to pay my commission. He was only on £500 a week at Southampton and had been suspended so often that season that he'd had to pay several large fines. In addition, there were other debts that needed settling with the signing on fee. I had got him his dream move and yet they did not want to pay me.

In the end, I deducted First Wave's fee from the car money and passed the rest on. This obviously upset Neil but we rubbed along fine for another year until, out of the blue, I got a letter from a well-known agent who had worked for a couple of high-profile players, informing me that Neil was now his client. I was hacked off that Neil hadn't told me but I suppose it was not unusual by the standards of the industry. But what really got my goat was the insinuation in the letter that I was a 'tame' agent, implying that my priority was to appease Venables rather than properly represent Neil. Moreover, the agent claimed that he would have got Neil £5000 a week if I hadn't sold him short. I reckoned it was an absolutely outrageous libel but when you are not used to reading such allegations it can be upsetting, even if they are wholly inaccurate. It really shook me up. Here was a guy who I knew to be powerful and influential, putting what in my view was such a stain on my character. Barbara had just been diagnosed with cancer and I was worried sick, so, in the state I was in, to get an accusation of being bent was the last thing I needed.

As luck would have it, a week or so later I was out jogging in the park near my house in Winchmore Hill when who should come running in the opposite direction but the man with the poison pen. I raced over and threatened to throw him in the lake for what he'd said. He claimed I'd misinterpreted it all, so I put him straight: Terry did not even want Neil at first, other clubs thought him a liability because of his disciplinary record yet I had got him a 500 per cent rise. How could I have misinterpreted what he said when it was written down in black and white? People like that are very brave behind their desks, dictating bile-filled letters and sending them out to put the wind up folk, disregarding how it might be taken by the recipient. I see now, of course, that he just wanted to poach our client and get me to roll over. And he succeeded in his plan because footballers will listen to any old pap. But I am pleased that I was able to give him a dose of his own medicine the day he was confronted by an enraged Scots jogger.

My involvement in the dispute between Terry Venables and Alan Sugar stemmed from my participation in Teddy

Sheringham's transfer from Nottingham Forest to Spurs. When Teddy joined Forest from Millwall I, naturally, accompanied him to the City Ground to do the deal with Brian Clough. As soon as we got there Cloughie famously asked Teddy what he liked to be called and obviously enough Sheringham said: 'Teddy.' Brian grimaced and, just to wind him up, said: 'I think I will call you Edward.' Teddy was bemused by that and, since he was almost as arrogant as Cloughie, it didn't get their relationship off on the soundest footing. While we were negotiating the package, Brian got up for a drink and put on a Sinatra record. I said that the particular track he had chosen was one of my favourites but he said: 'You don't like Sinatra,' and that I must be humouring him. So we had to break off while we had a who's the biggest Frank fan competition – we named track after track and then Cloughie insisted that I sing to him. We cemented Teddy's transfer by singing Sinatra standards together in his City Ground office and toasting Ol' Blue Eyes with brandy.

Sheringham's season with Forest was a huge success, and the twenty-one goals he scored in all competitions provoked interest from several other clubs. Teddy was missing his son, who had stayed in London, and asked me to see if a move south was at all possible. I never thought that Brian would let him go, but he had become even more volatile than usual in those last couple of seasons and was quite enigmatic when I asked him outright. 'Maybe,' he said, 'but I'd want more than my money back.' That meant he was looking for a fee in excess of £2,000,000. Maybe the drink had affected his judgement, but there was also the fact that he had never really taken to Teddy. Sheringham is like a Dutch player – he loves a debate, or even an argument, about tactics and football and was never the sort of person who would buckle to Brian's domineering personality.

As a Tottenham fan, Teddy made it quite clear that he wanted to go to White Hart Lane. This made my job as his agent both easy and difficult: easy because there was only one option; difficult because we did not have a position of strength from which to bargain. As soon as it became known that Cloughie was contemplating selling Sheringham I took a telephone call from the now late Jack Walker of Blackburn Rovers. He was offering an enormous package of wages, a huge signing on fee and bonuses – a far better deal than Tottenham ever put on the table – but Teddy was adamant about Spurs. It would have suited me better if he'd gone to Lancashire but I had to tell the Blackburn owner that my client would not be swayed.

Before the transfer went through, Tottenham had issued our agency with £50,000 plus VAT, in cash, as a settlement on money owed to us for work carried out on Sheringham's transfer as well as many other deals. I had agreed beforehand with Terry Venables that our fee was £50,000 inclusive of VAT so, a few days later we returned £8750 to Peter Barnes, the Tottenham Secretary. That could have been the end of it but a year on the whole issue exploded on the back pages when Alan Sugar dismissed Terry Venables from Spurs and the allegation was made that I had taken the £50,000 as a 'bung' to Cloughie to facilitate the transfer.

It subsequently became part of a broader FA Premier League inquiry into corruption, conducted by Robert Reid, Rick Parry and Steve Coppell. I was a witness in that inquiry and in a subsequent court case between Venables and Jeffrey Fugler, a former business associate of Terry. I said at the time: 'I had been working for Spurs for the best part of a year. The culmination of that work was signing Teddy Sheringham for the club. Other agents will tell you that you don't always get paid for the work you do for a club but that deal gave me the chance to put pressure on Spurs.' I know that it sounds fishy, but that's nothing more than innuendo.

The payment was authorised by Tottenham and I've admitted that part of the payment was for getting them Sheringham – a commission which was not technically legal at the time – and as I said in court, our invoice was misleading in that it did not mention the Sheringham deal but, I explained: 'This is used by a number of clubs to get out of what they consider to be the antiquated laws of the Football Association. Some agents call it merchandising and have done no work of that kind whatsoever, but we have at least done some genuine work, which we can prove . . . We are not breaking any rules because we are not governed by the FA. It is the clubs who are breaking the rules.'

I concede that using Teddy to lever the money we were owed was not an honourable thing to do, but speculation that we 'bunged' the money to Brian Clough called for a stout denial. The money was paid to us and we paid tax on it. Is it likely that we would pass on £50,000 and then stump up more than £20,000 to the Inland Revenue out of our own pockets to protect Clough? However, two members – Reid and Parry – of the Premier League inquiry team suggested that this had, indeed, been the case though that part of the report dealing with our involvement with Clough was never endorsed by Steve Coppell. This left me in no man's land with a slightly tarnished image and having to put up with taunts of: 'Have you got your brown paper bag with you, Frankie?' for the next couple of years.

An agent's job isn't just about negotiating wages and transfers. Part of it involves arranging friendly, and tour matches, taking managers out to games on the continent and actively scouting for players. Spurs wrote to First Wave, asking us to recruit players on their behalf and part of the payment we received was for expenses incurred bringing, at their request, Preki over from the United States for a trial. There were other instances of this over the years, not to mention all the videos and assessments provided on demand.

Finding myself in the middle of someone else's vicious dispute helped persuade me to get out of the agency business. I also didn't care for the commission element, as it's very difficult to make plans without a guaranteed income. It can be very frustrating, too, because you go up 100 roads and ninety-nine of them turn out to be dead ends. I would get a call from overseas about finding a player an English club; I'd get them to send over the tapes and I'd spend hours making my judgement about if he could fit in and which club might need a player of that type.

I tried to give an honest assessment every time. More than half of all the videos I watched I sent back and I refused to bombard clubs with dross and inappropriate recommendations. But when I did find a gem, I would go and see a manager and, still, he would wearily slip the tape onto a pile of fifty others. If I was lucky and the manager was interested I would get a phone call, maybe a fortnight later, to thank me for the tape and let me know that several other agents were offering the same player. It just became too frustrating as players did not keep to their word. They would authorise a whole host of agents to get them a club and go with the one with the best offer. I couldn't stand that any more, so I got out.

At the height of all the controversy raised by the Premier League's inquiry I was also concerned about my reputation and did not want my involvement in that business to define the rest of my life. In particular, I hated the thought that it might sour the good rapport I had with supporters, or ruin my credibility for the media work which I loved. When I stopped being an agent I threw myself back into punditry, enjoying my involvement with the best of football – the game itself, not its shady side.

I went to work for Capital Gold in the early nineties and, with Jonathan Pearce, Rodney Marsh and Alan Mullery, we had a good team there. We covered Euro 96, which was a fantastic experience, and had some great laughs along the way. My favourite story from my time there concerns Dave Clark, who now works at Sky Sports. God knows how, but he managed to get away with the following comment when he was running through the German team before a game: '. . . Bierhoff and Kuntz. Sounds like a good night out to me!'

Saturdays were quite exhausting, particularly if I was travelling up to Manchester or Newcastle. I'd get picked up by a car in Luton at eight o'clock in the morning and drive – with Pearcey pummelling my eardrums – for hours, do the match, then wait for the interviews and get home just before closing time. Richard Park inadvertently saved me from all that. He's now made a name for himself as the Mr Nasty on *Fame Academy* but before that he, a man commonly assumed to be in love with himself, was the programme director at Capital. During Euro 96 he proposed that we open a bottle of champagne and toast the best football audiences his station had ever enjoyed, along with the broadcasting team responsible for them. He promptly gave us the can before the next season had even begun, but Mullers, Rodney, Clarky and I all ended up at Sky so, as it turned out, he'd done us a favour.

These days, youngsters recognise me more for being on *Soccer Saturday* than for my distant playing career. We are all aware that Jeff Stelling makes the show; he has a phenomenal memory and is as sharp as they come. His bright and breezy personality sets such a wonderful jokey tone, which is incredible when you consider the constant talkback in his earpiece and the number of screens he has to monitor. It's great, too, that the viewers recognise how good he is and hold him in such affection. He really is a brilliant guy – just a bit short in stature. Footballers can be quite insular and cliquish to outsiders but he is very highly regarded by everyone for his charm and professionalism.

We have a great spirit of camaraderie on set which translates well to the viewers. The younger ex-players all call me Uncle Frank while the Scots guys call me 'Faither'. If I ever get tongue tied there are always quips about the onset of Alzheimer's. There's a lot of banter and sarcasm but there's plenty of insight, too, and it makes a potent mix. Rodney was happy to take on the role of the show's pantomime villain and his wind-ups got people tuning in to see what outrageous opinion he'd come out with next. We would bicker all the time about some preposterous statement or other and people tell me they loved our arguments.

Once, in Leeds, this chap came up to me at a dinner and said: 'Aye, that programme is great. I sit in front of the telly for six hours and my wife plays pop with me. My favourite bit is the fights you have with Rodney Marsh. You're brilliant. Mind you, it's crystal clear that neither of you knows fuck all about what you're talking about.' High praise indeed from our typically diplomatic Yorkshire fan club!

I genuinely love working on the show and was very upset when an inopportune comment of mine was taken out of context and threatened to jeopardise my relationship with Sky. I was working on the phone-in show with Rodney and Rob McCaffrey when the subject of Tottenham was raised. Spurs had made a big show of their management dream team – Frank Arnesen, Jacques Santini and Martin Jol – but Santini had resigned after only a handful of games.

Rod made a comment about one of them disappearing and that sparked a thought in my head about the plot of an Agatha Christie novel: 'It's like *Ten Little Niggers*,' I said. Not for a moment did I mean anything other than a reference to the novel I'd read forty years previously but, as soon as it came out of my mouth, I winced. I honestly didn't know that the book's title had been changed – and not once, but twice since I had last picked it up. But I had recognised that it was the wrong thing to say even in innocence and with no intention to cause offence.

I was mortified when complaints were made to Sky, and the press ran with it, but no one who knows me would accuse me of racism and Sky were very supportive, quickly confirming their view that it was not a malicious comment, merely an unwittingly foolish choice of words. But, and more so given the recent Ron Atkinson outburst, there was a great deal of understandable sensitivity about the issue. I apologised profusely and got a great deal of support from the viewers and people like Bobby Barnes from the PFA who knew what I had meant. I went through a few weeks of private terror and my pride was hurt that people could think badly of me but, fortunately, most soon accepted that my intentions had not been malign. I am thankful that it didn't end my career with Sky because it's been such a happy one. As I write I still have another year to go on my contract and I would love to carry on. I might be the oldest member of the panel but I am still enthralled by the game, and I don't think I'm like some of the old-timers who constantly hark back to the halcyon days.

Even though I am now aged sixty-five, I'm not ready to wind down just yet. I am still working full time in a security company in partnership with Ian Henderson and we are doing very well. And I'm clinging on to my ambition to get my golf handicap down to three. It's currently at seven but, with the help of the Swing Factory in Knightsbridge and my coach Bobby Mitchell at the South Herts Golf Club, I think I can do it. I've tried all sorts of techniques over the years and am now just modifying my take away. If I can reach my goal it wouldn't be a bad achievement for a man in his mid-sixties – I've not stopped trying to learn so I think I have a chance.

When you are as absorbed in your career as I was, you have to rely on your wife a lot. I'm close to my four boys, and I worry about them just as much now as I did when they were babies, but I missed out a lot in earlier years. I am trying to make up for that with my wonderful brood of grandchildren – Robyn, Ruby, Frankie, Ellis, Finlay and Thomas – and I love to take them up to the park on Sunday mornings. Barbara plays the grand matriarch to perfection, and we see a lot of our sons and their partners: Neil and Ruth, Iain and Joanne, Scott and Jo and Jamie and Mel. Neil, as I mentioned earlier, is an independent camera supervisor and has worked on everything from the World Cup to Live8 and *Top Gear*. Iain and Scott run a Cash Convertors in Edmonton which we've had for eleven years and they've made a great success of it. Our second-youngest son, Jamie, is a surveyor – he works in construction for plenty of large companies and in the future, to make the most of his expertise, I would like to get into property development with him.

If, as the old saying goes, everyone has to be the hero of their own story there still has to be a huge place in mine for Barbara. She has all the qualities I lack, particularly patience and calmness, and it's down to her that we have such a tremendous family. The boys worship her and she still fusses around them like a mother hen. She'll hate me for saying this, but I admire her formidable courage as she fought cancer four times in the past fifteen years. I don't like to face things like that, preferring to think of our best times, but I am so grateful that she has recovered so remarkably well. And I can't get jealous of the way the boys idolise her because she has been a devoted mother and the best wife I could have hoped for.

As I sit out in my conservatory and gaze across at the lawn that has taken me thirty years to get just the way I want it, I do feel an enormous sense of happiness and gratitude. I've made many mistakes and suffered my fair share of setbacks but I have always come back strong. That fighting spirit, born in the Gorbals tenements, continues to pulse through my veins as I reflect on a life full of pleasure beyond my wildest imaginings, and a future that still looks ripe for adventure.

CAREER STATISTICS

Francis McLintock, born Glasgow, 28 December 1939.
Career: Shawfield Juniors, Leicester City January 1957. First
team debut 14 September 1959 v Blackpool. Arsenal October
1964 £80,000, Queens Park Rangers June 1973 £25,000.
Honours:
9 full Scottish caps, 1 goal, 1 Under-23.
Arsenal Player of the Year 1967. Fairs Cup winners 1969-70.
Division 1 Champions 1970-71, FA Cup winners 1970-71.
Footballer of the Year 1971. Awarded MBE 1971. Leicester
City manager June 1977. Resigned April 1978. Youth team
coach Queens Park Rangers. Brentford manager February
1984 to January 1987. Millwall assistant manager July 1987
to February 1990.

FRANK McLINTOCK

SEASON	LEAGUE		FA CUP		LEAGUE CUP		EUROPEAN	
	Apps	Goals	Apps	Goals	Apps	Goals	Apps	Goals
LEICESTER CITY								
1959-60	17	2	1	-	-	-	-	-
1960-61	34	1	10	-	2	-	-	-
1961-62	30	6	2	-	1	-	1#	-
1962-63	42	4	6	-	2	-	-	-
1963-64	35	6	1	-	5	3	-	-
1964-65	10	6	-	-	1	-	-	-
ARSENAL								
1964-65	25	2	2	-	-	-	-	-
1965-66	36	2	1	-	-	-	-	-
1966-67	40	9	3	-	2	2	-	-
1967-68	38	4	5	-	8	2	-	-
1968-69	37	1	4	-	7	-	-	-
1969-70	30	-	-	-	4	-	7★	-
1970-71	42	5	9	-	5	-	7★	1
1971-72	37	3	9	-	4	-	5+	-
1972-73	29	-	3	1	4	-	-	-
QUEENS PARK RANGERS								
1973-74	26	1	6	-	3	-	-	-
1974-75	30	-	4	-	-	-	-	-
1975-76	35	2	2	-	4	-	-	-
1976-77	36	2	2	-	7	1	8★	-
Totals	609	56	70	1	59	8	28	1

European Cup Winners' Cup

★ UEFA (Fairs) Cup

+ European Cup

INTERNATIONALS
SCOTLAND

1963 v Norway (sub), Republic of Ireland, Spain (1 goal).

1964 v Northern Ireland.

1967 v USSR.

1970 v Northern Ireland.

1971 v Wales, Northern Ireland, England.

SCOTLAND UNDER-23

1962 v England.

INDEX

Note: 'FM' denotes Frank McLintock. Names of countries refer to national teams unless otherwise indicated. Subheadings for individuals are in chronological order.